I Wasn't Supposed
to Be Here

I Wasn't Supposed to Be Here

Finding My Voice,
Finding My People, Finding My Way

Jonathan Conyers

With Lori L. Tharps

LEGACY
LIT

New York Boston

Legacy Lit
Hachette Book Group
1290 Avenue of the Americas
New York, NY 10104
LegacyLitBooks.com
Twitter.com/LegacyLitBooks
Instagram.com/LegacyLitBooks
First Edition: September 2023

Legacy Lit is an imprint of Grand Central Publishing. The Legacy Lit name and logo are trademarks of Hachette Book Group, Inc.

The publisher is not responsible for websites (or their content) that are not owned by the publisher.

The Hachette Speakers Bureau provides a wide range of authors for speaking events. To find out more, go to hachettespeakersbureau.com or email HachetteSpeakers@hbgusa.com.

Legacy Lit books may be purchased in bulk for business, educational, or promotional use. For information, please contact your local bookseller or the Hachette Book Group Special Markets Department at special.markets@hbgusa.com.

All photos are from the author's collection.

Print book interior design by Jeff Stiefel

Library of Congress Control Number: 2023938065

ISBNs: 978-1-5387-4250-1 (hardcover), 978-1-5387-4252-5 (ebook)

Printed in the United States of America

LSC-C

Printing 1, 2023

*This book is dedicated to the three most powerful
women in my village:
My grandmother Gwendolyn Smith
My mother, Virginia Kim Conyers
My wife, Nicolette Conyers*

Contents

Introduction

There is an African proverb that says, "It takes a village to raise a child." I like to say it took a whole army to raise me because my village was so large, so strategic, and so ready to fight for me and my well-being.

The proverbial village that comes together to raise a child is usually made up of the aunties, neighbors, and teachers at school who regularly come in contact with the child. Whether they want to or not, they become part of a child's village simply because of their proximity or connection. But that's not how my village came to be.

For starters, my village is a chosen village. Chosen by me. Some people have a chosen family; I have a chosen village because the family I was born into couldn't be my village. They couldn't give me the resources, stability, support, and guidance I needed to get where I wanted to go in life. So, I had to build that village myself. I had to find the caretakers, guides, mentors, and teachers who could lift me up, hold me down, and light the path to my destiny. From the age of eleven, I knew instinctively I had to start assembling my village if I wanted to survive my circumstances.

Today, I can proudly say my village is made up of a diverse group of people who were fundamental to my success and who continue to be guideposts in my life. I know the only reason I am where I am in life is because I chose village members based on their knowledge, skills, and attributes rather than on where they came from or what they look like. I learned at an early age that people who could help me survive and thrive don't have to look like me or share the same background.

Therefore, my village includes people from every age, ethnicity, race, religion, sexual orientation, and gender identity. Rich and poor. Young and old. Able-bodied and differently abled, the members of my chosen village always brought something to my life that I needed at the time. Some of them continue to participate in my life, whereas others were part of the village for a season only. Even random strangers, those who passed through with words of wisdom or sage advice, are counted as honorary village members. Their contributions count because they made a lasting impact on my life.

My village members taught me how to act, how to be, and how to handle myself. They protected me, loved me, and kicked me in the butt when I started to lose my way. From teaching me how to tie a tie to teaching me how to use my voice to stand up for myself, the members of my chosen village provided me with the skills and life lessons that helped me be the husband, father, medical professional, and mentor I am today.

I wrote this book to show that opening yourself up to the kindness of strangers, to guidance from people who may have taken an unconventional path, and lessons from unlikely sources can lead to innumerable blessings and a life well lived. Because of my family circumstances, I had to rely on my chosen village as a matter of survival, but it doesn't have to be that way for everyone. You can build your village out of a sense of desperate need or because you're embarking on a new path in life, and you need a village to help show you the way.

The bottom line is, when choosing to build your own village, you will reap untold rewards, but it requires both strategy and humility. It took me a while to learn how to ask for help and then accept it when given. I had to learn how to recognize wisdom when it didn't come out of the mouth of someone who looked like me or who didn't look like society's version of "an expert." I had to go out into the world and find the people who could help me instead of waiting for someone to save me. Sometimes, I picked the wrong people to show me the way, but even still, I managed to learn something from the experience.

At the end of the day, we have to be the hero of our own stories, but I know from experience that even superheroes need their village. I have mine, and I want you to have one, too.

I Wasn't Supposed to Be Here

1

I Wasn't Supposed to Be Born

She's going to kill me," my father screamed, viciously banging on door after door down the hallway, begging for help. Alternating between yelling and sobbing, he brandished the butcher knife as both weapon and protection against his attacker. "Somebody help me!" he cried out again. "She's trying to kill me."

My mother tried desperately to snap out of her high and begged my father to calm down, but he continued yelling and screaming for help.

"Pumpkin," she tried again, using her pet name for my father. "Shut the hell up before someone calls the cops," she said. "You know if they call the cops, they gonna take the kids."

The kids—my siblings James Jr., Josh, Justin, and Helena—were hiding in a closet. Jay, which is what we called my eldest brother, was holding two-year-old Helena, while I laid in my mother's belly unaware of the turmoil around me.

The truth is, nobody was chasing my father. These paranoid episodes—brought on by the crack he had recently smoked—were common. My father would run around the house brandishing a knife, convinced someone was trying to kill him or his children. It would last about thirty minutes, and then he would snap back to reality. Afterward, everyone would pretend nothing happened. There was one time, though, when he did actually stab my mother in the chest to "defend himself," but on this night, he simply waved the knife around threatening the imagined enemies in our home.

By the next morning, life went on like always. I was still in my mother's belly, but I heard about this episode because it's part of my origin story. This was around the time my mother found out she was four months pregnant with me. She was using a lot during that time, as she had during all her pregnancies, except with Jay. According to my mother's telling of this story, once she found out she was pregnant with me, she had my father take her down to the Planned Parenthood clinic on Third Avenue in the Bronx and immediately asked for an abortion. With four kids and a drug habit, she couldn't afford another child. But Planned Parenthood refused to perform an abortion because she was so far along.

Still, my mother was determined to terminate the pregnancy. My father drove her to two other clinics and two different hospitals in New York, but everyone turned her away because my mother had a long history of medical issues that would have made an abortion dangerous at that point.

"I'm not driving you to any more clinics," my father finally announced after the last appointment. "This kid was obviously meant to be born."

My mother reluctantly agreed to keep the baby, but she didn't stop smoking crack. Neither did my father. Which is why I was born in Virginia instead of New York.

Two months before my birth, my parents gathered up my siblings and fled New York City in the dead of night, abandoning their government-subsidized apartment in the Bronx. My father hadn't paid his drug dealer, a dude named Hector. My dad owed Hector close to a thousand dollars, but he didn't have the money, and he couldn't keep stalling. So, my parents packed a few bags and hopped on a bus out of town, heading south. They got off in Virginia, where my father's mother, Corine, lived. My parents and my siblings crammed into my grandmother's already-crowded three-bedroom house and awaited my arrival.

I was born on October 23, 1994. I was my parents' fifth child. Unwanted and unplanned. Born into a family where violence, addiction, and dysfunction reigned. And yet, everyone always tells me that, even as a baby, I always had a smile on my face. Somehow, I must have known that if I managed to survive the circumstances surrounding my birth, I could survive anything.

My family returned to New York City soon after I was born. Life went back to "normal," except my parents now had an extra mouth to feed, their drug habit to satisfy, and no permanent housing. Having given up their apartment, we lived a chaotic and unstable life, always on the verge of being evicted from whatever temporary housing arrangement my parents managed to find. My memories of those early years are vague and tinged with trauma. I didn't understand the reasons we lived the way we did, why there was never enough food, or why our Christmas presents got stolen. I didn't know my parents had a drug problem. I just knew I never felt safe.

Five years later, we found ourselves back in Chesapeake. The move to Virginia was supposed to be the fresh start we all needed. A reset after five years of nonstop drama in New York. In Chesapeake, there were more job opportunities for my father and better schools for us kids. The cost of living was also lower. For the first year we were there, though, we shuttled between homeless shelters, temporary housing, and my grandmother's house before my father finally found a steady job doing ductwork for a big construction company, and my parents found a house they could afford to rent.

Our new home was a two-story, three-bedroom brick townhouse with a yellow door, which was attached to a row of similar houses that stretched down the block. It had a little front yard with two white plastic chairs and a paved driveway that led to a small backyard with dotted patches of grass. We even had a tree. As a kid who had never had a permanent home in New York, I was so excited to have our own house. Not an apartment. Not a crowded room in a shelter. Not the spare bedroom of my Grandmother Gwen's apartment in the Webster Projects. We had a home like the ones I saw on TV. A home where we could all live together—my parents, Jay, Josh, Justin, Helena, and me— like a normal family.

Our house was in Holly Cove. Back then, and still today, Holly Cove is considered one of the poorest neighborhoods in Chesapeake. Look it up. You'll probably find the words "gun violence" and "drugs" in every description, but Holly Cove was also on the right side of the catchment line to attend Chesapeake public schools, where fifty percent of the student population came from wealthy and middle-class white families. That's why my parents decided we should live there—they were determined that the Conyers kids would have "a rich white kid's education." My parents were always on the same page about school.

The Conyers kids would all go to college. My parents made it clear from the moment we could walk and talk that we were going to be somebody and have a better life than the one they had. Their addiction never diminished their commitment to supporting our education and setting us up for a successful future.

Raised by single mothers, my mom and dad grew up in the projects in the Bronx and they were both good students. There are a lot of layers to my parents that folks don't usually associate with Black people addicted to crack. That singular narrative about the victims of the 1980s crack epidemic doesn't tell a full story. My father graduated high school with an almost 4.0 GPA, and my mother attended Bronx Community College for two years, studying health sciences and human services. She had plans to get a nursing degree, but she got pregnant at age twenty with my brother Jay. Then, her addiction robbed her of her dreams. The same was true for my father. He dreamed of going pro with his boxing career and had the skills to do it. The drugs stole from them, dreams that they'd never get back, but that wouldn't be the case for their children. Their children would succeed where they had failed. Where drugs and poverty had forced them into a corner, the Conyers kids would take on the world.

My parents believed in education like other people believe in Jesus. Education was the way out and the way up. Grades before sports. Homework before fun. School over everything. That was how our household was run. My father made my brothers go

work construction with him during Virginia's hot, steamy summers just to make sure their hatred of manual labor was strong
enough to propel them to college.

When my brothers brought home a good report card, a gold
medal, or a trophy, my parents were their happiest.

So, you can imagine my mother's reaction when she registered
me for first grade in Virginia, and the school officials notified
her that I couldn't read at grade level—and that I would have
to repeat kindergarten. There was even talk of putting me in
special education classes.

"He doesn't know the alphabet, and he can't even spell his
own name," the reading specialist told my mother.

"You're not putting my baby in special ed," my mother told
the specialist, in her loud, raspy voice. "There's nothing wrong
with his ass." For the record, my mother always sounds like she's
yelling, and she uses curse words as adjectives, verbs, and nouns.
Probably because they were intimidated, the school officials
didn't argue with her.

"You'll see," my mother told the specialist as we got up to
leave. "I'll work with him and he'll catch up."

"You're not fucking stupid, Jonathan," Mommy told me as we
walked home along the highway because we didn't have a car or
money for the bus. "We'll show them." When we got home, she
told me I was going to learn how to read if it was the last thing
I did because nobody was going to label her child "special" and
put him in the system to rot.

My mom was good on her word. Every day during that first
year, when we were still hopscotching between homeless shelters
and my Grandma Corine's house, she would sit down with me
and help me learn the alphabet or read to me. The specialist
gave me homework, and my mom would help me complete it
correctly. By the time I finished kindergarten, I still couldn't
read, but I was getting the hang of things, and I had learned an
important lesson from my mother. Although I couldn't put it
into words as a five-year-old kid, I had witnessed my mom stand
up to authority and fight for my rights. She also taught me that

if I worked hard enough, I could achieve anything. That lesson would definitely come in handy later in my life.

In Holly Cove, people respected our family because we were a family of athletes. Jay was a varsity wrestler at the high school. He was so good there had even been a profile written about him in the local paper, and the article highlighted the athletic excellence that ran through the Conyers household. Justin was a star player on the middle school football team. Josh had broken the record in middle school for the most points scored in a single basketball game. Occasionally, my father would volunteer to ref Josh's games. Even the way we celebrated wins in the family was fun. When my brothers brought home a trophy or a gold medal, my father would take over the kitchen duties and he'd whip up a batch of his famous lasagna, and we'd devour it watching sports on TV. Watching my brothers succeed on the sports field and seeing all of the accolades they achieved for it, I couldn't wait to be a part of our family's sports tradition.

I was in first grade when I got my chance to start my football career. My best friend, Tevin, told me about his flag football team and begged me to join. I told my mom about the team, but she told me she didn't have enough money for me to play football, and we didn't have a car to get me to practice. I thought the dream was over, but it wasn't. Tevin's father came by our house one afternoon and offered to pick me up and take me home after every practice, and he told my mom that the coach would waive my fees.

"Well, in that case, you can play, Boo Boo," Mommy said.

I felt like all my dreams had come true. I was only seven, but I already loved the game—from listening to Justin talk about the sport every day and watching every collegiate and NFL game on TV with my brothers, football was my sport. Plus, I was big for my age, so everyone said I was going to be unstoppable on the football field. And as soon as I started, I proved them right. Our team won almost every game.

Still, my mother insisted that I had to do my homework

before football practice. I agreed to that, but many days I would skip my homework and go play football anyway. Then, I'd come home from practice at seven o'clock in the evening, ready to relax in front of the television. But my mom wasn't stupid. When I got home one evening, she was sitting on the couch, smoking a cigarette, with my book bag on her lap.

"Sit down," she said pointing at the cushion next to her. "You didn't do your homework before you left, did you?"

"Yes, I did," I lied.

"Oh, really," she'd say with a slow smile. "So, let's go over your spelling words then. How do you spell 'Jonathan,' your name?"

I still hadn't mastered that, but I wasn't going to admit it. Instead, I started spitting out letters that I was pretty sure were in my name and just prayed they were in the right order.

"J-O-E?"

SMACK. Her hand came across my face. "Boy, there's no 'e' in your name. Do it again!"

This became our routine every time I skipped my homework. But instead of doing my homework, I decided I could handle the smacks. After practice, I would just brace myself for the pain. I think I eventually learned to read just so I could put an end to my mother's "hands-on" approach to my education.

Once I graduated out of flag football, it was on to playing regular touch football with real equipment. Equipment my parents couldn't afford to buy, so my football career was over. Justin told me I'd just have to wait until I hit middle school, when I could play football for the school for free. I was disappointed, and it took me a few weeks to stop feeling sorry for myself, but I eventually got over it because that's what we did in our household. We got over our disappointments. And put on a happy face in public so everyone would believe the Conyers myth: we were just a normal happy family. I was too young to understand that what my parents did on the weekends would destroy that myth entirely.

Every Friday evening would start the same way. On Friday

nights, my brothers had sports practice or games to play, so they were rarely at home. That left Helena and me alone with my parents. My mother would dress up, meaning she'd abandon her daily sweatpants and T-shirt for a pair of jeans and a nice top. She would do her hair and put on lipstick. Then, she would put Marvin Gaye on the stereo, light some candles, and wait for my father to come home. While she waited, she'd smoke a cigarette and nurse an Olde English 40, a look of eager anticipation brightening her face.

Friday was payday, and my father, a man of few words and even fewer outward displays of emotion, would come home smiling and in a good mood, too. I loved to see him that way, so different from his Monday through Thursday stoic demeanor. Rather than fighting and screaming at each other, my parents would be grinning like teenagers getting ready for their Friday night fun.

"You two go upstairs and don't come back down," my father would tell Helena and me, sometimes bribing us with a new video game and take-out Chinese food to keep us occupied. One night, I decided not to stay in my room, and I slipped out and sat at the top of the stairs where my parents couldn't see me, but I could see them. I wanted to see what they were doing that made them so happy. I stayed still as I watched my dad light and then inhale the smoke from a small container that looked like a chemistry tube, and then pass it to my mom. Then, my father's eyes rolled back into his head. His tongue fell out of his mouth, dripping with strands of saliva. His hands started twitching. He started mumbling incoherently. On the TV, his pornography tapes played, creating a grotesque soundtrack to what I was witnessing. My mom just sat there, super relaxed, a lazy half smile on her face, with her eyes closed.

I ran back to the room with Helena.

"What's wrong with you?" Helena tore her eyes from the TV screen to look at me.

"I saw Mommy and Daddy smoking out of some strange bottle, and Daddy looked sick," I whispered.

Helena rolled her eyes and said, "That's crack they're smoking. It makes them crazy." Once again, Helena had all the answers.

"Are they going to die?" I asked, my heart beating uncontrollably.

"No, they're not going to die, stupid," Helena said. "But they shouldn't be doing it."

"So, why do they do it?"

"Because they're stupid." She shrugged. "I don't know."

And then she turned back to the TV.

That's how I found out my parents smoked crack.

I was young, but I knew smoking crack wasn't right. The word "crackhead" was thrown around my world all the time. Crackheads were the people I'd seen back in New York, sleeping in the streets, with ashy lips and uncombed hair, twitching and begging for money with empty eyes. That wasn't my parents. My mom was full-figured and beautiful. My dad was still in shape from his boxing days. There was no way they were crackheads, even though their Friday night fun often stretched into Sunday evening and, occasionally, they'd have "fun" during the week, too. My parents were too responsible. Too put together. Too normal in my eyes to be crackheads. But I didn't understand the connections between my parents getting happy on Friday nights and the part of our lives that we weren't supposed to talk about.

Sometimes, when my father smoked crack and his paranoia surfaced, he'd roam the house with his butcher knife. It wasn't uncommon for us to be awakened in the middle of the night by his insistent voice, demanding that all of us kids come downstairs and line up so he could ensure we were all there and accounted for. The next day, I'd be falling asleep in school at my desk and the teacher would call me out.

"Jonathan, class time is not nap time. Why are you so tired?"

I shrugged. "I don't know," I lied. "I'm sorry."

I knew better than to tell my teacher the truth. It was our family's secret and no one else's. One time, in first grade, I let something slip. "I didn't take a shower because we don't have any water." This prompted Mrs. Causey, the reading specialist who worked with me, to call home to check on things.

"You talk too damn much, Jonathan," Mommy yelled at me after she hung up the phone. "You're not supposed to be telling anybody, especially those white teachers at your school, about our situation. That's our business, not theirs."

I knew this and was sad to have broken our pact. Lying to my teachers was something I had to get good at. When my second-grade teacher asked me why I came to school smelling like pee, I didn't tell her I still wet the bed at night, but my parents didn't pay the water bill, so I couldn't wash myself before school. I didn't tell her there wasn't enough money to pay for more than a few pairs of underwear and two pairs of pants. I didn't tell her that we had to sneak across the street in the middle of the night and fill empty containers with water siphoned from an abandoned house to bathe, wash dishes, and flush our toilets. I didn't tell her any of that because my mom told me that was our business and not hers.

In addition to not paying the water bill, sometimes my parents didn't pay the electricity bill, either. My father would try to hack the meter in the back of the house and hotwire the transformers. Sometimes, it worked. Sometimes, it didn't. So, sometimes, we had heat and electricity, and, sometimes, we did our homework in the cold by candlelight.

Whatever money my father made at his job was never enough to pay for the things we needed as a family of seven and support my parents' drug habit. So, not only could we not depend on having things like water and electricity on a regular basis, but food also wasn't a guarantee. Sometimes, my father would ride his bike to the grocery store and steal food for us. He would come home smelling ripe with funk and sweat because he'd have to wear his big winter coat with lots of pockets so he'd have enough places to hide the food he swiped. Usually, it was bread and bologna, hot dogs, and Top Ramen noodles. Cheap food that could be hidden easily and carried home on his bike.

I didn't understand how we could be such a loving family, and yet have these terrible secrets. I didn't understand why my father worked so hard, sometimes picking up an extra part-time job at a restaurant, but still never had enough money for things other families had, like more than one pair of shoes, furniture in the house instead of milk crates to store everything, or a car so my mother didn't have to walk along the highway when she wanted to go somewhere.

But we didn't talk about those things. We didn't talk about real life. Our life. A life where my mom was constantly on the phone with her mother back in New York begging her to send money via Western Union unless she wanted to see her grandchildren living on the street.

My parents insisted that the way we lived was normal and demanded that we maintain that lie. And everyone had a part to play.

Us kids went to school and did our best. Mom made it to every parent-teacher conference. Dad was at work every day without fail. Even if he smoked crack all weekend long, my father would be up for work on Monday morning on time and clocked in. His work ethic was legendary. We spent Thanksgiving and Christmas at my Grandma Corine's house, and we went to church sometimes, especially when we needed an extra blessing from God.

My parents were so committed to maintaining the facade that we were a normal family, they decided that smoking crack in the house, in front of their children, was a better option than doing it outside the house where someone outside the family might see them.

There's a popular illustration that I first saw in college, of three monkeys labeled "See No Evil, Hear No Evil, Speak No Evil." One monkey covers his eyes, one covers his ears, and the third monkey covers his mouth. It reminded me of my family. All five of us kids became those monkeys.

As the youngest child in the family, I didn't know what my role was in our family's image of normalcy. Since I was just average in school, and I didn't play any sports after first grade, I decided that my role was to be the peacekeeper. Instinctively, I knew that if someone didn't diffuse the tension in our household, something terrible would happen. So, I took my job very seriously. If some issue exploded in the house, I'd follow it with a joke. I would do things to make Mommy smile. When she was happy, the house was peaceful. I tried not to let anyone anger her, including myself. I tried to be everybody's best friend and give them reasons to laugh. I told jokes and funny stories. But my parents only found joy on Friday nights. My brothers always seemed angry about our life; still, I tried to keep a smile on my face. It's what I was born to do.

But it wasn't enough.

Violence was also part of our family story. My great-great-grandfather on my father's side shot and killed a white man out of anger and was forced to flee his home. His parents never saw him again. That anger flows through my father's blood. He's calm at his base, but, if provoked, a switch turns on in his head that no one can turn off. At a very young age, my father learned to channel his rage in the boxing ring, but then he used those boxing skills to beat my mother. He started beating her before they were even married, but my mom married him anyway. My mother couldn't beat my father with her fists, so she lashed out with her tongue. She had scars on her body from all the places my father has punched, kicked, and, one time, stabbed her, but she made it clear to us kids that she would never leave him. Keeping her family together has always been her greatest ambition, since she grew up without a father. She takes her role as a mother seriously and that meant, above all, she would keep her kids together and stay with my father. Even if it, literally, killed her to do so. And for his part, my father swore he'd never be like his own father, who abandoned his wife and kids when my father was still a young boy. So, they were fated to stay with each other. And as of this writing, they still are.

As the peacemaker, I always took my mom's side in every fight they had. I had to protect her from him. As the peacemaker, I was her best friend and confidant. I loved my mother as hard as I could, even when she made it difficult.

My brothers did a better job standing up to my dad when he got aggressive with my mom, but they always seemed to be angry at both parents. Joshua and Justin, more than Jay, always had harsh words for my mom. They would slam doors in her face or suck their teeth at her when they were annoyed by something she said. They'd stay away from the house as much as they could, relying on their friends and their coaches to provide a home away from our home. But me, I'd try to cheer up my mom. She got so sad when my brothers yelled at her. She got sad when she and my dad fought. I'd shower her with affection. I told her I loved her. I snuggled with her on the couch and watched her favorite TV shows with her after school. But it wasn't enough to calm the storm that always seemed to be raging in our house.

Ironically, my father had no problem beating my mom, but he never beat us kids. Instead, he taught us how to fight.

When I was eight years old, it was my turn to learn this valuable lesson.

"What happened to you?" my father asked me on a Friday evening when he came home and saw that I had the hint of a black eye.

"I got in a fight," I said, unwilling to tell him that the fight had been about him. That two of the kids I liked to play with in Holly Cove told me that my father was a crackhead. They said their mother told them she had seen my father buying drugs.

They were brothers and younger than me and, before that moment, they had been my friends, but I knew I had to protect my parents. So, I threw a punch and then another. I fought them both, demanding that they take back what they said.

Even though I clearly felt I had won the fight, my father felt it was unacceptable that I came home with a "cookie" under my eye.

Without saying a word, my father left my room and then came back a minute later with a pair of boxing gloves in his hands.

"You're never going to embarrass yourself like that again and let some kid younger than you get in your face," he said, ignoring the fact that I had fought two kids at the same time.

Dad made me box with him every day for a couple of weeks when he came home from work. All three of my brothers had been coached by my father and knew how to fight. They were known to beat down anyone who messed with Helena or me. They didn't start fights, but they would raise hands to protect their family. I wanted to be like them so badly, I didn't even care that the only reason my father was teaching me to box was because he thought I'd let little kids beat me up. I also didn't care because, for the first time I could remember, I was more important to my dad than his usual Friday night binges with my mom. He was putting me first.

"Come on, Jon, get your gloves on," my dad would say, coming straight to my room after work, smelling like the sharp fumes from the construction site. He'd peel off his first layer of dusty work clothes and stand in my room sharing all of his wisdom from his days as an amateur fighter. He'd hold up his hands and make me punch and bob and weave, and shift my feet as I did it. I did my best to make him proud, to keep him talking and sharing stories of his life before he became the way he was now. Quiet and without stories, without affection. That was probably the closest I'd ever felt to my dad. Those weeks when he taught me how to fight.

When I was nine years old, I finally figured out how I could make a difference in our family. I was going to get a job and start earning money. Money was the one thing my parents were always fighting about. Money was the reason we didn't have enough of anything. I was just a kid but decided that I would get a job anyway.

I offered to help my friend David with his grass-cutting business. I told him we could split the work and split the funds. He agreed, so I started getting up early on Saturday mornings to go to David's house to pick up his mower and start cutting grass for the clients he had. That worked for a short while, but pretty soon David wanted to let me do *all* the cutting, but he gave me only *half* the money. We ended up arguing about it, and I walked off mad. When my father found out what happened, he took matters into his own hands.

"Jon, I see you working hard," my father said to me a few days after my fight with David. We were standing outside by the curb in front of the car my father was renting temporarily. "I figured if you had your own equipment, you could make your own money and not have to share it with anyone."

And then he surprised me by pulling a lawn mower out of the back of the car.

I couldn't believe it. *My very own lawn mower.* It was a secondhand gas-powered mower that I had to crank to start. It wasn't in the best shape—sometimes it took a few tries to get it running—but it was all mine, and once I got it going, it got the job done.

"Thanks, Dad," I said to my father, promising I would take good care of it.

"You better take care of it," my dad said in his typical gruff manner. But I could tell that not only was he proud of me, he was also proud of himself for buying me something of value.

With the solid work ethic I learned from my dad, I had my own grass-cutting clients in no time. And with the money I made from cutting the grass, I started buying chips, candy, and Yu-Gi-Oh! cards at the 7-Eleven to sell at my school. I was a little mogul in the making, but I wasn't trying to get rich, I just wanted to make sure Helena and I weren't going to bed hungry. I wanted to help my mom pay the bills so she didn't have to get on the phone and beg her mother for cash. I realized my brothers were probably mad a lot because they wanted to look nice for their girlfriends, but had no nice clothes. I wanted to help them, too. Sometimes, I would just give the money I earned to my father so he could buy food for us on his way home from work.

I wanted to be the hero but, soon, I learned those didn't exist in my world.

A few weeks after I started my business, I went to retrieve some of my lawn mowing money from the bag I kept under my bed, but the bag was empty. All of my money was gone. Nobody in the family wanted to admit what happened.

"Why would they take my money?" I asked Justin when he told me that our parents stole my cash. "I already give Mommy and Daddy most of my earnings so they can buy food."

Justin refused to meet my eyes. "That's who they are."

"But Daddy bought me the lawn mower, so he has his own money."

Justin started to fidget. "Look, Jon, I don't know what to tell you, except find a better hiding place." And with that, he left me alone in my room trying to fit together the complicated pieces of who our parents were.

When my money disappeared a second time, I stopped cutting grass. I didn't confront my parents about it, they never mentioned it, and some nights Helena and I went to bed hungry. The lights still didn't work. The water didn't come on and my brothers were still mad.

And I gradually started to learn that my parents' devotion to their drug habit was stronger than their devotion to me. Of course, they would never admit it—not to me or anyone else—but it became obvious that my happiness, and my safety, and my trust in them, was not top of mind for my parents. The two people who had taught me who I was and who wanted the best life for me, who were rooting the loudest for my survival, were not going to be the people to save me. It's a reality that many people must face about their parents. It can be the most painful truth to accept as a child—and as an adult. It was a truth that I'd have to revisit throughout my entire life, the lion that I'd wrestle with the most. But my parents had also instilled in me the belief that I could do and be anything I wanted. I was destined for more, even more than they could offer.

So, the village I had been born into was not the one I would grow in.

2

I Wasn't Suppposed to
See My Father Cry

The summer when I was ten years old, my mom started hanging out with her friend Sharon a lot more than usual. Sharon lived a few doors down from us in Holly Cove. She was a few years younger than my mom, and she was my mother's only friend in Virginia. Sharon was also the mother of my parents' drug dealers, Rashad and Alonzo. The thing is, although Sharon was slightly older than my mother, her sons weren't much older than my eldest brother, Jay. I knew Rashad and Alonzo because everyone in Holly Cove knew Rashad and Alonzo. They were the reason we didn't have money for groceries—because of the stuff they kept feeding my parents. They were also the same people who, sometimes, handed me twenty dollars so I could go buy snacks from Mr. Melvin's store. They respected my parents and how well they were raising us, so they helped us and took from us all at the same time.

One time, when he was selling to my mom, Rashad said, "Lady, you are the most high-functioning crackhead I have ever seen. Your kids are always on point with their sports games, and they're always out here being respectful."

To which my mother snapped, "Just because I do drugs don't mean I don't care about my kids."

And she stormed off in a huff.

Now, instead of dressing up on Friday nights to "party" with my father, my mom was changing into her fancy look as soon as my father left the house for work. "I'm going over to Sharon's," she'd holler when she left me home alone. And when she'd come back a couple of hours later, she'd remind me, "Don't say nothing to your father about where I've been."

And I never did. Even though I knew that Sharon worked during the days and wasn't even home when my mom was going to hang out with her.

I didn't say anything when my mother sent Alonzo's niece over to keep an eye on me whenever she went over to Sharon's house because she didn't want me to get into any trouble, and she didn't want me coming over there looking for her, either. At least that's what Alonzo's niece, Erica, told me when she came over.

"Your mama's over there with my uncle, and she told me to make sure you don't go nowhere," Erica said.

"Are you supposed to take care of me?" I said, looking Erica up and down. She was tall and skinny with smooth dark skin. She was taller than me but didn't seem much older.

Erica sucked her teeth. "Yeah, I'm here to watch you."

"How old are you?" I said, scratching my head.

"Fourteen," Erica said, looking around our sparsely furnished living room. "Let's go outside and play, it's boring in here."

We spent the next two hours horsing around in our front yard, playing tag and hide-and-seek, until my mom came home and told Erica her uncle was waiting for her back at Sharon's house.

The next time Erica came over, a few days later, instead of playing outside, she wanted a tour of the inside of our house. Because our house was so small, the tour didn't last long, but when we were in Jay's room, Erica turned to me and said, "Let's do something fun."

"Like what?" I said, trying to think of what kind of fun we could have in my brother's tiny room. The only thing in there was a twin bed and a desk. He'd taken his TV when he left for college that summer. The room still smelled like him, though, like sweat and a wet mop.

"You wanna play some video games?" I asked.

"No," she said. "I don't want to play no video games. I wanna play a different kind of game. But you have to pull down your pants first."

I made a face. "What? Why?"

"Just do it. I'm going to do something to you, and it's going to feel good."

I couldn't imagine what she was going to do, and I didn't want to take my pants down in front of a girl I barely knew. But then she came over to me, pulled down my pants, got on her knees, put her head between my legs, and put my penis in her mouth.

"What are you doing?" I yelped, squirming at the strange sensation while trying to pull away.

She grabbed me by the hips and held me still. "Stop moving. You're supposed to be a little man, you're supposed to like this. Stop playing, and let me finish."

I was so shocked; I couldn't believe what was happening. I didn't even know what was happening. This wasn't something anybody had ever told me that girls did. She wasn't hurting me, but it also felt strange to have somebody put their face in my privates.

I tried to say something, but Erica told me to be quiet, so I shut my mouth and squeezed my eyes shut, too, so I didn't have to see what was happening between my legs. I hoped it didn't smell bad down there.

When she was done, about five minutes later, Erica stood up and wiped her mouth and then told me to come downstairs so we could watch TV.

She left the room, and I pulled my pants up, sat on the bed, and tried to figure out what to do. What to think. What to feel. My emotions were popping with all sorts of feelings. Had I had done something wrong? What had Erica done to me? I lingered on the bed, waiting for the whirling questions in my head to stop and the waves of shame and confusion to subside. But then Erica called from downstairs, "Jonathan, come on, let's watch TV," so I slid off the bed, went downstairs, and watched TV with Erica until my mom came home.

We developed a pattern after that. Every time Mom went over to be with Alonzo, Erica came over and we "played" in

Jay's room. I hated it. And I was furious with my mother every time she left the house and sent Erica over.

One night before we went to bed, I told my brother Justin what was going on.

"Justin, this girl keeps, um, putting her face on my private parts."

Justin laughed. "Boy, you don't even have no private parts. Stop lying."

"I'm not lying," I whispered. "She keeps doing what those girls be doing to the men on Daddy's tapes."

Justin laughed again, louder this time. Like I was telling him some crazy joke.

But I wasn't laughing.

Finally, my brother stopped laughing long enough to offer some advice. He put his arm around me and pulled me close, like he was going to let me in on an important secret from his fifteen-year-old perspective. "Jon, listen, if a girl wants to put her face down there, it means she likes you. Guys love it when girls do that. So, don't worry about it. It's nothing bad."

"It isn't?" I said, needing reassurance. I didn't tell Justin that "this girl" was older than me. And I didn't tell him that she came over whenever Mom was hanging out with Alonzo.

"No," Justin said. "It's actually a good thing. So, don't worry about it."

Justin was the Conyers brother who was considered the best looking. He was the pretty boy. He was tall and slim, and everybody said he had nice hair. Even at fifteen, girls loved him, so I trusted what he said. I chose to believe him. So, every day after that, when Erica came over to "watch me," I reminded myself that Justin said it was a good thing. And I just prayed he was right. But I never told anybody else what Erica did to me.

And I never told my father where my mom spent most of her days that summer.

Later that same year, in the fall, Josh, Justin, and I were in our room, watching college football on a Saturday night. My parents were watching TV together in the living room downstairs. All of a sudden, we heard shots. *Boom, boom, boom, boom.* Josh grabbed me and threw me to the floor.

"Get down," he screamed at Justin. "Get away from the window."

Justin didn't move. He just sat there with a strange look on his face. And then he started shaking his head with his eyes closed. "I'm just so tired of all this," he said and stayed seated in his chair, almost as if he thought he could defy the laws of physics and avoid getting hit by a stray bullet by sheer force of will.

I covered my head with my hands and waited for the shots to subside. I heard my parents scrambling around downstairs, and then I heard someone come through the front door, followed by my mother screaming hysterically.

I ran to the top of the stairs and peeked down in the living room and saw Alonzo on our couch, laid out and bleeding. There was blood everywhere, a trail leading from the front door to the couch where my father stood over Alonzo, his hand desperately trying to stop the blood flowing out of the messy gunshot wound on his stomach.

"Jonathan!" Joshua was suddenly behind me. "Get away from there." He pushed me back into our room and surveyed the chaos in the living room below. "Justin, call Jay," he said, barricading himself across the door. "See if he can come get us."

I'll never forget my brother's eyes. I can still see them—years of terror had resurfaced in his eyes.

"What's going on, Josh?" I kept saying. "What's happening?"

Justin threw the phone down on the bed and sank to the floor. Jay had not answered his phone. We were stuck. "I can't take this shit anymore. I have to get out of here," Justin said.

The three of us sat in the room until we heard sirens approaching. Josh and I snuck back to the top of the stairs and watched the police, followed by EMTs, traipse through our living room. First they took Alonzo away in an ambulance, and then the police stood around and questioned my parents.

"We counted four bullet holes on the outside of your house," one of the officers said. "You got kids living here?"

"Yeah," Mom answered.

"Well, ma'am, they could have been killed by one of those bullets. Now, do you want to tell us why you let this man into your house when people were shooting at him?"

"Officer," my father said. "We didn't know what was going on. We heard shots and then the knocking at the door, so we opened up. We saw the man had been shot, and we were just trying to help out."

"It's true," my mother chimed in. "We didn't know who he was."

The next morning, I woke up to find my mom trying to scrub the bloodstains out of the carpet, but they wouldn't budge. Even with the evidence right there underfoot and bullet holes etched into the outside walls of our house, we didn't talk about what happened. Not even when Alonzo got out of the hospital and resumed his business relationship with my parents. We didn't ask, and my parents didn't tell. But I couldn't get the words the police officer said out of my head, *"Your kids could have been shot by one of those bullets,"* and the looks on my brothers' faces haunted me. My parents loved us, but they were willing to sacrifice our safety and well-being for their addiction. And as a child, I didn't understand addiction. I only understood that my parents kept putting our lives in danger.

And it kept getting worse.

My mother was caught stealing checks out of the mailbox of one of our neighbors, who just happened to be the mother of my good friend Khalil. When Khalil's mother discovered what my mother had been doing—because she did it more than once—everyone in the neighborhood found out, too.

"Bitch, I'm calling the cops and your thieving ass is going to jail. Rot in jail and see if I care!" Khalil's mother, Maxine, shouted across the street when she saw my mom coming into the house one day, not long after the shooting incident.

I heard everything from the living room, and I watched my mother rush back into the house, tears already in her eyes as she stood in the living room panting.

"Oh, Lord Jesus, I'm going to jail. They're going to take me to jail. Oh, God, help me."

My father came into the room, "Kim, what's going on?"

Mommy peeled herself off the door and came shuffling into the living room. She fell onto the couch sobbing and shaking.

"Maxine found out about the checks, Pumpkin," she told my father. And then she just kept repeating, "I shouldn't have done it. I shouldn't have done it."

My father looked neither worried nor surprised. "It's going to be okay, Kimmie," he said. "Stop all that crying. You know everything is going to be okay."

Gossip spread fast in Holly Cove, and soon everybody knew what my mother had done. Maxine kept threatening to call the cops on my mother, and every day I waited for the police cars to come and take her away. Like they did with my dad every Friday.

The year before, my father had been arrested and sentenced to four years in prison for driving with a suspended license—multiple times—and unpaid speeding tickets. Because he was the primary breadwinner in the family and had no other criminal offenses on his record, my dad was allowed to serve his time on the weekends. It was called the Weekender Program in Virginia, and it was created to accommodate nonviolent offenders who supported their families with legitimate jobs.

Every Friday, the cops would come to our house with their blue lights flashing, handcuff my dad, put him in the back seat of the car, and drive him off to prison. Monday morning he'd be dropped off at his job, and he'd come home Monday evening like he wasn't a prisoner, just an average dad doing a normal routine. With him behind bars every weekend, though, I felt less safe in our home. He was the man of the house, and he always made it clear that he would protect us with his life. He was tough on us and stoic in demeanor, but that's what a kid wanted in a protector. I know I did. I slept peacefully every night knowing my dad was there to handle anything bad that might happen. But now, on the weekends, that peace was gone.

And now, my mom might be joining him? Since she didn't have a job, I figured she wouldn't get the benefit of the Weekender Program, and Helena and I would be sent to foster care and our family would be destroyed. Mom had always said that the worst possible thing that could happen to our family would be for us kids to be taken away, split up, and sent to foster care. ACS (the Administration for Children's Services) was my childhood boogeyman. I had seen social workers show up unannounced and remove kids, kicking and screaming, from their mother's arms, so I knew the threat was real. And I knew that if my mother were sent to jail, ACS would come for us.

But it never happened. For all of her threats, Khalil's mom never called the cops, which meant the threat of my mother being sent to jail was no longer an issue, but it didn't take away what my mother did. And I couldn't forgive her.

My mom was the one who always told me to keep my mouth shut. To keep what happened in our home in our home. I did my part in maintaining the lie, never talking about all the things that went on in our home. But she didn't do her part. She took her bad behavior and made it public. And worst of all, she did it to one of my best friends.

"Why'd you have to steal from Khalil's mom?" I asked her, my eyes wet with tears. "Khalil is my friend. Or at least he was my friend."

"I'm sorry, Boo Boo." She started crying. "I don't know why I do these things. I'm so sorry."

For the first time, her tears didn't move me.

Nothing felt the same after that. It didn't matter anymore that we were the Conyers family. Jay was at college on a wrestling scholarship. Joshua had given up basketball and started singing opera. He now wore suits every day and his backpack was always stuffed with sheet music. His teachers all said he was really talented. Justin was still a star on the football field. But none of my brothers' good deeds mattered because my parents' bad behavior had been made public. Our perfect family image was gone, and all I wanted to do was disappear. I hated the way people looked at me now, at school and in the neighborhood, knowing who my parents were. I could feel the teachers looking at me with pity. Khalil wouldn't talk to me, and all of our mutual friends knew what happened.

I wanted to leave Virginia, start over where nobody knew our family. I hated the way we lived, but I was okay with it when people believed I came from a good family rather than what we truly were. Lying in my bed at night, I prayed for a way we could just press restart. Start over. Outrun the truth.

My prayers were answered about a year later when an eviction notice appeared on the front door of our home. It wasn't the way I wanted to start over but at least the process had begun. The notice was written with red letters and was big enough for everyone in our neighborhood to see and to know that my parents had failed to pay the rent. "Deadbeats" could now be added to our family's already-soiled reputation. The only thing that kept me moderately sane was knowing that, when we moved, we would be leaving behind all the faces of those who had seen our downfall. If we had to start over, I could go to a new school and find new friends. I could create a new story for myself and pretend that my parents weren't on drugs, that we didn't have to steal water from an abandoned house in the middle of the night, that my mother wasn't a thief and my father didn't have to go to prison on the weekends.

"Where are we going to go now?" I asked my mother that evening.

"I don't know, Boo Boo," she said, "but we'll figure something out." She gave me a little squeeze and said, "You know I always figure something out."

That was true. Even though she and my father were the reason we got evicted, I knew my mother would figure this out. She always did. She was the savior as much as she was a sinner.

My mother went to church to find answers to our housing crisis and befriended a church member with connections. Ms. Denise was only a little bit older than my parents, but she took it upon herself to save everybody's souls. She was the type to invite all the new church members to her home for dinner, and her husband would fry chicken while Ms. Denise read from The Word. It turned out, Ms. Denise was also the property manager at an apartment complex that wasn't too far from Holly Cove. She told my mother she could get us into an apartment if my mom promised to bring us back to church on a regular basis.

Mom agreed and quickly got on the phone to beg her mother to send us the money for the deposit on the new apartment.

"I know it's a lot of money, Ma, but we don't have any other options. They ain't got a shelter system here like they have in New York. You know that. This landlord ain't playing. We have thirty days to get out, so just send the money."

I always assumed my Grandmother Gwen was rich, considering how much money she sent my mother over the years to keep us afloat.

Within thirty days, we left our house with the yellow door in Holly Cove and moved into a two-bedroom apartment in nearby Wellington. Though it wasn't far from Holly Cove, it was far enough that I would have to go to a different school and start over. By this time, Josh had left for college on a full scholarship for singing. So, that left Justin and me to share a room. Helena had her own room, and my parents slept in the living room on an air mattress on the floor. Justin and I had to share a bed, too, which was also just a mattress on the floor. Helena was the only one with an actual bed frame. The few pieces of furniture we brought from the old house were worn and shabby, so the apartment didn't feel like a real home. Which was a good thing, because less than a year after we moved in, we got another eviction notice for failure to pay the rent.

Joshua was furious when he heard about the eviction. I didn't understand his reaction at first. He was visiting from college when we got the notice.

"How could you let this happen?" he hollered at my parents. Josh was the kid in our family with the worst temper, and everyone had always predicted he would end up in trouble with the law, rather than in college on a full-ride opera scholarship. "I sent you all of my refund checks from my school loans because you guys said you needed it to pay the rent and buy furniture for the kids, and y'all smoked it all up? How could you?" he raged, no longer willing to pretend away my parents' habit.

But my father wasn't having it. "Josh, remember who you're talking to," he warned. My father refused to let his children disrespect him. That was always his line in the sand.

"I know who I'm talking to," Josh said. "I'm talking to two of the most selfish people who ever walked the earth. And I'm done with you guys!" And with that, Joshua stormed out of the living room and went outside.

I followed him out and watched him just pace angrily back and forth on the sidewalk outside the building. I waited to see if he would calm down.

Finally, he stopped pacing and came over to me. "I'm so sorry, Jonathan. I really tried to help you and Helena," he said. "I sent them everything I had. Everything..."

It looked like he was going to cry.

"It's okay." I tried to console him. I had no idea he'd sent my parents all of his scholarship money, so it wasn't a loss I ever felt.

"I'm sorry you still have to deal with them, but I can't do this anymore," Josh said to me. "If you need anything from me, just call me, okay."

"Okay," I said, not understanding that Joshua was saying good-bye for a long time. Still, I hugged him extra hard before he left.

My parents never talked about what they did to Josh. Or that he said he was never coming back home. They just concentrated on what was next for the rest of us. And I never said anything about it, either. I had been conditioned not to confront my parents, and I had learned to hide everything, even my feelings, so that from the outside, it looked like I was okay with every-thing. I was used to not rocking the boat. Instead, I found ways to escape. I would just spend time in my imagination, creating a better life than the one I was living. Lucky for me, I found an escape in real life, thanks to a kid named Marcus, who lived in the apartment next door to ours.

Marcus was two years younger than me, but I still liked to play at his house anyway. He and his mother lived in a two-bedroom apartment that looked just like ours, except their apartment had furniture in it and art on the walls. Marcus had the new Nintendo console and all of the latest games, too. Whenever I'd go over there, his mother would buy us pizza and Capri Suns, and she'd ask me how I was and if I had a good day at school. She never cursed, and she didn't smoke. I didn't even like Marcus that much, but I loved his life, and I liked to pretend it was mine. So, I spent as much time as possible over there. After school and on weekends. Even when Justin yelled at me because he thought I was skipping football practice—I joined the team now that I was in middle school—just so I could play video games and eat pizza. He thought I was being lazy.

"Jonathan, you can't be a quitter, or you'll end up like Mom and Dad. You gotta work hard for the things you want," he warned.

Justin didn't realize that what I wanted was to feel like a normal kid, with a normal life, in a clean house with plenty of food, more than I wanted to play football. And if that made me a quitter, then I didn't care.

Once I'd found my comfort zone and great escape, either in my imagination or on Marcus's sofa, my parents announced that we were leaving the great state of Virginia.

They decided that the family would move back to New York City. My mother had been diagnosed with multiple sclerosis, and she needed treatments and medicines she couldn't afford in Virginia. In New York, her medication would be covered by Medicaid, so the decision was practically made for us. I had to leave Marcus and the pizza behind. Since my father still had to serve the rest of his prison sentence, my parents decided that my mother, Justin, Helena, and I would return to New York, and my father would join us as soon as he could.

As the weeks went by, the idea of leaving Virginia didn't bother me as much as I'd thought, until Justin announced that he wasn't coming with us.

"I'm not going to New York," he told my parents one night, a few weeks after they'd announced their decision. "I asked my friend Paul if I could live with him and his family for the rest of the school year, and his parents said yes. So, all you guys have to do is sign these papers of emancipation and then I can be responsible for myself."

He removed some papers from his backpack. Obviously, he had already thought this through and made his plans. Justin had just started his final year of high school. He wasn't willing to start over when college was less than a year away.

My mother wasn't having it. "My kids are staying together. Justin, you come with us to New York. We're a family and families stick together. They got good schools in New York."

Justin shook his head no. "No way. I'm staying here. I'm not moving anymore. I just want to be done. With all of it."

He didn't say, "with all of you," but I wondered if that's what he meant.

My mother started to argue, but my father put his hand up to silence her. "Let it go, Kimmie. If he doesn't want to go to New York, don't make him. Let him finish up here."

"But, Pumpkin, you want him to be down here all by himself?" my mother said.

"I'll still be here for a little while," my father reminded her. "And my mother's here if he needs something that Paul's family can't provide."

"I don't like the idea," Mommy sniffed. "It's not right."

My father sighed like the whole situation made him sad. "I don't like having the family split up, either, Kim, but Justin should be able to finish what he's started here. He's got a good thing going with football, and we can't take that away from him, too."

My mother acted annoyed, but she stopped trying to convince Justin to come with us. Just like that, she gave up! I couldn't believe it. My mother had always argued to keep us together. She said families were supposed to stick together, and yet she wasn't going to fight to keep Justin with us. I couldn't imagine going to New York without Justin. I was used to Jay not being around. But Josh had been gone only a little while, and now I was going to lose Justin, too? Just thinking about it made me feel hollow and cold inside. Like I was losing the warm, beating parts of myself. How was I supposed to survive in New York City without my brothers? How was I supposed to know how to act in a new environment? Who would protect me? Jay, Josh, and Justin were my models of who I was supposed to be. Without them, I would be lost.

These thoughts swirled around in my head, sowing seeds of fear that bloomed into anger. Justin seemed to have no problem leaving me with my parents when he knew what they were capable of doing. I wondered if he even thought about me when he was deciding not to come with us. But because old habits are hard to break, of course, I never asked him about his decision.

With the impending eviction hanging over our heads, my parents' focus turned to packing, buying bus tickets, and getting ready to head back up north. The fact that Helena and I were being pulled out of school before the first semester was even over didn't come up in any of the family discussions, other than when my mother told us that we'd be fine at the schools in the Bronx. "You two will be okay" was the beginning and the end of the discussion. The only person, besides Justin, who didn't think we should move back to New York was my Grandmother Corine. She invited us over for a farewell dinner to try to dissuade my parents from leaving.

"You take those kids back to New York," my grandmother warned my parents as she sat at the head of the dinner table, "they gonna get into drugs. They gonna be in a gang. They gonna be teenage parents. Don't say I didn't try to warn y'all"

My mother cut her eyes at my grandmother but didn't say anything. My father just reached for another piece of chicken and gave his usual response, "Everything will be okay, Ma."

Justin, Helena, and I just kept eating our food because we knew better than to talk back at my grandmother's table. Grandma sucked her teeth and stabbed at a chunk of sweet potato with her fork. "Don't say I didn't try to warn y'all," she repeated. "Mark my words."

On the day before our departure, my father came home from work and called Justin to the front door.

"Yo, Justin, follow me outside," he said. "I got something to show you."

My brother walked with him out of the apartment and to the front of our building. I followed right behind them, and we watched my father walk over to a beat-up, rusty blue car parked by the curb.

"Listen, son," he started, "you're going to need a car down here if you're going to be on your own. This is the best I could get for you, you know, given the circumstances. It's not fancy but the car works."

He handed my brother the keys and said, "I know it can't make up for everything, but I hope it helps." And then my father did something I'd never seen him do. He started to cry. He started to cry right there on the sidewalk, not caring who saw him. "I'm so tired of doing this to you all," he said through his tears. He dropped his head into his hands and continued to carry on, like he was confessing his sins to Jesus. "I'm really sorry I keep doing this. I wanna stop. I really do."

My brother and I looked at each other and then back at our father, who never showed us any real emotion. Never apologized for nothing. Never admitted that he made mistakes. Justin and I didn't know what to do or say. So, we just stood there and watched him spill his regret into the street.

When we arrived in Virginia, we came as a family of seven. When we left, we were only three. My father was trapped by the criminal justice system, but my brothers were free. Each one had followed my parents' advice and put their education first. And sure enough, it was education that gave them their ticket to freedom. Freedom from our family. Freedom from my parents. Freedom from dysfunction, violence, and chaos. They had liberated themselves from dependence on my parents so they could step into the world on their own.

I now had the blueprint for my future.

Justin showed me that, sometimes, you have to save yourself before you can save someone else. And later in his life, Justin would come back to save me. But at the time, his choice to leave us went against everything my mother had convinced me family was. Looking back, I know it hurt my parents to see Justin abandon the family unit, but at the same time, they knew they couldn't provide what he truly needed. Even though their addiction caused so much pain, my parents wanted what was best for their children, even when it meant letting us go so we could save ourselves. Sometimes, a hero has to leave.

Eventually, it would be my turn.

3

I Wasn't Supposed to Be
Set Free in the Bronx

The bus dropped us off in Chinatown in Lower Manhattan, and my mother hailed a gypsy cab that took the three of us up to the Bronx. As soon as we got out of the car in front of the projects where my Grandmother Gwen lived, my whole body tensed up. The air felt cold compared to the warmth we left behind in Chesapeake. The sounds of traffic and the distant rumble of the subway buzzed in the background. Nothing about the Webster Projects felt familiar to me, even though I'd spent much of my earliest years here, before Virginia. But those memories were hazy and jumbled in my mind, so I didn't trust them.

The Webster Projects are made up of six massive twenty-one-story red-brick buildings, connected by concrete pathways and tiny patches of playground space. Technically, my grandmother lives in the Butler Houses on Webster Avenue, but everybody just lumped the Butler Houses and the Webster Houses together, and the whole area was known as the Webster Projects. I tried to conjure up an image of my mother as a teenager running around these same paths, hanging with her girlfriends, meeting my father. My grandmother still lived in the exact same apartment where she'd raised my mother and her four siblings. It occurred to me then, as I took in the discarded plastic bags on the ground and the graffiti on the benches, that despite, or maybe because of, all the money she'd sent to my parents over the years, my grandmother was definitely not living large, as I had thought.

"Come on, Jon, help me with these bags," my mother yelled.

Helena and I grabbed the suitcases and trash bags from the trunk that contained the entire contents of our lives and stood there while my mom paid the driver.

When she was done, Mom led the way to my grandmother's building. I took note of the open bags of trash left near the entrance and the old Latino-looking man in a wheelchair who sat keeping watch at the front door.

"Hey, Scrappy," my mom greeted him like an old friend as we passed by.

Once inside, she turned to me and said, "That's Scrappy. He's paralyzed from the waist down, so don't worry, he's harmless."

"I wouldn't say 'harmless,' Mom," Helena corrected her. "I heard that if you come home too drunk or too high, Scrappy will empty your pockets." Helena spent some of her summers with my grandmother, so she knew the Webster Projects better than I did.

My mom laughed. "That's true. So, you better not come home fucked up, then."

I tried not to stare at Scrappy's legs as we passed by him, but I nodded hello out of respect. I needed someone like him to have my back in this new place, if I ever needed it.

"Come on, Jonathan. These bags are heavy," Mom said.

I raced to catch up.

My grandmother lived on the second floor, but since we had so much stuff to carry, we took the elevator. I held my breath the whole way up so I didn't have to breathe in the stench of what smelled like dried pee and garbage. We stepped off the elevator, and my mother turned to the left and started trudging down a long hallway with yellow-tiled walls and polished-linoleum floors. The fluorescent lights overhead flickered on and off as we made our way down the hall, casting our path in ominous shadows, reflecting my mood.

As soon as we got to my grandma's apartment, my mother barely had time to knock before the door swung open and my Grandmother Gwen was there, with her arms out to hug us, wearing her usual ankle-length denim skirt and long-sleeve shirt.

"Lord, have mercy, y'all made it," she said, taking her time to hug Helena first and then me. It always struck me that, even after living in New York City for over fifty years, my grandmother still retained her southern accent from Spring Hope, North Carolina.

"Hi, Grandma," I said, smiling into her beaming face. She was almost seventy years old, but her smooth, caramel-colored skin was wrinkle-free. It was only her long, gray hair that hinted at her age.

"Look how big you are," Grandma said, taking me all in. "Go on and get you something to eat, boy." She started nudging me toward the kitchen. "I know you're hungry."

I didn't have to be told twice. I knew her refrigerator would be full. She had diabetes and always kept a secret bag of chips, cookies, and candy around in case her sugars got low. So, I headed to the kitchen looking for her stash of snacks. I started opening cabinets but found nothing but a cockroach crawling near a box of crackers, so I turned my attention to the fridge instead. There, I found a slice of lemon cake and some milk and happily helped myself.

When I was done, as Mom got settled in, I went into the back bedroom to say hi to my Aunt Shaunie, who has an intellectual disability and is mute. My mom told me she was like that because she ate lead paint when she was little, so she's lived with my grandmother her whole life. I gave my aunt a gentle hug and she hugged me back, but she made it known that she didn't want me sitting with her, so I headed back into the living room where I found my Uncle Mark. It turned out Uncle Mark was also staying with my grandmother, along with his five kids, bringing the grand total to eleven people sleeping in my grandmother's three-bedroom apartment.

"How you doing, little homie?" my uncle asked, motioning for me to come sit beside him on the plastic-covered blue sofa.

"I'm good," I said, while trying to calculate where we were all going to sleep that night.

My mother was obviously thinking the same thing because she started yelling at my grandma about the limited space.

"You knew we were coming," my mother shouted. "Why would you let Mark and his kids all stay here?"

"Kimmie, Mark is my child, too, and he has the same right to stay here as you do," my grandmother said. "Now, we'll figure something out. The Lord always provides a way."

"Is the Lord going to provide us with an extra bedroom?" my mother responded, her hands on her hips. "Helena and Jonathan need to have a place to sleep, Ma. They gotta start school."

"Well, if it's too crowded for you, Kimmie, you better put yourself in the system and get on the list for housing as soon as you can," my grandmother said. "You know you guys always have a place here, but with all of your medical problems you gotta start doing things right. That's why you came back up here, ain't it?"

"I know, Ma," my mother snapped. "I just didn't realize we were going to be so crowded up in here while I tried to get us settled." She glared at my uncle.

"Sorry, Kimmie," my uncle said, shrugging his shoulders. "You know I don't want to be here right now, but times is tough, you know. But me and the kids will be outta here in a couple days. We're just waiting until our new place is ready."

Mom rolled her eyes.

Since I didn't want to watch a fight, I eased my way out of the room and went to find Helena. This new start in New York wasn't turning out like I'd hoped for. Everything felt messy and confusing. I missed Justin, and there was no place quiet to be alone in my grandmother's apartment. I felt like that little ball in a pinball machine, bumping up against the boundaries of my grandmother's apartment and not finding any place to land. And there was nobody to help me figure it out. As troubling and chaotic as our life in Virginia was, I knew who I was supposed to be. I was the youngest kid in the Conyers family. I was Jay, Josh, and Justin's little brother. And I didn't have to do much to play that role—other than do what my brothers told me to do and keep the family's business to myself. But now the family was all split apart. My brothers were gone, and we didn't even have a place to call our own.

That night, as I struggled to fall asleep on a pallet made of blankets on the living room floor, I allowed the tears that had been threatening to fall all day finally come out and soak the pillow underneath my head. But I didn't allow myself to cry aloud because I didn't want my sister to hear me. I knew she was sad, too. She missed her friends and her boyfriend back in Virginia. But Helena's way of dealing with things was to curse out everybody who wronged her and then move on. She didn't spend a lot of time feeling sorry for herself, and she told me to do the same. I promised her I would try, but so far it wasn't working. All I wanted was somebody to assure me that everything was going to be okay in New York. All I wanted was somebody to tell me how I was going to survive in this big, crazy city. All I wanted was somebody to tell me what version of Jonathan Conyers I was supposed to be now.

Three days later, I was dressed in khaki pants and a navy blue polo shirt, walking by myself to my new middle school, M.S. 219. The school was only a few blocks away from the Webster Projects, and my mother and I had walked the short distance together the day before to register me for sixth grade. Even still, I was nervous. I silently cursed Justin. He should have moved with us and been here to walk me to school on my first day. But he wasn't here and no amount of wishing was going to make him appear.

I arrived at M.S. 219's massive red brick building on Third Avenue. The school takes up almost an entire city block because it houses not just M.S. 219, but also two other schools—another middle school and a high school. When I walked into the school, I was greeted by two uniformed security guards who ushered me through a metal detector and then patted me down to make sure I wasn't carrying any weapons. Their hands on my body felt like a violation. I felt like I was walking into a jail instead of school.

The Black guard gave me a nod and told me to go straight to the cafeteria, where I could get breakfast and wait for the bell to ring. "Yes, sir," I said as I picked my book bag off the table.

I walked slowly down the long hallway, passing classrooms and the school's administrative offices. I couldn't stop myself from comparing everything to the way things were in Virginia. In Virginia, all of my schools were in large, modern buildings and space was never an issue in suburban Chesapeake. We had plenty of room for our academic buildings and sports fields, without having to share. Everything I saw here looked crowded and old. But I tried to keep an open mind.

When I got to the doors of the cafeteria, I had to brace myself for whatever awaited me on the other side. "You can do this, Jonathan," I whispered quietly to myself. "It's just a cafeteria."

I pulled open the doors and was greeted by a rush of noise. It took a minute for my ears to recognize the sing-songy sound of Spanish being spoken, mixed in with the staccato rhythms of the New York City accent. Everyone was talking at fast-forward speeds. I studied the scene for a moment, trying to determine who was in charge, but the only adults I saw seemed to be too busy talking to each other to care about what was happening with me. Kids were seated at tables and on the tables, some kids were running around the room, and the older kids were huddled in groups along the perimeter, talking.

I stayed rooted in one spot without making any attempt to wade into the madness. Everyone was wearing the required uniform of khaki pants and a blue shirt. But I couldn't believe these were only sixth, seventh, and eighth graders. Some of the boys had full beards, and some of the girls had the bodies of grown women. But that wasn't the only thing that stood out to me. As I looked around the room, I realized that what was visually different between this school and my school back in Virginia was that there were no white people in sight. No white kids. No white teachers. No white cafeteria workers. Coming from Chesapeake, where the student body at my school was fifty/fifty white and Black, and most of the teachers were white, it felt strange to be surrounded only by Black and brown people in a school setting. Technically, I should have felt more at ease surrounded by my people, but everything was so intense, matching skin tones wasn't enough to put me at ease. I felt like I had stepped into an entirely different world where the kids talked different. They looked different. They moved different. And to my country ears, it sounded like somebody had turned up the volume and intensity level on everything. I felt like that country mouse in that kids' book who was dropped into the big city and overwhelmed by everything he heard and saw.

And just like that little mouse, all I wanted to do was turn around and run back to my grandmother's apartment. Actually, I wanted to run all the way back to Virginia, back to a life that I understood, but then I remembered that that life didn't exist anymore. It had been destroyed by my parents, and there was nothing I could do about it. So, this was my life now.

With a deep sigh, I pushed aside my thoughts of escape, went to grab a carton of milk, found a seat at an empty table, and sat down. The smell of weed, sweat, and industrial disinfectant hovered in the air. As I sipped from my milk carton, I tried not to make eye contact with anybody.

Then, I noticed a girl squinting her eyes and looking me up and down. She approached my table and asked my name and where I was from. I told her and, suddenly, a look of recognition crossed her face.

"Wait a minute, did you used to go to P.S. 55 and you had long hair?" she said.

"Yeah," I said as the memories flooded back. In kindergarten in the Bronx the kids had teased me about my hair because my mother refused to cut it, claiming I had good hair and should show it off.

"Boy, I remember you," the girl said, and for a moment I wondered if the teasing would resume. Thankfully, it didn't. The girl told me her name was Chantal and she called her friends Sherida and Tiffany over who remembered me, too. They started talking about my hair and my southern accent. "Your accent is cute, V-A," Chantal said, and as more kids came over, they all started calling me that: V-A. The nickname would stick.

The bell rang soon after, and we were released from the

cafeteria and sent to our classrooms. I gathered my things and joined the river of students exiting the room.

My homeroom teacher's name was Mrs. Green, and she welcomed me to her class and told me to find a seat. I stared at the desks in front of me, most of them with students already in them, and wrestled with the decision of where to sit. I knew that simple act could set the tone for the rest of the year.

Thankfully, I didn't have to make the choice on my own because a kid came up to me and threw his arm around my shoulders and said, "Yo, what up, V-A? You from Virginia, right, bro?"

"Yeah," I said.

"That's fire, bro," the boy said, looking me over as if he was trying to figure out what kind of kid I was. Whatever he was trying to assess, I obviously passed because he steered me toward the back of the room and said, "Yo, you with me now, V-A. You can hang with the gang."

He showed me a desk and told me to sit, and then he slid into the desk alongside me. "My name is Marquise," he said, and then he pointed to two other boys. "That's Omari, and that's Shaun. They cool, too."

I looked at Omari and Shaun. Omari was about my height, with light skin and a round baby face. He had a big diamond in his left ear. Shaun was at least a foot taller than me and had cornrows that reached down his back. Later, I found out that Shaun was fourteen and should have been in eighth grade, but he had been held back twice because he couldn't read.

I turned my attention to Marquise, then. He was shorter than me and had a spark of mischief in his eyes. Just from the way he moved around the room, it was clear to me that Marquise was a confident kid and the other students all seemed to like him, so I wasn't sure why he wanted to be my friend. My survival instincts kicked in as I tried to figure out if Marquise was just being nice or if he was messing with me. I wasn't sure yet if he seemed like the kind of guy I wanted to align myself with. But, according to the teacher, that's exactly what I shouldn't do.

"Hey, new boy," Mrs. Green shouted over the noise of the classroom. "You better not sit with them bad motherfuckers! You'll be in trouble before the day is over." I whipped my head around in shock and just stared at Mrs. Green. Did she just curse in front of the whole class—and diss a kid at the same time? I stole a glance at my fellow classmates to see if anyone else was as shocked as I was by our teacher's behavior, but nobody seemed to even notice or care. Not even Marquise.

"Come on, Mrs. Green," Marquise said, his hand over his heart like he'd been wounded. "Why you gonna do me like that? I thought we were cool. I thought we were family."

Mrs. Green rolled her eyes and shuffled over to her desk. "Marquise, please."

And then she pointed a finger in my direction. "Don't say I didn't warn you."

"Yes, ma'am," I said, stealing a glance at Marquise, who was now busy laughing with Omari and Shaun.

Before I could decide whether I should get up and find another place to sit, Mrs. Green told everybody to stand up for the Pledge of Allegiance.

Everybody stood slowly and without a whole lot of enthusiasm. A scratchy noise came over the PA system followed by the voice of a woman who told us to pledge allegiance to the United States of America. As I recited the words, my right hand on my chest, I checked out the other twenty-nine kids in the classroom. Some of them were reciting the words like me, some were talking to their friends, and some just stood there staring out the window. Marquise and his friends didn't even bother to stand up. None of that would have been tolerated at my school in Virginia, where allegiance to the flag was almost as important as allegiance to football.

It took another five minutes after the pledge was over to get everybody to stop talking, and then Mrs. Green went over to the board and started writing instructions for what we were supposed to read in our language arts textbooks. But before she could begin explaining the lesson, the door swung open and a tall Black man with a fresh cut and designer glasses sauntered into the room. My first thought was that this man, who looked to be in his fifties or sixties, with his crisp dress pants, button-down shirt, and flashy jewelry, looked like Denzel Washington's older brother. Before I could lean over and ask someone who he was, he bellowed at the top of his voice, "Who's ready?"

"We are!" everybody screamed back.

Mrs. Green rolled her eyes and sat down at her desk with a sigh of resignation.

Marquise leaned over and whispered to me with a grin, "Get ready, bro, shit's about to get crazy because we're about to do the pledge. Mr. Marshall is the man."

"I thought we just did the pledge," I whispered back.

Mr. Marshall's voice pulled me back to attention.

"Ya'll ready to do the *real* pledge?" Mr. Marshall shouted, sounding every bit like a preacher praising the Holy Ghost.

"Yeahhhh!" everyone in the class yelled back.

"Then, stand up, let's go," Mr. Marshall said, planting himself in front of Mrs. Green's desk.

Everybody stood up, and I waited to see what was about to happen.

"I will NOT do drugs!" Mr. Marshall barked at the top of his lungs like a drill sergeant.

All the kids in the class shouted back at him. "I will not do drugs!"

"I WILL go to college," his pledge continued, and the students repeated after him.

"I will take care of MY neighborhood, MY community, and MY family."

Mr. Marshall's pledge went on like this, where he extolled the virtues he obviously felt we needed, and the kids parroted it all back to him. Even Marquise, Omari, and Shaun were laser focused on Mr. Marshall. Spitting his affirmations back to him.

I started to feel the energy and joined in the chanting.

"I will BE somebody!" Mr. Marshall said as his final maxim.

And all the students responded, "Because I AM somebody!"

"That's what I'm talking about," Mr. Marshall concluded with a clap of his hands and nod to us all. And then, inexplicably, he yelled, "Like hot buttered popcorn!"

And every kid yelled back, "Like hot buttered popcorn!" and then Mr. Marshall pulled a bag of popcorn out of his jacket pocket and said, "Pow! Like that!" And he calmly started to munch on his popcorn. And that's when the class exploded into laughter and shouts of triumph, high-fiving each other and pumping fists like it was game day.

"Alright, then," Mr. Marshall drawled, "you children have a blessed day." And he walked out of the classroom, leaving Mrs. Green with a room full of superhyped students to get back in order.

Everyone was laughing and talking about crazy Mr. Marshall, while I tried to figure out what I had just witnessed. And what did hot buttered popcorn have to do with anything?

Everything about M.S. 219 was different from Western Branch Middle School in Chesapeake. School in Virginia had always been the place where I could expect structure and discipline. It was the antidote to all the chaos at home. But at my new school, Mrs. Green spent a lot of time just trying to get the kids to stop talking, stop fighting, or stop walking around the classroom. Everything felt out of control, and unsafe, on the first day.

When Mrs. Green called on me to read from the textbook, and I made it through my two paragraphs without stumbling over any of the big words, Marquise slapped me on the back and said, "Yo, V-A is smart." He did the same thing again when I answered a math question correctly later in the day. "Go 'head, V-A."

I wasn't sure if he was making fun of me, so I just kept my antennae up as I tried to get through the day without making a fool of myself, or making any enemies.

When the bell rang, signaling the school day was over, I felt like I had been holding my breath the whole time. I walked out of the building, heading back to the Webster Projects, and finally let myself exhale.

Two weeks after arriving in the Bronx, my mother, Helena, and I had to leave my grandmother's apartment. In order to get all the government assistance we needed, food stamps, Medicaid, and our own apartment, we had to let the city of New York know we were officially homeless, which meant moving into the shelter system. Staying at my grandmother's apartment would suggest we had other options for housing and we'd never be prioritized for getting our own place. Only after they processed our case would we be put on the list for government-subsidized housing. Although I enjoyed being surrounded by family and knowing there would always be food in the refrigerator, hot water for showers, and electricity and heat, the prospect of getting our own place was very attractive to me. But the closer we got to moving out, the less excited I got.

I could tell my mother was getting nervous about the whole thing. She was agitated and picking more fights with my grandmother than usual. On the Saturday morning when we were due to leave, my grandmother got up early and made us pancakes and sausages and demanded we eat.

"Ya'll need to put something in your stomachs before you go," she said, acting like we were taking a long trip instead of going down to a government office for assistance.

"Ma, we don't got time to eat. The earlier we get there, the faster we get waited on," my mom said.

My grandmother pushed Helena and me to sit at the kitchen table and forced us to eat anyway. "Ya'll better eat some of this food I made. Lord knows, I can't afford to be wasting good food."

"Jesus, Ma," my mom said, but she sat down, too, and ate quickly, telling Helena and me between bites to hurry up. I barely had time to wipe the syrup off my lips before my mother shuffled us back to the bedroom to pick up the black trash bags with all of our stuff—clothes and the few things that mattered to us. I had my anatomy book my Grandmother Corine had bought me. Helena had pictures of her friends from Virginia.

"Come on," my mom yelled. "Let's go!"

My grandma rode the elevator down with us, and she hailed us a gypsy cab. She stood on the side of the curb and watched as we all slid into the back seat of the car. The night before, I had been excited to get out of the projects, but looking at the worry on my grandmother's face made me worry now, too.

"It's going to be alright." My grandmother leaned into the window of the back of the car.

"Bye, Ma," my mother said as she pushed the button to roll up the window.

As the car pulled away, I watched my grandmother turn and head back to her building.

Getting "into the system" to get an affordable apartment in New York City requires a lot of sitting and waiting. But there aren't enough chairs for all the people who need an apartment in New York, so Helena and I sat on the floor in a corner of the waiting room while we watched our mother sign paperwork, go outside to smoke cigarettes, sign more paperwork, and then sit like everybody else, waiting for someone to call her back up and tell her what the next steps in this process would be.

Everybody in that sterile waiting room with beige plastic chairs and a linoleum floor was just like us. Waiting for a place to live. But most of them seemed more in need than we were. I mean, we had just left my grandmother's apartment and had pancakes. Helena showered before we left, and my grandmother made sure my shirt was pressed so we "didn't look like we came from nothing," she said.

Kids in that room had holes in their pants. There were adults wearing, what looked like, every piece of clothing they owned. I knew we were poor—that had been clear to me my entire life— but the people waiting with us made me feel like we'd been living large. We had lived in a house in Virginia. We weren't really homeless like the people who lived on the streets, carrying their belongings in grocery carts. Our homelessness was more of a technicality. It didn't define us. I didn't think we were *that* poor. In some ways, I still believed in the fairy-tale version of our family that my parents had spun for us. We were a normal family. I didn't think we belonged here.

"How long do we gotta sit here and wait?" I whined after what felt like hours.

"I don't know, Jonathan," my mother snapped. "All I know is that we gotta sit here until they find us somewhere to go," she said.

She stood up then. "I gotta go smoke a cigarette, but they got sandwiches in the other room. Why don't you guys go get you something to eat."

Helena turned up her nose. "What kind of sandwiches?"

"Listen, Ms. Thing. I don't know what they're serving," my mother answered. "This ain't no restaurant. But if you're hungry, go on over there and find out. But take your brother. Don't leave him by hisself. And take your bags with you, otherwise they might not be here when you get back."

"Come on," Helena said to me as she stood up. "Let's go."

Anything was better than sitting on the cold, hard floor, so I followed my sister to where they had a table with brown paper lunch bags and crates with milk.

"Y'all want a sandwich?" a Black lady with an Afro streaked with gray asked us. She was standing behind the table handing out lunch bags to anyone who asked for one.

"What kind are they?" Helena asked.

"We got ham or bologna," the woman said.

My sister took a bag with a ham sandwich, and I took bologna.

There still weren't any seats, so we went back to our corner and ate our sandwiches on the floor.

The sun had already set when we finally arrived at our temporary apartment after an entire day of sitting and waiting. My mother had tried to explain how the system worked while we were riding in the van that ferried us across the city, but I was too tired to take in the details. What I understood was that this place, where we would be sleeping tonight, would not be our permanent home.

We were dropped off in front of a building somewhere in

Manhattan, in a neighborhood I didn't know. From the outside, it was just a brick building. Once we were inside, though, it was clear we had stepped into government property. Just like at my school, we were greeted by a security guard, and my mother had to sign us in at the front desk.

I stood close to my mother while she put her name on more forms. I read all the signs plastered on the walls behind the desk: No smoking. No alcohol. No visitors. No drugs. No weapons. No profanity. There were also signs reminding residents always to sign in and sign out and that curfew was at 9 p.m. The guard said we had to be inside the building by 9 p.m., or we wouldn't be allowed in for the night. Then, he gave my mother her key and wished us a good night.

When we got up to our apartment on the third floor, my mother opened the door slowly, peeked her head in, and exclaimed, "Oh, this is nice!"

Helena and I walked in behind my mother and took it all in. It was one room, set up like a hotel room. There was a double bed, a couch, and a small table with a chair.

My mother walked around and checked out the bathroom. "Y'all, this place is real nice. Much better than a lot of the other places I've had to stay in, for sure."

Helena and I just stared at her. I don't know what my sister was thinking, but living in one room with three people did not seem nice to me. But I knew better than to open my mouth and say that out loud.

"Y'all put down your stuff." My mother laughed at us. "And be happy ya'll have a decent place to sleep tonight. It could have been much worse. Y'all motherfuckas don't even know." She walked around the room once more. "Hey, Boo Boo," she said to me, "at least they don't got no roaches," and then she busted out laughing.

Two days later, on Monday morning, my mother didn't think our little hotel room apartment was so nice anymore because she had to get up at the crack of dawn and take two buses and the subway to get me back to school up in the Bronx.

After a week of doing that, my mother was pissed. "This is some bullshit," she said when she came to pick me up, and we had to reverse the process to go home. "I'm going back to the housing office and telling them they have to get us something in the Bronx. I can't keep doing this every damn day," she huffed.

I don't know if it was because she went to complain or if that's just the way the process worked, but within a couple weeks, we had to leave our little shelter apartment in Midtown and move into another temporary place. But we still didn't make it back to the Bronx. We just kept getting shuffled around from one shelter in Manhattan to another. Some of them were closer to my school, or at least closer to a bus that would take me directly to school. Sometimes, my mother would put me on the bus by myself; sometimes, she would come with me. After a while, my mother decided that if the shelter was just too far from my school, anything that required more than a single subway or bus ride, she would let me stay with my grandmother. It was technically illegal for me not to stay with my mom in the shelter system, but my mom said she didn't care. "Stupid rules are meant to be broken, Boo Boo," Mommy said. "You're better off at your grandmother's than at a shelter anyway."

I knew my mom was trying her best to get Helena and me settled. So, I didn't tell her I was scared to ride the bus by myself. And I didn't tell her that I was scared to stay at the Webster Projects without her, too. I also didn't mention that my school sucked. I didn't think my mother had space to handle my fears and issues along with everything else weighing her down. Sometimes, I'd come home from school and she'd be crying, saying she was sorry she'd done this to us. "Ya'll know it's only because I got multiple sclerosis that we had to come back to New York, right," she'd say tearfully. "I didn't want to make you and Helena have to live like this," she'd add, pulling me into a hug. And I'd hug her back and tell her it was okay because I didn't want her multiple sclerosis to get worse. I was the one who had seen her falling for no reason in Virginia, and I was the one who had to help her turn on the stove and open jars when her fingers would get stuck and wouldn't move right. I was the one she showed her brain scans to, the ones with the big white holes where pieces of her brain were supposed to be.

I wanted my mother to get to the doctor and take care of herself. I wanted the doctors to take her pain away. I also secretly hoped that the doctors would tell her she had to stop smoking crack and that she'd listen to them because, being away from my father, I thought my mother might actually be able to quit. And then if she got clean, she would leave my father, and we could finally live in peace.

"You don't have to worry about me, Mommy," I said. "I can handle myself."

And that made her smile. "That's my Boo Boo," she said. "You so grown. I know I can always count on you."

Inside, I didn't feel grown, not by a long shot, but New York was the kind of place that forced you to grow up. Ready or not.

"Yo, Jon," Marquise said to me as we were leaning against the playground fence at recess. "You see that girl over there standing next to Sherida, with the long braids?"

"Yeah," I said.

"I'm gonna fuck her before the year is over, you watch."

Before I could get my mask of indifference firmly in place, Marquise peeped my shock.

"What's a matter, nigga, you ain't never fucked a girl yet?"

"Look at his face." Omari jumped in laughing. "Jon, you still a virgin, man?"

I felt my cheeks burn hot. I didn't know what to say. After what happened with Erica, I wasn't sure if I was a virgin. And I wasn't about to ask Marquise and them to help me figure it out. That was a secret I wasn't sharing with anyone. And, in the meantime, I wasn't thinking about having sex with anyone in my class. We were too young. And I didn't think any girl looked at me *that* way. I was chubby and still had a baby face at twelve. The whole conversation made me uncomfortable, but I tried to act like I was cool with it.

Once again, Marquise came to my rescue. He put his arm around my shoulders and said, "It's okay, V-A, you stick with us, and you'll definitely get some by the end of sixth grade. We got you, bro."

"But listen," Shaun interrupted, "V-A, you gotta stop all that southern hospitality with these hoes. Sherida gonna be pregnant by the ninth grade. She a hoe, and you need to stay away from girls like that."

"Aight," I said, smiling on the outside, while something inside of me felt like it was twisting in my guts. I was getting used to that feeling, the more I hung out with Marquise and his friends. I was slowly learning the rules of the South Bronx, with the first one being learning not to care. Or maybe it was just acting like you don't care—about anything. That's how you protected yourself from getting hurt. The other thing I learned was that humor was an excellent way to make people ignore their pain. My mother always said I talked too much, and my elementary school teachers always called me a class clown, so I used that to my advantage and eased my way into Marquise's crew with my mouth and my jokes.

Marquise always had jokes, too, and he could make anybody laugh. In the classroom, in the cafeteria, and on the basketball courts after school, Marquise was always on. Even the teachers couldn't help themselves sometimes and laughed at Marquise's antics, even as they were sending him out of the room for being disruptive. We had fun together, and I liked hanging with him and his friends because everybody respected Marquise.

But there was another version of Marquise that I discovered, too. A quieter more somber version. Marquise's mom wasn't around, and he never met his father, so he lived with his uncle. They lived just a few blocks away from the Webster Projects, so on the days when I was staying with my grandma, Marquise and I would walk home together and talk. I never told him I stayed with my grandmother because we were homeless. I never told him my parents smoked crack. But Marquise understood my silences, and I understood his. Especially after his uncle came to school one day because Marquise got caught stealing somebody's lunch money. His uncle showed up, came into Mrs. Green's room, and smacked the shit out of Marquise in front of the whole class. "And your Black ass better not even think about stealing from anyone again," he said before leaving the room. Marquise sat there after his uncle left, his eyes glassy with tears he refused to release, but with a blank expression that said he couldn't care less about what had just happened. He had that trick down perfectly.

It was a trick I was still learning to master. The blank expression when something is tearing you up inside. Acting like you don't care when all you want to do is scream and cry and beg for something different or something better. Sometimes, I wished I didn't have to learn these tricks. I wished I really could be indifferent about the things my parents did. To us. And to themselves. But I couldn't. It still hurt every time. So, I resolved to get better at pretending. I had to because certain things were never going to change.

My mother was still smoking crack in New York. I knew because, after years of watching her get high with my father, I recognized the signs—how her voice changed and how she moved in her body when she was high. But now, instead of smoking in front of Helena and me, and running the risk of getting us kicked out of whatever shelter we were currently staying in, she'd go to her friend Carmen's house to smoke. She'd do it when we were at school or on weekends if we were out playing with friends. It was weird that my mother wanted to hide her habit now, after all the years of doing it in our faces, but it did make it easier for all of us to act like things were going to get better.

I don't know if I was pretending or hoping. Sometimes, on the nights in the shelter when it was cold and there was no heat, and it was dark because lights-out was enforced by turning off all the lights in the apartments, I would lie in my bed and allow myself to hope that our next placement would be the permanent one. Sometimes, I would imagine the apartment we would get would be as big as my grandmother's in the Webster Projects, with three bedrooms, but it would be in a nice neighborhood where I could go outside and play without worry about getting into a fight or something popping off. And there would be a good school in the neighborhood that I could walk to and learn things about science and history, rather than what was happening at M.S. 219, which was basically nothing as far as academics went. I didn't know this at the time, but less than 10 percent of the student body at M.S. 219 was performing at grade level for math, and only 12 percent could read at grade level. I didn't have those statistics in front of me, but it was obvious that the education I was receiving was nowhere near the quality I'd had in Chesapeake. I was now getting all A's at school because most of the work we were doing in class, I had already done in fourth grade in Virginia.

There were so many doubts and worries and questions in my head about school. About my friendships. About girls. About the effects of crack on multiple sclerosis. But I kept my worries to myself because I didn't want to be the kid who was a burden. My mom needed me to be grown, and that's what I was going to continue to be. But I was raising myself, and I was worried about that, too. Maybe, if I had just opened my mouth and talked to my mother and shared just a little bit of what was on my mind, she could have stepped in and helped me sort things out. Make some better decisions. Choose a different path. But I didn't say anything to my mom. I told her everything was fine when she asked. And that's why things happened the way they did.

One Friday afternoon after school, Marquise and I were standing on the corner of 167th Street trying to decide which courts to go to to shoot hoops, even though it was too cold to be playing outside. But we didn't have anywhere else to be. And nobody was waiting for us at home.

I started to suggest we go to the courts by my grandmother's apartment so we could get a snack or maybe even dinner afterward. My grandmother was always happy to feed me, and she didn't mind if I brought Marquise with me. Especially when I told her that Marquise was lucky if he got a bag of potato chips for dinner. She warned me that Marquise was a little too street-wise for her taste, but he'd gotten on her good side by agreeing to let her read him Bible stories whenever he came over.

"What do you think?" I said to Marquise.

Rather than answer me, Marquise turned and looked at the commotion across the way. Two guys were yelling at each other, and things were getting heated.

"Damn," I said to Marquise, "brothers always gotta be fighting about something."

"Yeah," Marquise said, but he wasn't really paying attention to me, his eyes were fixed on the fight.

"You think it's about a girl or something?" I said, trying to sound like I knew something. "My brothers always told me never to let a girl—" but before I could finish my sentence, Marquise yelled at me to get down.

"They got guns, Jon!" And with that, Marquise tackled me to the ground and pulled me over behind a parked car where we'd be protected from the bullets now flying through the air.

I covered my head with my hands, but my mind went blank, and that's when I felt Marquise put his whole body over mine, protecting me with his life. Like my life was more important than his. I felt tears in my eyes, and I prayed to Jesus as hard as I could to save me. To save us.

When the shooting finally stopped, Marquise stood up and peered around the side of the car. "Come on, Jon, those dummies are both running scared down the block." He reached his hand down and helped me up. He turned to look at me and joked, "Damn, them niggas don't even know how to shoot." And then, without missing a beat, he said, "You still wanna play ball?"

I knew I was supposed to jump up off the ground and laugh with Marquise. I knew I wasn't supposed to be shook by the fact that we could have died standing on the corner minding our own business. I wasn't supposed to care. But I did. I almost peed my pants. I wanted to cry. I wanted to talk about what happened. I wanted a grown-up. I wanted someone to hug me and tell me it would be okay, but Marquise had already moved on, so I pushed my feelings down and moved on, too. Or at least I pretended to.

"Yeah, let's go play," I said. "I'll race you to the courts."

That night, I didn't tell my mother about almost getting shot. She wouldn't have anything to say about it anyway. Not because she didn't care, but because, that day, she'd messed up her medications for her MS and was knocked out on the couch. This had happened a couple of times as she tried to get used to all the different pills she had to take. Helena was staying at her friend's house, so I tried to call Justin to tell him what happened, but he didn't answer his phone. So, I sat in my bed and tried to figure out what I was supposed to do with the fear that was still pulsing throughout my body. How was I supposed to get up the next day and go out and act like I was going to be safe when I now had hard proof that I could get shot just standing on the corner?

"Don't be a follower, be a leader, Boo Boo" is what my mother always told me. "Don't let anyone make you do anything you ain't wanna do," she'd say. And I had never had a problem with doing my own thing. But after almost losing my life for no reason other than being in the wrong place at the wrong time, I decided it was time to be a follower. I needed to follow Marquise and do whatever he told me to do. He was the only reason I hadn't gotten shot. I would have never seen those bullets coming and wouldn't have known to get under that car. I needed someone to look out for me and show me how to survive. My mother wasn't reliable. My brothers weren't around. And my father was serving time in Virginia.

It was now crystal clear to me that being smart and doing sports weren't going to keep me safe or alive in the South Bronx. Those rules were outdated and irrelevant in my new reality. Instead of trying to be like my brothers, I realized I needed to be like Marquise. I needed to stop caring about so many things. I needed to stop being afraid. I needed to toughen up. I wanted people to respect me like they respected Marquise, and that meant I had to prove myself worthy of respect.

That night, I fell asleep resolved to change my focus. I was going to model myself after Marquise to give myself the best chance of surviving the circumstances where I now found myself. Looking back on my life now, this would be the point when I intentionally started to assemble my village, when I started looking beyond my family members for guidance on how to live my life, to guarantee the best possible outcome. To survive.

Not too long after the shooting, I got my first chance to prove I could be like Marquise. In front of an audience of my peers. During recess, a kid came up to Marquise, pointing at me, and said, "Yo, I wanna fight your boy."

Fighting at recess meant one thing, slap-boxing. Just like it sounds, slap-boxing uses the principles of boxing, but you slap your opponent in the face instead of punching him. Even though I had participated in my fair share of fights in Virginia, in the Bronx, I quickly realized a fistfight could easily turn into a shoot-out or getting your face slashed with a knife. But in the schoolyard at M.S. 219, where the options for recess were limited to basketball and talking trash, slap-boxing was considered an acceptable playground sport. The teachers didn't bother to intervene, so I figured this was my moment.

But Marquise answered for me. "Nah, he don't fight," he said, eyeing the kid who was in the seventh grade. He was taller than me by a few inches. Up until this point, Marquise had appointed himself my protector, but I was ready to show him— and everybody else watching—that I could protect myself.

"It's okay, I'll fight," I said.

"You don't have to do this, bro," Marquise said. "It don't mean nothing."

"Nah, I'm good, bro. I can handle this," I said, sizing the kid up.

I felt Marquise look at me with fresh eyes. "You deadass, bro! Let's go," Marquise said, clapping me on the back.

A few kids were already standing around, and now a few more gathered as they waited to watch us fight.

The other kid stared at me and probably thought, because I was fat, that I couldn't move much. But I was light on my feet. And my father had taught me how to use my hands appropriately. Fast and quick.

As soon as Marquise gave the signal to begin, I smacked the other kid across his right cheek. *Crack!* He never saw my hand coming.

And then I followed up with another whack on the left cheek before he had time to recover.

"Oh, shit, Jon's hands is different!" Marquise hollered, and the kids all around us whooped in approval.

Pumped up on their praise, I went in for one more slap, and I tapped the kid on his forehead. But then I put my hands down. I clearly won and didn't need to prove anything else. I ran a quick circle of triumph with my arms up in the air like Rocky Balboa.

"Yo, bro, I had no idea you could move like that," Marquise shouted with glee. "You smart, and you can fight, yo! That's dope!"

Omari and Shaun also started running around the yard gassing me up, shouting, "Our boy Jon studies all day and fights crime at night!" Marquise joined in their chanting. "Jon is the head ass nigga!"

I didn't often thank my dad for much, but as I stood there on the playground that day listening to these kids big me up, I gave thanks for those afternoon boxing lessons in Virginia. I knew my dad wasn't a role model I wanted to follow as far as parenting was concerned, but I was happy to follow in his footsteps when it came down to whipping somebody's ass.

My father resurfaced in January. He finished serving his prison sentence and came back to New York so we could be a family again. That's what my mom said to Helena and me when we came home and saw our father sitting on the couch in our apartment, like he had always been there. We had finally gotten a long-term shelter apartment in the Bronx. Rather than having to move every couple of weeks, we were allowed to stay for at least six months while we looked for an affordable government-subsidized apartment. Our apartment was tiny, but it actually had a separate bedroom with two twin beds for Helena and me. My mother slept in the living room on the couch. We had just gotten settled in, and things had been pretty calm for the three of us, so I wasn't exactly thrilled to see my father. I could only imagine what his presence would mean for the fragile peace we'd constructed. Especially in such a tiny space.

Within days of arriving, my dad found a job washing dishes at a restaurant. What that meant was that he could now come home on payday, and he and my mother could resume their Friday night fun together. Crack was so convenient in New York, just like the corner bodegas. It was cheap and easy to find, so there were no limits to their "fun," except the size of my father's paycheck. It was just like in Virginia, only this time, there was no upstairs for Helena and me to escape to, just three hundred square feet of space for us to watch them smoke away any dreams we had of ever getting to a better life.

And then, it got worse.

THWACK! The sound pulled me out of my dreams.

"Pumpkin, I said I was sorry. What else do you want me to do?"

"You not sorry, Kim!"

And then I heard the unmistakable sound of my father's fists making contact with my mother's body. Again.

I looked over at my sister in her bed and saw she held her pillow tightly over her head.

I did the same and tried to ignore the sound of what had become a nightly ritual ever since my father found out my mother had cheated on him with Alonzo, in Virginia. I don't know how he found out, but when he confronted her about it a couple weeks after he got back, she admitted it was true. And now, my father decided to punish my mother on a regular basis for her infidelity.

When it first started, Helena told me to ignore them. "They gonna fight, and Mommy's never going to leave him, so we can't do nothing."

But I couldn't do nothing when I could hear my mom

screaming in pain. So, I threw off my covers, ran into the living room, and did what Marquise had done for me. I threw my body over my mother's and begged my father to stop beating her. My father would hit my mother, but he rarely laid a hand on us kids. So, he walked away from the both of us and quietly left the apartment.

I felt my mother trembling beneath me. Her cries had subsided, but she was breathing heavy, and her tears soaked through my pajamas. So did the blood dripping from her mouth.

"Why did he have to come back?" I cried to my mother. "We don't need him. Why don't you just divorce him?"

My mother sat up then and wiped at her eyes with the sleeve of her sweatshirt. Then, she looked at me and said, "That's your father, Jonathan. What goes on between me and him is our business."

"But, Mommy, he could kill you," I shouted. "Don't you even care?"

"Boo Boo, you don't understand," she said as she tried to pull herself off the couch. Then, "Go to bed, Jonathan," my mother said wearily.

I shook my head, wiping my tears and wanting to say more, but not knowing what to say to make my mother understand. And then I remembered what Jay had told me a long time ago when I thought I could convince my parents to stop smoking crack. *"You're never going to change Mommy and Daddy, Jon. Just work on yourself. Be about you."*

I didn't want to believe him when he told me that, but now it was pretty obvious. People don't change because you ask them to; they change only because they want to or they have to. It seemed my parents weren't interested in either option. And that just made me sad, but also, at that moment, I wanted to cut the blood ties that connected my parents' behavior with my own well-being. I wanted to divorce myself from their inevitable downfall. But I didn't know how to do that at twelve years old.

I tiptoed back into the bedroom, trying not to bother my

sister. But she was already awake. "I told you to ignore them," she said. "But you don't listen."

After that, I tried to stay away from home in an effort to stop caring. I couldn't stand to see my mother with a black eye or a fat lip. Sometimes, I could barely stand to be in the same room with my father. Helena made herself scarce, too. She had a new boyfriend and spent most of her time with him. My parents were too engrossed in their own drama, or too interested in getting to their next high, to care where Helena and I were or what we were doing. Some kids might have been thrilled to have that much freedom, but I would have traded that freedom any day for two parents who paid attention to what was going on in my life. But since they didn't, I did pretty much whatever I wanted to do—increasingly, that meant hanging with Marquise.

I got bolder and braver with Marquise. Maybe you could say I was getting more reckless, too. Or maybe I was just being stupid. But I told myself that wherever Marquise would lead, I would follow. And I was all in. We'd race into the corner bodega and grab a bag of chips or an iced tea and run out without paying. We'd jump a kid and steal their phone. We'd cut school occasionally and just hang out and play ball. And I enjoyed every minute of it. Hanging with Marquise, Omari, and Shaun felt like having my own band of brothers. We had wild fun together. We looked out for one another. We laughed together. And, unlike my parents, I could count on them to be there for me, no matter what. They made me feel safe, and that's what I wanted more than anything else.

As Marquise and I became closer friends, I learned that he was already involved in low-level gang activity in our neighborhood. Sometimes, he'd hold a gun for someone. Sometimes, he had to run errands for people. He never got into specifics about who he was working for or the extent of what he was doing, but he always made it clear that even though I was with him, I wasn't going to get involved with anything gang related. "Leave Jonathan out of it," Marquise would tell anybody who tried to pressure me into something I wasn't willing to do. Even when, in my eagerness to be accepted and show my loyalty, I would offer to do something that could get me into real trouble, Marquise would stop me. "You not like us," he would say to me. "You're smart, bro." And that would be that.

I didn't think I was that smart, but I was smart enough to get what I wanted. In school, I did everything I was supposed to do and didn't cause any trouble. It wasn't hard to stay on the teachers' good sides because, even with minimal effort, I was a straight-A student. I turned in all of my homework assignments and did well on my tests. My goal, as far as school was concerned, was to give the teachers and administrators no reason to suspect I lived in a homeless shelter, that my parents used crack, or that I was practically raising myself. I didn't want any calls to protective services, or any calls home that would bring my mother to school to check up on me. I quickly realized that being a perfect student kept all eyes off me. That way, after school and on weekends, I could do whatever I wanted to with Marquise with zero consequences from school or my family.

On the first Saturday of summer, when sixth grade was officially over, Marquise and I were hanging out together in the park on Washington Avenue. That was our spot. We'd already played basketball and were just walking around eating chips and drinking AriZona iced tea, looking for something else to do to fill the long, hot hours before sundown. Marquise was in a mood, so we weren't talking much.

"What do you wanna do now?" I broke the silence.

Marquise barely looked at me and shrugged. "Fuck you asking me for?"

By this point, I knew Marquise could fall into dark places sometimes, and I just had to let him work through whatever was bothering him. And when he was done, he'd start joking again, and we'd get busy with our next adventure. So, we kept walking without talking.

As we made our way out of the park and past the high school, we found ourselves on a block with a row of connected single-family townhouses. We passed by them almost every day and always remarked that whoever lived in the two-story homes had to be rich since they didn't have to live in the projects like everyone else we knew.

"Yo, Jon," Marquise finally perked up. "Let's break into one of these houses and get some quick money."

I willed my face to remain calm, but inside my heartbeat quickened, and I could feel my palms go cold. This wasn't our usual thing. Breaking into a house was a real crime. This wasn't stealing chips from the bodega on the corner.

"Nah, bro, I don't want to do that," I said, hoping the idea would pop out of Marquise's head as quickly as it had popped in. That happened a lot with Marquise. He'd say some crazy stuff, and then, ten seconds later, be on to the next thing.

Marquise stopped walking and looked me straight in the eye. "Come on, Jon, you ain't gotta be scared. We'll be in and out in a second. We'll get some money and be out."

I looked up and down the block, trying to assess the danger I was about to put myself in. There was nobody walking around at that moment, and Marquise always seemed to get away with everything, so I agreed.

"Aight, let's do it," I said, while ignoring the warning bells going off in my head.

I followed Marquise as he ran up onto the porch of the house in the middle of the row. I noticed there were no cars in the driveway, but there were cars in the neighbors' yards on either side.

Marquise quickly tried the front windows and was able to jimmy one up while I kept watch. He climbed through and then opened the front door for me since I couldn't fit through the tiny window.

The house was dark inside, and it took a moment for our eyes to adjust. Marquise took the lead and immediately started running from room to room on the first floor looking for cash.

He ran toward the stairs and shouted at me, "Start looking for money, Jon! Don't just stand there!"

"Okay," I said, but I was so scared we were going to get caught. Maybe somebody was in the house just waiting to take out their gun to shoot us. I walked slowly around the living room without touching anything. The furniture looked shabby, and there was an empty coffee cup on the table in front of the couch. The couch itself was covered in plastic. Like my grandmother's. *Oh, damn, we're robbing somebody's grandmother,* I thought. And I suddenly felt a wave of guilt crash over me.

Just then, I heard Marquise yell, "Fuck yeah, bro," and he ran back downstairs to flash twenty-five dollars and some loose change in my face.

"Can we go now?" I whispered, desperately wanting to leave.

"Yeah, bro, let's get outta here," Marquise said, and I breathed a sigh of relief. We ran back to the front of the house and walked right out the front door. That's when we heard the sirens. Marquise told me to run. "Get out of here V-A!" he yelled as he sprinted away. I turned and ran the other way, as fast as my legs could carry me. I realized I was close to my mother's friend Carmen's apartment building, so I decided to run there. It was only two blocks down, and I figured if I could make it there Carmen would let me in, and the cops would never know which floor I was on, or which apartment I was in.

I willed my legs to go faster. I cursed all the extra weight on my body that was slowing me down.

"Police! Stop!"

I heard the command, but I kept running because I had only one more block to go. I was almost there.

But then the sounds of fast-moving footsteps were right behind me, and I went down as an officer tackled me to the ground. He rolled off me quickly and pulled me up to face him. He was holding me tightly with both arms and forced me to look him in the face. I was relieved for just a brief moment that it was a Black face I was looking into, but my relief didn't last.

"What are you doing, kid? I told you to stop. Why you

running, man?" He sounded like my father when I did something stupid.

People were starting to gather around, and even though I was totally freaking out, I refused to break down in public.

"I know you robbed that house," the cop said to me. "What did you take? What do you have on you?" he demanded.

"I didn't take nothing, I swear," I said.

"You're already in trouble, kid, don't lie to me," the officer said, still holding me by my arms.

"I'm not lying. I swear. I ain't got nothing. I didn't take anything. You can check my pockets," I offered, hoping he would let me go.

At that, he patted me down. I was wearing only shorts and a T-shirt, so it didn't take him long to figure out I was telling the truth. But he wasn't done with me yet.

"Who were you with, kid? Where's your friend? We know you were with somebody," he asked in a calmer tone of voice, now that he realized I had no contraband on my body.

My mind immediately went to the code of the streets. I wasn't about to snitch. "He's not my friend," I said, trying to sound believable. "I don't even know him," I added.

That seemed to make the officer mad, and he went from being a stern father figure back to a cop.

"Oh, now you're going to lie to me?" he said, shaking his head like I was the stupid one. "Fine. You're under arrest." And with that, he spun me around and put handcuffs on me and then called his partner. Within moments, a blue-and-white NYPD police car pulled up. I expected to see Marquise inside but the back seat was empty, which made me think, maybe, Marquise had gotten away. I hoped so, even though I didn't know what that would mean for me.

From the back seat of the police car, I tried to hold myself together. Tried to tell myself that I didn't care about what was happening. "Just so you know, kid, we already picked up your friend, and he's going to tell us everything," the officer driving the car told me. The fact that he was also Black didn't make me feel any safer or put me at ease.

"You want to get a head start and tell us your version of things?" he asked.

My friends at M.S. 219 had told me never talk to the cops. Never turn on a friend. Never share anything with the law. This wasn't new information. I knew that snitches got worse than stitches in my neighborhood, so I wasn't about to tell this police officer anything. So, I just kept my mouth shut.

Once we got to the police station, I was taken into a room that was pretty bare except for a metal table and two chairs. The same officer who arrested me came into the room and repeated what he told me before, but this time with more details.

"Look, Jonathan, we picked up your friend Marquise, and he's in another room just like this one, telling us everything we need to know. He's probably telling my friend that it was all your idea to go into that house. That you wanted to break in and steal some stuff. And that means you're going to take the rap for this and end up locked up. Is that what you want?"

I shook my head no, but didn't say a word. I had to work hard to keep my face a blank mask.

"You know, there's been a bunch of robberies in this neighborhood, maybe you and your partner are responsible for all of them," the cop said. "If you're not talking, maybe it's because you got something to hide."

I hung my head, shaking it back and forth, no. No, we didn't do those things. No, I'm not a criminal. No, I'm still not talking.

When the officer realized I wasn't going to say anything, he told me to follow him, and he led me back into the main room of the precinct and told me to sit in a chair and wait. Wait for what I didn't know, but I did what I was told and tried to figure out where Marquise was and what he was going through.

I didn't have long to think, though, because my grandmother showed up a few minutes later.

"Lord Jesus, what in the name of heaven?"

I heard her before I saw her. She was in her customary long skirt and long sleeves, even though it was full-on summer.

Maybe because she thought the police would give her more respect, my grandma had added one of her church hats to her outfit. I groaned inside but I was happy to see a familiar face. When asked, I'd given the officers my grandmother's phone number because she lived only a few blocks from the precinct, and I knew she'd be home, whereas my parents might have been high. So, I decided my grandmother was my safest bet to call, but she wasn't going to be quiet about it.

She rushed over and laid her hands on my head and shouted, "I rebuke you Satan, get thee away from this child." And then she mumbled some holy words I could barely understand.

"Grandma, stop," I whined.

And that's when she grabbed me by the ear and pulled me up to a standing position so she could yell at me properly.

"You telling me to stop, boy? Jonathan, have you lost your entire mind?" she screeched, and then shook her head like she was completely overdone. "Jesus! Jesus! Jesus!" my grandmother lamented. "What in the world were you thinking, Jonathan?" And then she answered her own question. "Obviously, you weren't thinking. Lord have mercy on this child for he knows not what to do."

I started to think I should have called my mother instead of my grandmother.

The cop who arrested me came over to where we were standing.

"Ma'am, are you the grandmother?"

"Yes, Officer," she said.

"Well, you should know we caught your grandson fleeing from the scene of a robbery. We didn't find anything on him, but he won't talk to us or tell us anything. We caught his friend, too," he said as he looked down at his paperwork. "His name is Marquise. We got him in a different room."

My grandmother turned to me then. "I told you to be careful with that boy. Didn't I?"

"Grandma, stop," I said again.

She ignored me and turned back to the cop. "Officer, you

take him back now. He's going to talk to you and tell you everything you need to know. Go on, Jonathan."

I looked at my grandmother as if she were the crazy one. She expected me to rat out my best friend? She was telling me to be a snitch?

Before I could protest, though, my grandmother pointed her finger in my face and said, "You better tell 'em everything they wanna hear, right now. This ain't no game. This is your life, Jon."

I was ashamed of what I'd done. And I was sorry that my grandmother had to come down to the police station to deal with all of this. But I still wasn't about to betray Marquise.

The officer led me back to the interrogation room and told me to get my story straight because, when he came back, he was going to be taking my official statement.

He left me alone in the room, and I had to sit in silence, with only my conscience tormenting me about what I would say when he came back. My mind refused to settle on one thing; my thoughts and emotions were ping-ponging all over the place. I was ashamed of myself for letting my brothers down. They had suffered through a long list of horrible experiences with my parents and none of them had ever turned to crime, or gotten arrested. That made me think about my parents and my shame morphed into a familiar anger. If my parents weren't addicted to crack, I reasoned, then they could actually provide a good life for me, instead of leaving me out in the streets without any supervision. Sitting there stewing in my thoughts, it was easier to blame them than to take responsibility for what I'd just done. But blaming my parents wasn't going to help me figure out what to say to the police about what happened. I couldn't rat out Marquise. If he got in trouble, all I could think about was what his uncle would do to him. But I wasn't trying to go to jail, either. I didn't know what to do.

When the officer came back to the room for my statement, I still had no idea what to say.

It turned out I didn't have to explain anything.

"You can go," the officer said without sitting down. He stood by the door, holding it open. "Your grandmother is waiting for you."

"What do you mean I can go?" I said. "What happened?"

"Your friend told us everything," the officer started. "He said you had nothing to do with the robbery. He said it was all his idea, and that you didn't take anything or break anything. So, you're free to go, Jonathan. But you got lucky this time. If this happens again, you're definitely going in the system, and you'll just be another Black kid with a record, so you better make sure there isn't a next time."

"But where's Marquise? What's going to happen to him?" I said, rooted to my seat, in shock that Marquise was still protecting me.

"Your friend is going to get sent somewhere for juvenile offenders because he broke the law," the officer said. Then, he gave me a pointed look. "Do you have any other questions?"

"No, sir," I said as I scrambled out of my chair and hustled to find my grandmother in the waiting room. The cop followed behind me.

"Praise the Lord," my grandma said when she saw me. "Is he free to go?" she asked the officer.

"Yeah, you can take him home. But let me tell you both something. I called over to one of my contacts at M.S. 219 to ask about you, Jonathan. They told me you were a good kid. Smart. New to the city."

"Yeah, he just moved here from Virginia," my grandma said. "It's been hard to adjust, and his parents are having a hard time finding a place to live—"

The cop interrupted her. "I understand, ma'am. I get it." But then he turned to me. "Look, Jonathan, I meant what I said back there. Don't be another Black kid who gets caught up in the system. You don't have to live this life. You have choices."

"God bless you, Officer," my grandmother said with tears in her eyes. "Jonathan is a good boy. All his brothers are in college. He's just hanging out with the wrong kids."

I felt the dam inside of me burst at my grandmother's words, and I couldn't stop myself from crying. Being Marquise's friend wasn't a mistake, it was just complicated, and I didn't know how to handle those complications at the time. Marquise understood how the world worked, a testament to the fact that he was forced to leapfrog over childhood and act like an adult before he'd even sprouted chin hair. What I still don't understand is what Marquise saw in me that made him take me under his wing, protect me, and regularly remind me that "I was different and destined for something better than the streets." Every hero has their sidekick who is always overlooked because he's too short, too poor, or comes from the wrong side of the tracks—even though he is wiser than the hero. Marquise was that for me. He was smarter than me in so many ways, but, because of his circumstances, he gave me the best he had to offer, almost as if he knew that if I succeeded, he would succeed as well. I don't know what would have become of me if I hadn't picked Marquise as the first member of my chosen village. But I'm really glad I did. Despite what happened that summer. I learned that the people you bring into your village don't have to be perfect—sometimes, they just have to see the perfection in you.

My grandmother wrapped her arms around me as I sobbed into her. "Come on, baby, let's get you home."

After that, my grandmother decided she had to do more to keep an eye on me. She said my parents weren't doing a good enough job keeping tabs on me, so I was to stay with her at her apartment more often.

I didn't see Marquise for the rest of the summer.

4

I Wasn't Supposed to Be
Making Difficult Decisions

How was your summer, Mr. Conyers?"

Mr. Marshall had pulled me out of class. We were standing in the hallway. So we could "have a little talk," he'd said. The hallway was Mr. Marshall's favorite place to have heart-to-heart conversations. The hallway was his second office.

"My summer was okay," I said with a shrug. "I didn't do anything special."

Mr. Marshall raised an eyebrow and made a noise in the back of his throat. "I heard you and your friend Marquise got yourselves into some trouble over the summer," he said. "You wanna talk about it?"

"How'd you find out about that?" I blurted out.

"Mr. Conyers, I make it my business to know about everything that goes on with my students," he said. "I got eyes and ears all over this neighborhood."

My mind jumped back to the police station. Was Mr. Marshall the "contact" the cop who arrested me had called? If so, that meant I owed Mr. Marshall a lot.

"So, you sure you don't want to talk about what happened?" Mr. Marshall tried again.

I considered my options. I liked Mr. Marshall. He was definitely the man around M.S. 219. He wasn't like any of the other teachers. I still didn't even know what his official job was at the school. Everybody just knew Mr. Marshall was the guy who roamed the hallways and kept things in order. He always looked sharp and had his walkie-talkie ready for action. He was like a guidance counselor, security guard, and your favorite uncle all in one. He lived in the neighborhood, too, so it was hard to get over on him.

"Mr. Conyers," Mr. Marshall said. "Remember I told you, you have to be careful who you surround yourself with. There are a lot of Black men in jail right now who are not bad people, they just chose to hang around the wrong people. I don't want to see you making that same mistake."

I felt the need to defend my friend. "Marquise isn't bad, Mr. Marshall. He just doesn't have anybody looking out for him," I said.

"But you do, don't you?"

"Yes, sir," I admitted, thinking about my grandmother.

"Listen, son," Mr. Marshall said as he leaned against the wall, "you're not going to be able to save Marquise. Be his friend, okay—but you can't save him. What you can do, though, is save yourself. Get your education. Go to college and then come back here and see the changes you can make. But right now, Jonathan, the only thing you're going to do if you try to hold on to Marquise is sink with him. You understand me?"

I nodded. "Yes, sir," I said again. "It just makes me depressed to think about what Marquise has to go through." I hesitated for a second, and then I confessed what had been weighing me down all summer. "I feel guilty that he got punished for what we did, and I didn't." Once the words were out of my mouth, I felt myself starting to tear up. All the guilt I had for getting to go home with my grandmother while Marquise was sent off to who knows where came rushing to the surface. But now I couldn't stop. It was 10:30 a.m. on a Wednesday, and I was blubbering in the hallway outside of my seventh-grade science class.

"Jonathan," Mr. Marshall said, "I'm going to say it again. You are not responsible for Marquise. He makes his own decisions and you make yours. You understand me?"

I nodded, but I couldn't say anything else because I was crying so hard.

Mr. Marshall put his arm around me and told me to let it out. And I did. I cried for Marquise because I had no way to contact him. No way of knowing where he was or if he was okay. I had no idea if he hated me because I was free and he was serving time somewhere. I didn't say any of this aloud, though. I just slobbered all over Mr. Marshall's silk shirt, and he kept telling me it would be okay.

"Alright now," Mr. Marshall eventually said, "that's enough. Why don't you go to the restroom and clean your face. I'll tell your teacher you'll be right back to class."

"Okay," I said, still snuffling, feeling embarrassed about crying but, at the same time, also a sense of relief after holding all that in for so long.

Mr. Marshall patted me on the back. "You're going to be okay, Mr. Conyers. And remember, I'm always here if you want to talk about anything."

"Thank you, sir," I said as I headed to the bathroom.

It was only the second week of seventh grade, but I had already decided that this year was going to be different. Talking to Mr. Marshall only confirmed what I already knew: I couldn't be following Marquise around and expect to stay out of trouble. Even though I had fun with Marquise, my mother was right. I had to be a leader, not a follower. I had to do what I knew was right. And my brothers had laid out the path for me so I had no excuses—education and sports were enough to get them out of living in Holly Cove. Got them to college. Got them away from my parents. I could do the same thing. I just had to stick to the original plan. Lucky for me, Mr. Marshall was there to keep me on track. Mr. Marshall was the father figure my own father couldn't be. And he reminded me that I had choices, too. Marquise was definitely the right person to follow to help me survive the streets, but Mr. Marshall could help me escape the streets. And that's what I wanted. That's what I needed.

It wasn't that hard to get back to the Conyers game plan

because Marquise didn't come back to M.S. 219. Nobody had seen or heard from him since summer. So, rather than sitting in the back of the classroom cracking jokes, I sat closer to the front and did my best to focus on learning. But it was often hard to concentrate during class because there was always something going on. My teacher, Mrs. Brown, had to spend so much time trying to stop classroom antics, we'd have less than half the class time to spend actually learning. Then, there was the issue of the difference in academic abilities among students. Some kids were still struggling to read at grade level, so Mrs. Brown had her hands full. I quickly realized that if I wanted to get a good education, I would have to take matters into my own hands.

In the mornings, I would get to school early, but I refused to go to the cafeteria like I was supposed to. Over the last year, I'd learned that the cafeteria was a breeding ground for bullshit, gangs, and negativity. So, I spent as little time there as possible. I'd grab my milk and a piece of fruit and head straight upstairs to my homeroom with Mrs. Brown. And that's when I'd get the attention I couldn't get during the regular school day. Mrs. Brown was always happy to see me, and she would look over my homework assignments and answer any questions I might have. My friends would tease me, saying I had a crush on Mrs. Brown, since I preferred her classroom to breakfast in the cafeteria. Sometimes, she would recommend a book she thought I would like, and we'd get lost in an animated conversation. I looked forward to those thirty minutes every morning.

I also started going to the after-school program at my school. Directions For Our Youth (DFOY) was located on the first floor of M.S. 219. DFOY had tutors—high school students from our neighborhoods—to help us with our homework, and in turn, we helped younger kids with their homework. Just seeing kids older than me who were into their academics excited me. It was proof I had options. The DFOY program was about speaking life into us and making us feel as though we mattered, which was completely different messaging from what we got from the rest of the world. It was too easy to believe that we didn't matter. To anyone.

I also joined M.S. 219's basketball team. I wasn't the best player, but the coach said he loved my positive attitude and wanted me at practices and the games. He told me I always motivated the other players, which made them try harder. And, because kids couldn't play basketball if they weren't doing well in school, I became a tutor for some of my teammates.

My friends, my teachers, the staff at DFOY, and especially Mr. Marshall, kept telling me I was smart, but I had a hard time believing it. My early struggles with reading had left a residue of insecurity. Now, I was rising to the top and could help other kids learn. I liked watching them go from not understanding something to getting it. For the first time in my life, I started to think maybe I *was* smart. And I started to think that maybe being smart could be my thing. My brothers Justin and Jay were athletes. Josh had opera. Maybe excelling at school was what *I* was going to be good at.

Between playing basketball and hanging at DFOY, I made new friends who weren't into gang stuff. My life was starting to look like a normal seventh grader's. My new friend Terrence was a preacher's kid. Dwayne was focused on making the NBA, and Melvin was just a cool regular guy who didn't get into trouble, but like me, happened to have a mother who was addicted to drugs. The three of us would hang at DFOY until they closed their doors every evening.

Melvin lived out on Staten Island and I would sometimes go to his house on weekends and help him take care of his little brothers and sisters. His mother was never around and, even if she was, she was often laid out in the bed, sleeping off her latest high. Melvin had to change diapers and cook meals for his siblings. Sometimes, he wouldn't even make it to school because he was too busy taking care of his family. I went to Melvin's house because I wanted to be a good friend, but also, deep down, seeing how Melvin lived and what he had to deal with made me feel just a little bit better about my situation.

Sometimes, seeing Melvin's mother made me appreciate my mother more. Knowing that Melvin had to do all the work of a grown man because he didn't have a father made me grateful for my father. Even with all of his flaws. And there were many.

My father was still fixated on my mother's infidelity. And although my mother had spent a lifetime taking my father's blows, now that her body had been weakened by multiple sclerosis, she couldn't recover from the beatings as quickly as she used to. Watching her wince in pain as she walked across a room, or seeing her skin discolored from the bruises my father inflicted, filled me with rage. But I didn't know who I was madder at, my mother for staying with my father, or my father for inflicting the abuse. And to make matters worse, my parents' fighting, coupled with the fact that they were both caught violating the shelter's "no drugs" policy, meant we were dropped down the list for getting a real apartment, and we had to return to hopscotching between temporary placements, moving every couple of weeks.

One evening in October, my parents and I were sitting around a small plastic table in yet another anonymous shelter. Dinner was Oodles of Noodles out of Styrofoam cups, and we were eating with the plastic forks my father brought home from his job. I don't know why I opened my mouth at that moment, but I did. "Why didn't you guys try harder to abort me? Your lives would have been easier," I said.

Both of my parents stopped eating.

"What the hell?" my father said. And then he turned to my mother. "Kimmie, what did you tell him?"

My mother glared at me. And then said, "I just told him the truth. That when I first found out I was pregnant with him, I tried to get an abortion."

"Why would you tell him that?" my father said.

"Listen," my mother said, putting her hand up. "Don't start with me. I told Jonathan that because I wanted him to know I was so happy I wasn't able to have the abortion. I told him that because I love him, and I wanted him to know how happy I was to have my Boo Boo in my life." And then she turned to me. "Not because I don't want you. Jesus, Jonathan!"

"Well, you guys don't act like you want me."

"Boo Boo, you know that's not true," my mother said. "Tell him, Pumpkin."

"I'm not telling him anything," my father said dismissively. "You're the one filling his head with that shit about an abortion. I don't know why you always gotta be opening your mouth."

"Don't you even start with me," my mother said. "I am not going to listen to you start."

"Can you guys please stop?" I said. "This is what I mean."

"Boy, eat your noodles," my father said. "I don't need to hear any more from you."

That night, my parents fought about me. I don't think either one of them heard me crying.

The next day, I decided to stay at my grandmother's apartment. Lying in her guest bed that evening, I could hear the sounds of other people's lives in the apartments above, below, and alongside my grandmother's. Babies crying. People watching movies. Drug dealers joking around outside. Doors slamming. But at least within the four walls of my grandmother's house, it was peaceful, the only sounds being the thrum of gospel music and Jimmy Swaggart's voice on the TV.

"Grandma, do you think I could stay here with you for a while, like I did this summer?" I asked the following morning.

"Of course, you can, Jonathan. You know Grandma always has space for you."

Thanks to my grandmother and Mr. Marshall, I felt like I had at least two adults in my life I could count on if I needed help. But my grandmother was old and relied too much on Jesus to offer much practical advice on navigating the life I was living, and Mr. Marshall had 298 other students to keep track of, and I couldn't be his priority. So, I pretty much felt like I was on my own most of the time. College, a career, and a life far away from poverty, the projects, drugs, and my parents was all I thought about.

"What do you want to be when you grow up, Mr. Conyers?"

Mr. Marshall and I were having lunch together. He knew I tried to avoid the cafeteria at all costs, so he had invited me to eat with him in his office.

I shifted in my seat. It had been a long time since anybody asked me that question. But I decided to be honest. "I want to be a doctor," I said.

Mr. Marshall whistled and then smacked his hand on his thigh. "Well, go ahead, son. That's fantastic. We need more Black doctors, and I'm sure you'll make it all the way."

I smiled in response. "Thank you, sir," I said as a feeling of pride washed over me.

"What kind of doctor you think you want to be?" Mr. Marshall asked, as he munched on a carrot stick.

Nobody had ever asked me that question. I had to take a moment to consider. "I don't know exactly. I just know that when my mother got diagnosed with multiple sclerosis, when I was nine, I decided I was going to be a doctor so I could help her." I shrugged. "And I still want to do that. I want to help people."

Mr. Marshall finished chewing and then said, "Mr. Conyers, I'm going to do everything I can to make sure you get to be a doctor. You know it's never too early to work on your future. If you stay ready, you don't have to get ready when opportunity comes your way."

I smiled. "Thanks, Mr. Marshall," I said. "And I'm definitely going to be ready."

"That's my boy," he said, clapping me on the back.

Even though I knew my father would never abandon our family, I still needed a father figure like Mr. Marshall in my life. He was my first village elder. He had that paternal instinct I craved, and I could count on him to provide a shoulder to cry on, a pat on the back to tell me I did a good job, and high expectations for me to work toward. Like Marquise, Mr. Marshall saw something special in me that I still didn't see in myself, but his consistent care gave me hope for my future.

In early November, Marquise came back to school. He just showed up on a Monday morning like he hadn't been gone for the entire first quarter of school.

When I saw him sitting in the cafeteria, I ran right up to him. It was like one of those commercials where you see someone you haven't seen in a long time. I was all ready to hug Marquise and tell him I missed him and that I was glad to see him alive. But when I got a look at the expression on his face, I stopped. He didn't look happy to see me. He wasn't smiling. He didn't look angry. He just looked hard. His mask was in place. He didn't care.

"What up, bro?" I said, testing the waters. "You back!"

"That's right. I'm back. Ya'll miss me?" he said with the hint of a grin.

I laughed. "Nah, I didn't miss you, nigga. I barely noticed you were gone," I joked.

Marquise cocked an eyebrow but didn't laugh. I rushed to assure him I was joking, and then I tried to get to what I really wanted to say.

"Marquise," I started. "Yo, man, I'm really sorry for what happened to you . . ."

He cut me off. "Don't worry about it, man. We cool."

"For real?" I said. "I mean, where'd you have to go? What'd you have to do?"

Marquise shook his head and drew in a deep breath. "I don't want to talk about it, okay."

"Okay, fine," I said, "but what you did for me—"

Marquise cut me off again. "Yo, Jon." He waved off my gratitude. "I told you we cool. Let's move on."

"Aight, bro," I said. "But if you ever wanna talk about it or something."

"Nigga, are you deaf?" Marquise said, raising his voice. "There's nothing to talk about."

"Whatever you say, bro," I said, and I went to get my milk so I could go upstairs with Mrs. Brown.

Marquise was different. He looked the same, but there was a hardness to him that wasn't there before. No longer was it just a blank mask. His jokes were meaner. He laughed less. Whatever innocence Marquise had once held on to was now gone, and I once again felt guilty that he had suffered while I had not.

But just when I got used to Marquise being back, he disappeared again. He'd been at school for only about a month, and poof, he was gone. For two weeks nobody saw him at M.S. 219 or around the neighborhood. And then, with no explanation, he came back. Just like before, I found him in the cafeteria like nothing had happened.

Marquise had a fresh cut and was sitting at a table by himself.

I sauntered over. "Yo, bro, what the hell?" is how I greeted him. "Where you been? How come you can't tell anybody where you're going or nothing?" I pulled out my new Dwyane Wade Limited Edition Sidekick 3—proud to show it off. "My grandmother bought me a phone, so you could have texted me or something."

Marquise didn't respond. He just sat there drinking his milk.

"Yo, bro, what's up? Why you ain't talking?" I said, grabbing a seat next to him. "You went on some supersecret vacation and can't talk about it?" I said, trying to make him laugh. "You a celebrity or something?"

Marquise stood up. "Oh, my mother dying is a fucking vacation to you, bro?"

I was shocked, but I didn't have time to process what Marquise said. He looked so mad, like he wanted to fight me. I stood up, too. "Chill out, man! I was just joking."

Marquise cocked his head and curled his lip. "Yo, now you think my mother dying is funny? This a joke to you?"

"Bro, back up," I said, putting my hands up in defense. But Marquise just sucked his teeth and walked away.

At recess, Marquise found me on the playground. "Yo, I'm

sorry, man, you know, I shouldn't have come at you like that," he said.

"It's okay, bro," I said. I looked down at my sneakers and then said, "I'm sorry about your mom."

Marquise sighed real heavy. "Yeah, she died a couple of weeks ago, and I had to go to South Carolina for her funeral."

Marquise never talked about his family. I had no idea his mother even lived down South.

Marquise put his hands in the pocket of his hoodie and pulled out a wallet-size picture and handed it to me. "This my mom," he said. "It's the only picture I have of her."

I looked down at what looked like a high school photo of a brown-skinned girl with big brown eyes and a nose I recognized from Marquise's face. She wasn't smiling in the picture. "She looks nice," I said, handing the photo back to Marquise.

He shrugged. "She wasn't nice to me, but she was my mom. And now she's dead, so it's just me out here now."

Marquise shoved the photo back into his pocket then and turned to face the street. He eyed the metal fence that kept us in and the neighborhood out.

He put his fingers through the holes of the fence and said, "Yo, man, this place feels like a fucking prison!"

Marquise stopped coming to school on a regular basis after that. When he did show up, we all acted like everything was normal, and he'd hang with me and my new friends, and we'd have mad fun together. But whenever he wanted us to follow him into something dangerous, I refused.

One time, Marquise wanted me to hold a gun for him, but I wouldn't do it. He got mad at me after that, and we stopped talking for a while, but I had to shrug it off. I felt like I owed Marquise my life, but I wasn't prepared to give up my life for him. I knew I couldn't save Marquise from the path he was on, but I refused to be yet another person in his life who abandoned him. The way I looked at it, Marquise didn't have anyone who really cared about him, except me.

Sometimes, I'd try to talk him out of doing something stupid, like fighting someone or jumping a kid to steal their kicks or a phone. Marquise could never ask his uncle for anything, so if he ever wanted something, he had to get it himself. Rather than help Marquise jump the kid, I pulled off the pair of boots my mother had recently bought me, and I walked home with no shoes on. I knew my grandmother could take me to Payless and get me another pair of boots. They wouldn't be anything fancy, but it would mean Marquise wouldn't get in trouble for at least one more day.

And that's how we played it for the rest of seventh grade.

The summer before eighth grade, my grandmother and I got into a fight.

"Grandma, your daughter is a crackhead," I had said. It was the argument that had ended it all. After living with my grandmother for almost all of seventh grade, I was "getting sassy," as she said. And I needed to go to church. Also her words, not mine.

The thing was, as much as I loved my grandmother, I could no longer keep my mouth shut about her hypocrisy when it came to my mother.

"Boy, you better watch your mouth," my grandma said after the crackhead comment.

My mother had just left my grandmother's apartment with my grandmother's last one hundred dollars in her pocket. She'd demanded that my grandmother give it to her so she could pay her phone bill, otherwise she wouldn't be able to call her doctors.

And my grandmother handed over the cash.

After my mother stormed out of the apartment, acting like she had the right to be indignant that my grandma hadn't wanted to give her all her money, I turned to my grandmother and said, "Why did you give her that money? You know she's going to smoke it, right?"

"I don't know what you're talking about," my grandma said and then went to turn up her gospel music on the radio.

And that's when I made the crackhead statement. Followed up by, "And you keep giving her the money to fund her habit."

"Jesus, Jesus, Jesus," my grandmother said, fluttering around the room with her broom, acting like she just *had* to sweep the floors at that exact moment.

"Grandma, you know I'm right," I said. "And no amount of praying or pretending is going to make her habit disappear."

"That is no way for a child to talk about his mother," my grandmother said, shaking her head like she couldn't believe I could make up such lies.

So, I tried a different tactic. "Isn't it a sin in your church to do drugs, Grandma?"

"Yeah," she said, squinting her eyes at me, like she thought I was trying to trick her somehow with my words.

"Well then, aren't you sinning by paying for your daughter's drugs?" I said. "That's the devil right there at work."

"Jesus! Jesus! Jesus!" my grandmother screeched. "You got a wicked tongue, little boy, and you will not speak to me like that in my own home!" And then she stomped away from me, went to her bedroom, and slammed the door.

I knew I had gone too far, but I was so frustrated living with my grandma. All day long she talked about how good God was and ignored everything bad. I guess it was too much to expect her to tell my parents that what they were doing was wrong. That they weren't being good parents. That they were selfish and mean. That their children needed them. I needed them. I didn't want my grandmother to rescue me from my parents, I wanted her to fix them. I wanted her to shame my mother into doing the right thing. Sometimes, I think I just wanted her to acknowledge the truth so I could talk about the pain I was in, but because she wouldn't even admit that my mother had a problem, there was nowhere to take my pain. As generous and giving as my grandmother was, she couldn't give me what I wanted and what I needed most. She could not, or she would not. And I wouldn't let it go. So, we came to an impasse.

When my grandmother came out of her room that night, she said curtly, "Until you apologize for what you said to me, you cannot stay here."

I refused to apologize, so I packed up my things and went "home."

Home was another tiny, temporary shelter. The good thing was, the shelter was on Tremont Avenue in the Bronx, so I was close enough to school that I didn't have to take two buses and a subway. The bad news was, it was a tiny homeless shelter apartment, and I had to live there with three other people—my parents and my sister.

Eighth grade didn't start on a positive note.

"Wherever you go to high school is gonna determine the course of the rest of your life," Mr. Marshall said from the podium in the cafeteria, where all of us eighth graders were assembled on the second day of school after summer break.

This was how the school administrators welcomed us back to our final year at M.S. 219. The principal had already given his short, but dramatic, speech about how critical the high school selection process was and how important it was for us to stay on schedule with all of our applications and requirements to get into the school of our choice. The whole process was foreign to me, as I had watched all three of my brothers simply go to the high school they were assigned based on our zip code in Holly Cove. In New York, public school students have to apply to get into high school, even if the school was around the corner from where you lived. The process included filling out forms, sending in a transcript of your grades from the past two years, and, if the high school was of high caliber or had a specialty like the arts or technology, you also had to take a test or perform an audition on top of everything else. It all sounded like a lot of work just to get into high school.

Since statistics showed that most of the student population at M.S. 219 would not go on to college, where they went to high school really mattered.

"Now, listen," Mr. Marshall said, leaning into the microphone, "you kids really have to think about what school you're going to go to because, you know, a lot of these high schools are run by gangs, and they will try to recruit you as soon as you set foot inside the door."

As soon as he said that, kids started talking among themselves. Some joked about joining the Bloods and the Crips, some acted like they didn't care, and some kids looked genuinely scared.

"Settle down, now," Mr. Marshall said with his hands up. "Let me finish." He cleared his throat and then went on. "You all have one year left here, and your teachers, and me, and Principal Johnson are all going to be here to help you with this transition. We're going to get you ready, but you have to get yourselves ready, too. You have to get your minds right and not be falling susceptible to everything that everybody else is doing out there. We don't want you girls getting pregnant, and we don't want you boys gangbanging and selling drugs."

"Dag, Mr. Marshall, what you think we gonna do in high school?" a girl named Taneesha called out, and everybody laughed. "You make it sound like we going to war or something."

Mr. Marshall gave Taneesha a bittersweet smile. "Taneesha, it is going to be war. We already know we're going to lose some of you to violence, to gangs, to parenthood too early, which is why we're talking about this now and why this year is going to be all about making sure each and every one of you is ready for battle."

At first I thought Mr. Marshall and some of the other teachers were exaggerating. But I did notice there were already two pregnant girls in the high school that shared the building with us, and hanging with Marquise, I knew that gang members were always looking for new recruits. But I didn't think high school was going to be the battleground Mr. Marshall was predicting. I hoped he was just exaggerating to grab our attention.

My friends and I decided together that we would all apply to this relatively new high school called Mott Hall Bronx High School. It was the school closest to us and where a bunch of kids from M.S. 219 wanted to go. It was the logical place if you lived in the area, and it was in a brand-new modern building that looked more like a New Age art museum than a typical New York City public school. Even Marquise, on the days he still showed up to school, said that he was thinking about applying there. You didn't have to take a test to get into Mott Hall, so I was pretty sure we would all get accepted, and we could keep the good times rolling. Terrence, Dwayne, Melvin, and I made all kinds of plans for how we would take our crew to high school, get girlfriends, and run the place. We were full of ourselves, but we knew if we were all together, we'd be okay.

Mr. Marshall didn't see things the same way. He pulled me out of class as soon as he got word about my high school plans.

"Jonathan, what's this I hear that you're only applying to Mott Hall? You know you can do so much better than that, son."

"What's wrong with Mott Hall?" I asked. "It seems like a good school, and everything looks new over there."

Mr. Marshall gave me a thin smile. "I'm not saying something is wrong with Mott Hall, Jonathan. I'm saying you have the grades and the intelligence to get into one of the top high schools in the city. And that's what you should be doing."

I made a face. "I'd rather go to a school close to where I live and be with my friends, Mr. Marshall," I said. "I don't want to have to take a million buses and the subway just to go to school every day. I promise, I'll keep my grades up, and I'm still going to college."

Mr. Marshall shook his head and kissed his teeth. "It doesn't work like that, Jonathan. You can't throw away a chance to go to one of these special admit schools because you want to go hang out with your friends. And you're too lazy to take a bus in the mornings."

I hated when people called me lazy, so I asked, "Where are these special schools you're talking about?"

"They're all over the city, in all of the boroughs," Mr. Marshall said. "You need to go sit down with Mrs. Givens in the office. She's in charge of submitting all of the high school applications. She'll tell you what all your options are. And what you have to do. Can you do that for me?"

"Okay," I said, without a lot of enthusiasm.

Mr. Marshall narrowed his eyes and said, "Now, listen, Jonathan, I'm going to keep checking with you until you do it. I'm not going to let you lose out on a lifetime opportunity. You got that?"

"Got it, Mr. Marshall," I said.

He smiled then. "That's what I like to hear. Hot buttered popcorn!"

I had to wait until lunchtime before I could tell my friends about my conversation with Mr. Marshall. I had been tracked into different classes because of my good grades, so I saw Melvin, Dwayne, and Terrence only at lunchtime and recess.

"What did you tell him?" Dwayne asked.

"I told him I'd go talk to Mrs. Givens," I answered.

"Are you going to?" Melvin asked.

"I mean, I guess I have to," I said. "But, you guys know, I'm down for Mott Hall. All the way."

Melvin gave me a dap. "Ride or die, Jon. Ride or die."

There were very few things I could count on in my life. Stability wasn't something I had an abundance of, so when I had it, I grabbed hold and held on like a drowning man hanging on to a lifeboat. My parents couldn't be counted on for anything. My brothers and sister were too busy leading their own lives to be steady figures in my world, so I had my friends. I had school. And I had my grandmother. Those were the consistent forces in my life. The things that didn't change. So, I wanted to protect them and keep them close. That was the real reason I wanted to go to Mott Hall. I craved consistency and resisted change. My instinct was to preserve what I had. Don't move too much. Don't ask for too much. Don't stray too far from what you know and can handle. Mr. Marshall didn't know that was why I wanted to stay in the Bronx, because I didn't tell him. And I didn't tell him because, at the time, I felt these things but didn't know how to put the feelings into words. I'm sure, to Mr. Marshall, I just seemed like a stubborn kid who refused to take his education seriously. Lucky for me, Mr. Marshall believed in me more than I believed in myself.

When the whole high school process started, I decided I wouldn't bother mentioning it to my family. There was no point. Considering everything else going on in our lives, where I chose to go to high school hardly seemed like a priority. Soon after Helena started eleventh grade—the same year I started eighth grade—she came home and announced that she was pregnant. My dad was so pissed that his only daughter was going to be a teen mother. But the way he dealt with his anger, after initially screaming and yelling, was to fall into one of his characteristic silences and smoke weed to obliterate his feelings. My mother was suffering from a painful multiple sclerosis flare-up when my sister shared her news, so my mother's response was, "At least I'll get to see one grandbaby before I die."

There was also nobody in my household who could actually offer me any useful advice on the high school entry process. Helena had transferred into her high school from Virginia, so she didn't know much about it. My brothers had all finished school in Chesapeake, so they couldn't help me, either. And my parents had gone to high school in New York so long ago, whatever information they might have had would be outdated anyway.

The decision was mine to make, and I'd figure out where to go to high school on my own. I knew what I wanted and what I didn't. I knew what mattered and what didn't. I just had to convince Mr. Marshall that I knew, not him, what was best for *me*.

"Jonathan." Mr. Marshall caught me one day in the hall between classes. "We need to talk."

"What is it, Mr. Marshall?" I said, trying to keep the tone respectful.

"Mrs. Givens told me you haven't been in to see her yet. The test for the specialized high school admittance is at the end of October, so you're running out of time to register for the exam."

"I don't think I really want to go to any of those schools, Mr. Marshall," I said. "I thought about it, and Mott Hall still seems like the best option for me."

"Jonathan," Mr. Marshall said with a labored sigh, "Dwayne and them don't have a future like you do. You have to think about you. You got something special, boy. I'm looking at your grades. I'm looking at everything you're doing at DFOY, tutoring the other kids and all of that. I've talked to your teachers, and they've all told me you're barely tapping your potential here. You can't just be following your friends around, Jonathan. You're at a different level than a lot of them. They don't have what you have."

I wanted to believe what Mr. Marshall said. What my teachers said—about me being smart—but I didn't trust it. Maybe I was smart only in comparison to the kids at M.S. 219. Put me at one of these special admittance schools for smart kids, and I might fail. I didn't think the risk was worth it.

"You could thrive at a school like Stuyvesant. You'll be surrounded by kids who are just as smart as you are, with teachers who will challenge you in the classroom with new textbooks and good technology. And if you graduate from Stuyvesant, all the best colleges will be throwing their doors wide open for you."

Because I didn't say anything, Mr. Marshall asked me a question.

"Last year, you told me you wanted to be a doctor. Is that still true?"

"Yeah," I said.

"Well, Jonathan, getting into Stuyvesant, or any of these other high-caliber schools, would be a right step in that direction."

"But, Mr. Marshall, if I can get good grades here and stay out of trouble here, which I did all last year, then I can do the same thing at Mott Hall. Why do I need to go to some school on the other side of the city to do that? It's not necessary."

Mr. Marshall shook his head. "Listen, I don't make the rules that the world runs on. I wish I could say that every school offered the same opportunities, but they don't. In New York, it's not fair, but these special admit schools are going to give you a leg up. They have the resources and the reputation that will take you wherever you want to go. The academics would really challenge you, and you wouldn't have to pretend not to care about being into your schoolwork and come in early just so you can get attention from the teachers. You can just go there and focus on getting the best education possible."

For just a second, I imagined myself at a high school with clean classrooms and fancy new science equipment, and kids who wanted to learn. I imagined myself raising my hand in class because I knew the answer and not being embarrassed to let my classmates know it. Mr. Marshall was right. I did sometimes dumb myself down in class at M.S. 219 because I didn't want to seem too nerdy. Too eager to learn.

"When's the test?" I asked quietly.

"Hot buttered popcorn!" Mr. Marshall shouted in triumph. "Let's go see Mrs. Givens and get you signed up."

It turned out, I had only three weeks before the entrance exam for Stuyvesant. I found out that some kids started preparing for this test in sixth grade, but I had only three weeks. I didn't make a big deal about it to my friends, but Mr. Marshall's speech and encouragement had me daydreaming about the possibility of going to this famous school. Once I looked up Stuyvesant online and saw everything the school had to offer, I gave myself permission to get excited, even though I kept that excitement to myself. I knew my friends wouldn't understand. But every day, seated at the small plastic table in our apartment, I pored over the study guides Mrs. Givens had given me and prayed that I really was smart.

After I took the test to get into Stuyvesant, I had to wait several months before the results would be in. In the meantime, there was still more to do to get ready for high school. Every day there was another essay to write or a test to take. Mrs. Givens and Mr. Marshall kept finding schools for me to apply to, with an urgency that left me dizzy and, oftentimes, confused as I tried to navigate this whole process on my own.

"Jonathan, with your grades and your aptitude, there are so many options you should consider for high school," Mrs. Givens said to me, on one of my now-frequent visits to her office. She paused for a moment and shuffled through some papers on her desk. "There's a boarding school that I think you should apply to. It's in Upstate New York and, if you do well enough on the entrance exam, you can qualify for a full scholarship."

"Where's the school at?" I asked, not even knowing what "boarding school" meant.

"It's somewhere in the Hudson Valley," Mrs. Givens said, as if that would mean something to me. "One of our students was accepted there last year, and I think you'd have a good chance of getting in, too. His family was from Cameroon, and they said Carlton loves it up there."

"I don't know," I said, scratching my head, as I tried to remember the few interactions I had with Carlton and whether the fact that he loved this place should mean anything to me.

"How about we do this, Jonathan. You go home and talk to your parents about boarding school, and I'll see what you have to do to apply. Come talk to me tomorrow, and tell me what your parents think, and we'll go from there. How does that sound?"

"Fine," I said with a sigh. "I'll ask my mom about it."

"Mom, what's boarding school?" I asked that night.

"I don't know, nigga," my mom answered, and went back to watching TV. And that was our discussion about boarding school.

The next day, Mrs. Givens tried to fill in the missing pieces.

"Like I said, the school is in Upstate New York, and you would live up there on the campus with the other boarding students."

"Wait, I gotta live up there?" I said. "Up in the woods?"

"It's not in the woods, but yes, you live and go to school there. I don't know much more about it, but it's a very prestigious school with an excellent reputation. If you got a scholarship to go there, it would be like winning the lottery."

Before I could formulate the questions I needed to ask about boarding school, Mrs. Givens was already moving on to the next thing. Like every other adult at the school, Mrs. Givens was doing the job of three people, not just high school admissions, so she always seemed rushed and in a hurry.

"You don't have to decide now whether you want to go or not, but you do have to take a test to get in, but you can take it here at school. I'll get that set up for you. And, in the meantime, Mr. Marshall wants you to apply to this other private high school in the city that he thinks you'd be perfect for. They offer scholarships, too."

"What's the school called?" I asked, trying to keep all these different options straight in my mind.

Mrs. Givens started shuffling through more papers, looking for something she couldn't find.

"I don't have the details here right now, Jonathan, but I'll get everything all straightened out for you. I think you have to write an essay as part of the application process. But your job is just to do your best. Come see me after school today, and I'll have more information for you then."

"Okay," I said, my head spinning with everything I was supposed to be keeping track of and yearning again for the simplicity my brothers had in Virginia. Sometimes, my mind dipped into jealousy and anger that my life didn't look like theirs. All they had to do was stay focused. They didn't have to apply for high school. They didn't have to think about boarding schools and private schools. Plus, they had their coaches and their friends' parents to help guide them on their paths. I had so many questions and concerns. One minute I'd think going to private school sounded cool, but the next minute I'd see myself surrounded by some stuck-up rich kids and know I didn't belong in a place like that. Sometimes, I'd look at the empty drug vials beneath my feet when I walked home, and all I could think about was how much I wanted to escape—but the courage to go from that dream to the reality of leaving the comfort of my familiar wasn't in me. Deep down, I knew fear was the thing that was really holding me back, but rather than face that fear, I simply added it to my collection of untouched emotions.

I certainly wasn't the only eighth grader feeling overwhelmed. We all felt the pressure from our teachers who kept warning us that high school was going to be the defining moment for our future. I think we all would have been happy to just pump the brakes and slow everything down. Just have a moment to breathe and be kids and not have to worry about our future every, single, minute of the day. So, when Melvin and Dwayne sometimes wanted to skip class just so we could hang out, I was right there with them. When Dwayne pulled out his rolling papers and rolled a joint on a Friday after school, I said no like I always did, out of habit. I had always told myself that I would never do drugs because I was terrified I would end up like my parents. But my whole world was changing, and I could barely keep up. Nothing was easy anymore. Nothing seemed fair. So, I decided, what the hell? Why not?

We started smoking in the park regularly after school. Getting high took the edge off my anxiety about all the looming changes and expectations weighing on me. For a few brief moments, my mind would be at peace, and I luxuriated in the feeling. It was such welcome relief from the racing thoughts that occupied my brain, twenty-four seven. School, my parents, my sister, my future. All of that was on me, and I carried the responsibility to make the right decision like a fifty-pound weight on my back. Most of the time, I was overwhelmed with my feelings of helplessness, which would then turn to anger and sometimes just darkness. But the weed made all those feelings go away. And that's when I understood why my parents did drugs. They wanted to be free from all of their worries and pain. I wanted that freedom, too.

Hanging out with Marquise was, once again, my other escape. Being with Marquise meant following him into whatever adventures he had planned. No thinking for me. No decisions. Just following. I was tired of trying to be a leader. That's why I went with him to Harlem one day, after skipping out on the last two classes at school. There was no real plan. We were just going to hang out, check the new sneaker store that had opened, and maybe get some fries. Marquise didn't have an agenda, and that suited me just fine. Once we got to Harlem, though, Marquise told me he wanted to go find some of his friends.

"They about to get out of school. Let's go over there and catch them," he said.

"Aight, bro, let's go," I said.

We walked over to the school and waited in the park across the street for a few minutes until kids started to spill out of the school.

"I'm gonna go over there and see where these guys are," Marquise said. "Just wait for me here."

I watched Marquise disappear into the crowd of kids, and I lost sight of him for a while. And then I saw him. Actually, I heard him first. The sound of his voice cursing out someone was unmistakable. I stood up and walked over to the curb to see what was going on. That's when I saw Marquise in another kid's face. I couldn't make out exactly what they were saying, but it was obvious it wasn't good. I ran to the corner to cross the street to see what was up, but by the time the light changed and I ran over, Marquise and this other kid were already fighting. Fists were flying, and it was hard to distinguish one body from the other.

I pushed myself to the front of the circle of kids surrounding the fight and tried to see if Marquise needed my help. Tried to see if I should put myself in this fight.

Before I could decide, another kid came in and started pounding on Marquise. And without thinking, I jumped in. I got in only one or two punches before I heard whistles being blown and the school security guards came charging down the steps. The two kids we had been fighting jumped away, and Marquise told me to run.

Without saying anything, we both ran back to the subway and jumped on the first train we saw.

It wasn't until we were safely back in the Bronx that Marquise told me that the kid he was fighting ran with known gang members.

"I didn't mean to get you involved with all that, Jon," he said. "But, for your own safety, I suggest you stay out of Harlem for a while. I don't want anyone to recognize you."

My heart sped up. "For real, man?"

"Look, V-A, you know I always got your back. And probably ain't nothing going to happen. But just be cool and don't go down there for a while. Whatchu need to do in Harlem anyway? They ain't got nothing we don't have in the Bronx."

I tried to play it cool. "That's right, bro," I said. "I don't fuck with Harlem anyway."

Marquise got suspended for cutting school that day because it was the third time he got caught. I didn't get suspended, but I had to stay after school for detention. A weird part of me was good with it—it would prove to Mr. Marshall that I wasn't so different from my friends. My parents were addicted to drugs. My sister was pregnant, and I was getting into trouble left and right. I wanted to make it obvious that I was like everyone else. And I belonged at the same school they did. If the choice was taken away from me, then there would be no choice to make. I got caught smoking weed at school, and my grades started slipping. Mott Hall would be my only option, and that's just where I would have to go to high school. But the more trouble I got into, the more determined Mr. Marshall became to get me into a school away from the Bronx. So, I did what I had to do. I deliberately failed the tests or botched the interviews with any private or boarding schools that he sent me to apply to.

So, Mr. Marshall did what *he* had to do. He called my mother and told her everything. He told her I came to school high. He told her about cutting classes and my grades sliding. He told her I deliberately sabotaged my opportunities to go to two excellent schools. He told her I was ruining my chances of getting into a good college. And that's all it took. My mother would always pull herself together when the school called to say something was wrong with one of her kids. That was her line in the sand that we kids knew not to cross.

After talking to Mr. Marshall, she was mad. Getting caught

smoking weed was just dumb, she said. But ruining my chances to go to a fancy private school on purpose? That was another whole level of stupid, she told me.

"You better not try that shit again. You hear me, Jonathan?" she said. "If somebody is going to pay for you to go to a private school, you better take that chance and run with it. You're too smart to play dumb."

Even my father had something to say. "Boy, don't you ever walk away from an opportunity for a free education. That's the stupidest thing you could ever do."

Even if they would never win a Parents of the Year Award, my parents never wavered on their belief that getting a good education was the most important thing in life. So, I promised them that I wouldn't mess up anymore, but the truth was, there were no more opportunities to mess up. It was time to turn in my high school application form to Mrs. Givens. Like my friends, the only school I applied to was Mott Hall. If I got into Stuyvesant, I promised Mr. Marshall I would consider it. But if I didn't get in, there was just one place I would end up.

For the next three months, there was an air of calmness at school because there was nothing to do but wait for our high school placements to arrive. When the high school letters finally came in March, there were no big surprises. I didn't get into Stuyvesant, but I missed the qualifying score by only one point. I didn't say it aloud, but I was amazed I did that well, considering I had only three weeks to study. When I scanned the page to find my acceptance to Mott Hall, it wasn't there. For some reason, it said I had been accepted to a school in Harlem called Frederick Douglass Academy. I had never heard of it, and I certainly hadn't marked it on my application.

"What the heck is this?" I said, when I read the notice at my grandmother's house. I had used her address since I didn't trust our temporary address at a homeless shelter.

First thing next morning, I went straight to Mrs. Givens' office to find out what was going on.

"Mrs. Givens," I said when she called me into her office.

"Can you help me figure this out?" I pulled the letter out of my book bag and showed her what it said. "How could I be assigned to a school I didn't apply to? I don't even know what that school is."

Mrs. Givens looked over my paper, and she smiled, but then she quickly pulled it back.

"Have a seat, Jonathan," she said.

I sat down.

"I just want you to know," she started, "that what I did, I did in consultation with your teachers and Mr. Marshall because we thought it was best for you to have an opportunity to really succeed."

"What do you mean?"

Mrs. Givens cleared her throat. She wouldn't look me in the eye. "I changed your application when you handed it in. Instead of Mott Hall Bronx High School, I put your number-one choice as Frederick Douglass Academy."

"I can't believe you fucking did that," I said, jumping up from my chair. "Are you fucking stupid?" I shouted. "You must think I'm some kind of punk, doing some shit like that."

"It's an amazing school in Harlem, Jonathan—"

"This is my life," I cried.

"A high percentage of their student body goes to college. Going there could really give you an advantage. . . ."

I shook my head no. I stopped listening.

Mr. Marshall must have heard the commotion, and he came running into the office shouting, "Have you lost your gotdamn mind, Jonathan? Sit your ass in that chair and apologize to Mrs. Givens right now!"

I sat down quickly and put my hands over my face.

This woman had totally ruined my life. I wouldn't be with my friends. There was no way to get into Mott Hall now that final decisions had been made. And Harlem? Of all places? According to Marquise, I could get killed showing my face in Harlem.

"Jonathan, please trust me," Mrs. Givens pleaded, walking over to my chair. She put her hand on my shoulder. "I understand you're upset, and you have every right to be, but I think, when you calm down, you'll realize this is a good thing."

I didn't say anything.

"Mr. Marshall and I did this for your own good," she said. "You weren't willing to consider any other options besides Mott Hall, so we did this for you."

"That's right, son," Mr. Marshall confirmed. "We were only thinking about you and what you needed. And don't be mad at Mrs. Givens—it was my idea."

"I'm sorry for talking to you like that, Mrs. Givens," I said, trying to collect myself, "but you can't just change what I put on my application. That's illegal. I could call the board of education and report this."

Mrs. Givens actually looked a little nervous then. She glanced over at Mr. Marshall, and he just shook his head like he couldn't believe my ungrateful attitude. She tried again to convince me.

"I think if you just go take a look at FDA and meet with the principal, you might change your mind."

"No way," I said, my anger lighting up again. "The only thing that better change is my high school assignment. You better find out how to fix this, or I'm going to have my parents call the board of education and report you both."

And with that, I stormed out of the room.

"Jonathan Conyers, please come to the office," the voice rang over the PA system later that same afternoon.

"Go ahead down, Jonathan," my teacher said, motioning me toward the door. I dropped off my assignment at her desk, grabbed my backpack, and left the room. I assumed I was going downstairs to hear Mrs. Givens tell me that she had fixed everything and gotten me placed at Mott Hall. I prayed that my threats to report her had worked. I knew she could legit lose her job for tampering with my paperwork.

When I got to the administrative offices, I told Mrs. Campbell, the secretary, I was there to see Mrs. Givens.

"Yeah, they're waiting for you," Mrs. Campbell said.

Who was "they?" I wondered.

When I stepped into Mrs. Givens' office, she was sitting in there with my mother.

"Hey, Boo Boo," my mom said when she saw me. "What's going on?"

I looked at Mrs. Givens, but she didn't speak. So, I filled my mom in on the details of what my counselor had done.

"They took away my freedom," I said to my mom, even though I was looking dead at Mrs. Givens when I said it. "And they better fix it, or we're going to report them to the board of ed."

"Mrs. Conyers, I want you to know that what I did was not appropriate," Mrs. Givens said, pleading with her eyes, "but I did it for the right reasons. I told Jonathan that many of the kids who go to that school go on to prestigious four-year colleges."

"I don't care about that," I said, cutting her off. "You can't just be changing things because you think you know better than me. You're not my mother!"

"Shut up, and let the lady finish," my mother said, giving me a look.

Mrs. Givens nodded. "Your son needs to trust me," she started. "What the principal at FDA is doing over there is truly amazing. They call that school the Black Mecca because he's all about proving that Black kids, particularly Black boys, can excel if they're given the right resources."

Mrs. Givens looked at me and said, "They're taking kids to Japan. They offer, like, four or five different languages to study. They even have a fencing team."

"What the heck is fencing? Whatever it is, I don't want to do it," I said, folding my arms across my chest.

Mrs. Givens turned back to my mother. "I want you guys to go over to the school and meet Dr. Hodge, the principal. They're having Orientation this weekend for all admitted students, and Dr. Hodge is really excited to meet Jonathan."

I had heard enough. "I'm not going to any FDA. You and Mr. Marshall went behind my back and made this choice without even asking me what I wanted. I've already told you

I want to go to Mott Hall with my friends. I'm not going to go over there and start selling drugs. I'm not going to join a gang. I'm going to go there and do my work and go to college. I don't need to go to no school in Harlem just to do the same thing."

"Shut the fuck up, Jonathan, and let the lady talk," my mother said.

Mrs. Givens' eyes grew wide at my mother's language, but she continued on.

"Mrs. Conyers, we're all worried about the recent changes we've been seeing in Jonathan and, quite frankly, we're worried that if he stays in this environment, he's not going to succeed. Mott Hall is a relatively new school right down the block where all of Jonathan's friends live. We're not saying Mott Hall is a bad school. We just think we need to get Jonathan away from this neighborhood for high school. And, quite frankly, with the high score he achieved on the test for Stuyvesant, he could have been accepted at several other top schools, but he filled out the forms wrong."

My mother shook her head like she couldn't believe what an idiot I was.

"I didn't know I was supposed to fill in other options on that form," I said in my own defense.

"All of us here know that if Jonathan's in the right environment, he's going to excel. But he just can't do that at Mott Hall."

"Yes, I can," I shouted.

"Shut. Up. Jonathan!" My mother turned to me. "You done already fucked up enough. If these people at Frederick Douglass are willing to take your ass, and it's as good of a school as Mrs. Givens says, then that's where you're going to go."

Mrs. Givens gave a tense little smile, and then she pulled out a brochure and a flyer and passed them to my mother. "Orientation is on Saturday, and I think Jonathan will have to take a test to see if he can handle the work there. The academics are serious."

"I ain't doing it," I said stubbornly. "I'm not going there."

My mother turned around then and lit into me. "Listen, we're

going to the goddamn school. You're going to pass that goddamn test, and you not calling any goddam board of ed because
these people are trying to help you, Jonathan. You're not going
to end up running in the streets with your little friends. You're
going to go to this FDA and get a good education and go to
college just like your brothers. The End." And with that, she
stood up, thanked Mrs. Givens, and headed out of the office.

"Let's go!" she hollered at me.

Defeated, I followed her out the door.

Frederick Douglass Academy is on Adam Clayton Powell Jr.
Boulevard in Harlem. My mother and I had to take two buses on
a Saturday morning to arrive on time. There were signs outside
the building that said "Orientation," and an older Black woman
was in the lobby checking people in. My mother marched right
up to her and told her my name. The woman told me where to
go to take the test. Before I left, Mom whispered to me, "You
better not fuck up, or I'll beat your ass." And then she wished
me luck.

When I finished, I was sent back downstairs to the lobby.
"How was it?" my mother asked me.

I shrugged. "It was easy."

"That's my Boo Boo." She beamed. "See, you belong at this
school."

"Whatever," I said. From what I could see, FDA looked like
every other public school in New York. Old brick building,
drafty, dark hallways, and linoleum floors.

As the rest of the kids came trickling down from the test room,
everyone was told to gather in the auditorium for a presentation
and a tour. My mother and I started following along, but the
lady from the front door stopped us.

"Mrs. Conyers," she started. "Dr. Hodge would like to meet
with you and Jonathan in his office. Would you mind following me?"

"I hope we're not in trouble already," my mother said with a smile.

"No, no, no," the woman rushed to assure her. "That's not it at all. Dr. Hodge just wants to meet you and Jonathan." And with that, she led us down the hall to Dr. Hodge's office.

She knocked on the door, and we heard a gruff "Come in."

The woman opened the door and introduced us to Dr. Hodge. He stood up from behind his desk and walked around to shake our hands. He was a short, chubby, white man with thick, black hair streaked with gray, and a fat mustache that reminded me of Mario from the video game. My first thought was that he looked like an Oompa-Loompa from *Charlie and the Chocolate Factory*. But he wore dress pants and a tie, which made him seem more professional.

"Have a seat," he said, gesturing to the two chairs in front of his desk. I noticed a twin bed in his office, but I didn't ask why it was there. "I already know who you are, so it seems only fitting that I introduce myself. My name is Dr. Hodge, and I'm the principal here at Frederick Douglass Academy."

"Nice to meet you, Dr. Hodge," my mother said.

"It's nice to meet both of you, too," Dr. Hodge said, taking his seat again behind his desk. "Believe it or not, Jonathan, I already know a lot about you."

"Like what?" I asked, surprised.

"Well, I know you're a supersmart kid who lives in the Bronx. You currently attend M.S. 219, and you've had some troubles here and there. I know there was some incident with the law in sixth grade. I know your teachers are worried about you getting into trouble if you stay in the Bronx. And I know that you didn't really want to come here. But here you are. And that's what's important."

"That's right, Dr. Hodge," my mother said, nodding.

I rolled my eyes. It sounded like Dr. Hodge had spoken to Mr. Marshall. That man was doing everything to make sure I ended up at this school. He was relentless.

"Listen, Jonathan," Dr. Hodge continued, "I am certain you

will do well here. But I run a very tight ship. You wanna know why I have a bed in my office? Because I sleep here most nights. I don't rest until I know everything that is supposed to be done here is done. And I have the same expectations for my students."

After that, he ran through all of the accomplishments of the school, the same ones Mrs. Givens had told me, plus some. "We offer ten AP classes. We have a fencing club and a robotics club. You play chess? We have a chess club. Everything that a Black school isn't supposed to have, we have—and it's all free," he said proudly. "The only thing we ask you to do is take advantage of everything we offer. You are required to pick at least one after-school activity to participate in and that choice must be made in the first week of school. We don't play around with that."

"This *is* serious," my mother said with admiration in her voice.

"I'm dead serious," Dr. Hodge confirmed. "You will not be going to the Bronx after school every day so you can get into trouble," he continued. "You will live here. You will breathe here. We will be your new family, and *I* will be your daddy."

This man had some nerve, but I just listened. He turned to the bookshelf behind his desk, pulled out a book, and handed it to me. It was a copy of *Narrative of the Life of Frederick Douglass*.

"This is your summer reading assignment. Make sure you read it before you come back, and you have to write a book report about it." He handed me a paper with the requirements for the assignment written out, and then he gave my mother a list of all the rules and regulations for the school, including wearing a uniform with a tie.

"Why do we gotta wear a uniform?" I said, frowning. "It's high school."

"Boy, shut up," my mother said. "You gotta wear a uniform because it's a serious school."

"It's alright, Mrs. Conyers," Dr. Hodge said. "I can answer the question." And then he turned his steely-eyed gaze to me. "When you come to my school, Jonathan, you will do whatever

I say. I make the rules, and you have to follow them whether you agree with them or not.

"But I'll tell you why we wear uniforms here. We wear uniforms at FDA because most of the students at this school don't have money to buy the latest fashions. So, what I won't allow is kids bullying other kids because this one's got the latest look and this one doesn't. You're all gonna look the same so everybody can focus on their schoolwork, which is why we're here. And by the way, Mr. Conyers, when you come to FDA, your uniform better be ironed and neat, shirt tucked in. And you better not come in my building without a belt."

"Oh, Jonathan will be here on point, Dr. Hodge," my mother promised him. "You have my word he will be ready to go come September."

Now, Dr. Hodge turned to my mother. "I'm glad to hear you say that, Mrs. Conyers, because you have a job to do here, too. We all do. These kids can't do it all by themselves. You have to help your son succeed. You have to make his life easier at home so he can focus at school. I don't just hold these kids accountable. I'm gonna hold you accountable, too," he said. "Because if you're not doing your job, *I* have to work harder to make up for what you're not doing at home."

For a minute, I thought my mother was going to start crying because we both knew she wasn't making my life easier at home, but she held it together and said, "Don't worry, Dr. Hodge. I'm going to do my best for Jonathan." And then she added, "All three of Jonathan's brothers got into college, and we expect the same of him."

I wanted to tell Dr. Hodge that my brothers made it to college in spite of my parents *not* because of them, but years of keeping my mouth shut prevented me from shaming our family and telling that truth.

Dr. Hodge clapped his hands in glee. "Well, that's good to hear. And I appreciate your attitude, Mrs. Conyers." He stood up then, indicating that our meeting was over. As he walked around his desk to shake our hands again, he said to me, "'If there is no struggle there is no progress.' Do you know who said that, young man?"

I shook my head no.

"Frederick Douglass, the man for whom this school is named. Make sure you read that book."

"Oh, he'll read it, Dr. Hodge," my mother said.

I was getting so mad at my mom. She was so eager to do what this man said. She didn't even ask me why I wanted to go to Mott Hall. She didn't care that I'd have to haul my ass every day to Harlem.

"Don't forget to stop by the student store and purchase a uniform," Dr. Hodge said as we were heading out. As soon as he said that, I knew I had my chance.

"We can't afford to buy a uniform," I said triumphantly, knowing my mother didn't have more than our bus fare in her pocket.

Dr. Hodge looked me over, then walked back into his office, over to a cabinet in a corner. He pulled out a plastic bundle and brought it over to me. "You can have this uniform for free," he said. "See you in September, Mr. Conyers."

Walking back to the bus stop, I held tight to my anger. In my mind, I just kept telling myself, I wasn't going to FDA, and if I had to figure out how to get myself enrolled at Mott Hall on my own, I would. Meanwhile, my mother rambled on and on all the way to the bus stop about how great FDA seemed.

"You're going to FDA, whether you like it or not," she said to me, right before we got on the bus. "So, get used to it."

On Monday at school, Mr. Marshall found me in the hallway.

"How'd you like FDA?" he asked me with a hopeful smile on his face.

"I didn't like it," I said bluntly.

Mr. Marshall sighed. "Well, you don't have to 'like it,' I guess, as long as you go there and get yourself a good education, that's what matters. I expect to be calling on Dr. Conyers one day."

I rolled my eyes. "Whatever, Mr. Marshall."

And I left him there in the hallway and went to my class.

Melvin and Dwayne asked me about FDA, too. At lunch. "Yo, that school ain't special," I said. "It's just another school in the 'hood."

"I know that's right, bro," Melvin said.

"Plus, folks be tripping if they think I'm taking two buses every day just to go to Harlem. Nah, son. I don't think so. Next year, my Black ass will be right here with you guys in the Bronx where I belong."

I ended eighth grade bitter and angry at Mr. Marshall for what I felt was his betrayal in forcing me to go to FDA. It would take a couple of years before I recognized that his "betrayal" saved my life. I loved Mr. Marshall when he was cheering for my hopes and dreams, but it was the fact that he never gave up on me that made him an invaluable member of my village. Everybody needs someone who will fight for you when you're too dumb, or too weak, or too scared to fight for yourself. Someone who will continuously be the mirror to remind you of who you really are. Mr. Marshall was that champion for me, even though I didn't see it that way when I left M.S. 219. It is one of my greatest regrets in life that I didn't thank Mr. Marshall when I had the chance.

5

I Wasn't Supposed to Be in High School in Harlem

At 6 a.m., I was standing at the bus stop, waiting for the Bx41 and cursing Dr. Hodge for making a tie a required part of the FDA uniform. I was already riddled with anxiety about starting a new school, but the tie was just making it worse. Every time I tried to tie the thing, it ended up looking like my shoelaces, or just a messy knot under my chin.

"Shit!" I exclaimed for probably the one hundredth time in less than a minute.

My father worked construction and restaurant jobs, and I'd never seen him wear a tie in my life. Josh used to wear ties when he was singing, but he never taught me how to tie one, so I stood there fussing with the thing and cursing the fact there was nobody in my life to teach me something that seemed so basic. Even though I should have been used to that reality by now, the pinging disappointment could still bring me to tears, but I refused to let myself cry over a stupid tie on a street corner in the Bronx.

Suddenly, an old Black man wearing disheveled clothes, who smelled stale and musty, shuffled over to me and made like he was going to grab me around the neck. On instinct, my hands went up to defend myself.

"Put your hands down, boy," he barked at me. "Let me show you how to tie that tie."

I was so surprised, my hands dropped to my sides, and I

watched the man start to undo the messy knot I had been trying to wrangle into place.

"You're a Black boy outside struggling to tie a tie. What's wrong with you? You don't got no daddy?" the man said while he worked. He started humming a tune and the tip of his tongue peeked out from the side of his mouth. I didn't bother to respond to his question. Besides, what would I have said, *"Yeah, I got a daddy, but he never taught me anything, except how to fight."*

I kept my mouth shut and watched the man, trying not to make eye contact, in case he took it as an invitation to ask me more questions.

"There," he said when he was finished. "That's how you tie a tie."

"Thank you," I said, in a tone that probably expressed the fact that I was both grateful and embarrassed. Because I was more embarrassed, I turned to walk away to avoid any awkward follow-up conversation with the strange man, but he stopped me by reaching for my neck again, to untie the tie.

"We not done until you can do this yourself," he said, pointing a finger at me. Then, he reached up and undid his work and took the tie off my neck and said, "Now, you do it."

Without thinking, I grabbed the tie and quickly tried to re-create the steps I had just seen the old man do, but I messed up. A few people were now clustered at the bus stop, and I felt ridiculous. The man didn't seem to notice or care, and he showed me again how to do it.

"Try again," he said.

This time, I blocked out the people around me. I couldn't be late to school on my first day, so I needed to get this done before the bus arrived. I focused solely on getting the movements right. "Alright," the man said when I was done. "You got it. Now, just keep practicing, and you'll never forget how to tie your tie." Then, he clapped me on the back, said, "Have a good day," and just walked away.

At the time, the shame of being in public having a homeless man help me get dressed, quickly transformed into frustration with my father for not being there for me. For not teaching me the things I needed to know to succeed. It was a vicious cycle that I'd circle through mentally when caught in moments of need like this. If my tie wasn't tied correctly, I wouldn't be let into school—and those times of stressful constraint always led back to the resentment regarding my parents.

Only later would I be able to look back at that moment and be thankful for that old man's presence in my life for those few minutes. I consider him a temporary visitor in my village. His motive was pure and clean—simply to help a kid in need. The thing is, we're taught to move through the world with boundaries up and to be afraid of each other, especially when a person doesn't look like our expectation of a blessing. So, I could have missed out on receiving his gifts. I could have pushed him away. Instead, I thank whatever it was in me that day that allowed me to accept help from a stranger, rather than letting my pride or my ego shun his goodwill because of the way he looked, or smelled, for that matter. It was a valuable lesson I had to be taught a few more times before it stuck, but it is a habit I have learned to cultivate: to stay open and accept help from the most unexpected people and places.

When I arrived at FDA, Dr. Hodge was standing in front of the building, welcoming all the students—something I would come to learn he did every single day—and making sure everyone was in uniform and looking sharp. When he saw me, he smiled, and said, "Good morning, Mr. Conyers. I thought you weren't coming back."

I just glared at him in response. I couldn't believe he was going to throw that in my face. And then, to make it worse, he said, "Mr. Conyers, hold up. I don't like what I'm seeing." He ran his eyes over my body from head to toe. "I might need to send you home, young man."

"What are you talking about?" I said, looking down at my

clothing. I had my uniform dress pants on, my white shirt was pressed, and, thanks to the old man, my tie was tied properly.

"Why don't you have on a belt?" Dr. Hodge said, pointing to my waist. "A man never leaves the house without a belt."

I couldn't believe I was going to have to go all the way back to the Bronx just to get a belt. This man was crazy.

"Listen, go to my office," Dr. Hodge started, "and I'll be in there shortly to get you a belt you can borrow for the day."

I stormed into the school and headed to the office. I told the secretary what had happened, and she told me to go have a seat in Dr. Hodge's office. "Don't worry," she said, "Dr. Hodge is a little tough, but you'll be okay." I ignored her and sat in Dr. Hodge's office stewing for twenty minutes until he came back, acting like we were old friends. He made small talk while he fumbled around in the cabinet behind his desk.

"Here," he said, handing me a belt. "You're fat like me, so this will probably fit you."

I couldn't believe this man called me fat, but I put on the belt and kept my mouth shut. Because it was true. I was fat. But I didn't need anyone to remind me. Dr. Hodge acted like he didn't notice my discomfort.

"You missed breakfast, so you can have mine," he said, tossing me the plastic-wrapped muffin on his desk. "Now, go to your first class."

"I don't even know where my first class is," I practically shouted. It wasn't even 9 a.m., and already I felt like I'd lived a whole day.

Dr. Hodge was not feeling my pain. "Well, wander the halls until you find it," he said. "All freshman classes are on the second floor. You'll figure it out," he said.

I grabbed the muffin and left the room thinking Dr. Hodge was a total nut case. And mean. But, as I walked down the hallway of the second floor, looking for my English class, my annoyance slowly dissolved as I took in everything around me. I passed dance studios and a classroom where students were building robots. Lining the walls were the pictures and names of former students posted with their academic achievements, interspersed with photographs and images of famous Black historical figures.

That feeling continued when I finally found my classroom. English was one of my favorite subjects because I loved to read. As soon as I settled into a chair in the back of the room, I noticed how quiet it was when the teacher spoke. The other kids weren't talking. Nobody was goofing off. I couldn't believe the order and respect the teacher had in the classroom. And nobody was being sent to the principal's office.

After English, I had global studies with Mr. Murphy. Apparently, he was a legend at FDA. Standing just over five feet tall, with slicked-back gray hair, he ran his classroom with military precision. Skipping over first-day niceties, Mr. Murphy launched right into drilling us on what we needed to do to get into college, starting with taking AP classes. I didn't even know what an AP class was, and I was too embarrassed to raise my hand and ask. But I started taking furious notes because everyone else was, and I didn't want to get left behind. By the end of the day, I realized that going to school at FDA was going to challenge me in ways I'd never experienced at M.S. 219 or at my schools in Virginia. I just prayed I could handle it.

I kept to myself the whole first week of school. I went to class and went home, hating the hour-long commute every day. I toyed with the idea of trying to find some kind of way to transfer into Mott Hall. But I didn't have the energy to figure out how to start that process. I told myself I just had to deal with FDA. I'd get through it somehow. Someway.

During the second week of school, Dr. Hodge called me into his office and threatened to suspend me.

"What did I do?" I cried, racking my brain trying to figure out what rule I had broken to be threatened with suspension. I hadn't even been at the school long enough to cause any real trouble.

"We had an agreement, young man," Dr. Hodge said, pointing his finger in my direction. "I promised your mother that you would not be leaving this school building until 6 p.m. You were supposed to choose an after-school activity by the end of last week."

"Dr. Hodge," I said, "I don't fence. I'm not good enough to join the basketball team. You don't have a football team, and I'm not playing chess. So, what am I supposed to do?"

Dr. Hodge leaned back in his chair and said, "I can tell you what you're not going to do and that is leave this building at 3 p.m. If you can't find a club or a team you want to join, then you may wander the halls until six o'clock or sit here in my office. But you can't leave this building until six o'clock, unless you want to get suspended."

"Are you serious?" I asked.

"As a heart attack," Dr. Hodge responded with a sly grin. "Now, go back to class."

I hated to be forced into doing something I didn't want to do, so I wandered the hallways of FDA after school and just wasted time until 6 p.m. I wasn't going to join the chess team just because Dr. Hodge said so. I didn't think that was even legal. And it wasn't my fault that FDA didn't have any teams or after-school activities that interested me. I would have been thrilled to play football, but a football team in Harlem was highly unlikely because no school had the space to build a football field in Harlem.

Wandering the halls at FDA became a specialty of mine because I'd also started wandering the hallways during lunch hour. I hated sitting in the cafeteria by myself. Everybody else had their friend groups, since a lot of the kids at FDA had been there since the sixth grade. Rather than waiting for someone to invite me to eat with them, I preferred to skip lunch and just walk up and down the hallways, trying to look like I was going somewhere so I wouldn't get sent back to the cafeteria.

On a Monday, when I should have been at lunch, I was strolling the hallways peeking into rooms and reading the posters on the walls when I heard a teacher asking her students, "What is your *why*? Why do you care?" It was the sound of her voice that stopped me. There was something so dramatic in her tone. She sounded like an actor in a movie or something.

I peeked into the room and saw what looked like a class of older kids. I knew they had to be at least juniors because freshmen and sophomores were all in the cafeteria. The teacher was a young, white lady with long, dark hair and glasses. She was wearing a dark skirt and a simple blouse. Her voice sounded older than she looked.

"Can I help you with something?" She caught me lingering in the doorway.

I don't know why, but I opened my mouth and blurted out, "Can I sit in the back of the class here?"

The teacher looked at me funny at first, but then she shrugged her shoulders and said, "Sure, you can sit right there," and she pointed at a desk and a chair in the back of the room. The twenty-five other students gave me a quick glance, but then returned their attention to the teacher.

"You guys finish reading the end of the chapter, and then we're going to discuss it," the teacher said before coming back to talk to me.

"What's your name?" she asked me, lowering her voice. I told her, and she said her name was Ms. Dicolandrea, but everyone just called her Ms. DiCo.

"Are you a freshman?" she asked as I settled into my seat.

"Yes, ma'am."

"Why aren't you going to lunch? This is your lunch period, you know."

"Yeah, I know," I started. "I just don't like, um..." I didn't know how to explain it without sounding like a baby. She quickly filled in the empty space.

"Don't worry about it," she said. "This is a senior elective class on debate, so you might be a little bored, but you can sit here as long as you want to." And then she went back to teaching. I knew the seniors were allowed to choose some of their classes instead of being forced to take a full menu of required science, math, history, and English. The electives I'd heard of were for cool classes like dance and robotics. But debate? I had no idea what a debate class was supposed to be about, but anything was better than sitting in the cafeteria by myself, so I decided to settle in and figure it out.

I came back the next day and the day after that, and I decided debate class meant talking about real life issues and then discussing them in a philosophical way that Ms. DiCo taught the students. Instead of textbooks, the students were reading a book called *Justice* by Michael Sandel, a Harvard professor who was masterful at breaking down social issues using philosophical paradigms. She also had the students read articles from the *New York Times* and news magazines like *Time* and the *Atlantic*. After reading the articles, they would have a discussion where Ms. DiCo would ask the students their opinions about what they read. Even if a student couldn't provide a specific example from the article to prove their point, it was okay if they talked about their personal experiences or opinions on the topic, as long as they could defend their argument.

Far from bored, I was hooked right away because it seemed like the whole point of the class was to learn how to argue. If there was one thing I knew I was good at, it was talking and arguing. Also, Ms. DiCo was one of those teachers who bounced around the room and got super animated when she spoke. She, literally, got excited every time a student raised their hand and said something. She was like that parent who thought everything their kid said was brilliant, but every student in the class was her kid. It was hard not to feed off her energy, as well as the energy of the other kids in the class. It was an elective class, so everybody in the room wanted to be there.

Four days later, I'd made it to every one of Ms. DiCo's lunchtime classes. There had been a few times when I'd been tempted to raise my hand and say something, but I chickened out. But, on this day, the discussion was about poverty and, so far, the conversation had been all theoretical based on the articles Ms. DiCo had assigned. People were talking about government policies and the wealth gap between Black and white America.

And then this one kid raised his hand to share his thoughts about what was wrong with the welfare system.

"Look, I know I'm not supposed to say this, but I think people on welfare are just abusing the system. They don't want to work. They're lazy, and they just want to collect a check. And, sometimes, people that live in the projects are living better than people who have to pull regular New York City rent prices. So, we have to be careful when we're talking about who is really poor and who isn't."

Before I could stop myself, my hand shot up.

"Yes, Jonathan," Ms. DiCo called on me. She sounded surprised that I had raised my hand.

I stood up before I could lose my nerve. I said to the kid who had just made that statement. "Kevin, do I look lazy to you? Because I've lived off welfare my whole entire life and I don't think I'm lazy."

Kevin looked alarmed. But I wasn't done. I was so triggered by what he'd said, like he knew something about the life I had been living.

"Kevin, do you know what it's like to feel like the only thing you can do to guarantee that you're going to eat in a day is to steal a loaf of bread and packet of bologna?"

"No," Kevin said.

"Well, I do, and I can tell you it's not because I'm lazy or I'm trying to game some system or because I don't want to work. And I can also tell you that my grandmother lives in the projects, and the projects literally smell like shit, and they're infested with rats and roaches, even though my grandma scrubs her apartment from top to bottom every day, and she is not living the high life you seem to think she is."

I stopped talking. My heart was racing, and I felt my face grow hot. My mind was suddenly spinning. *Why did I just say all that in front of these people? Why did I let that out?* I quickly sat back down and kept my head down.

Nobody said anything. I had to fight the urge to jump up and run out of the room.

Finally, Ms. DiCo spoke. "Thank you for sharing, Jonathan. That was very brave of you, and you shared in a way that really made us think deeper about how poverty truly affects people."

Then, she turned to the class and asked, "Any comments?"

Kevin raised his hand. "Yo, bro, I'm sorry for what I said. I'm sorry I sounded ignorant."

"It's okay," I mumbled, still not wanting to look up and see them looking at me with pity or contempt.

Luckily, the bell rang at just that moment, releasing me from the agony of sitting in that room any longer.

But, instead of hustling out of the classroom like they usually did, all the students came over to me and patted me on the back, saying things like, "Thanks for sharing, man" and "You're going to be okay." One girl said, "You know, you're not the only one at this school whose family is struggling, so don't be too hard on yourself, okay?"

I looked up then and realized nobody was making fun of me, or looking at me like some charity case. I felt my embarrassment start to dissolve.

The last kid to approach me on his way out was Malcolm. He always spoke up in class. He reminded me of Justin in a way because he was always super confident and he liked sports, too. "Yo, bro, we Black Kings," he said to me, patting me on the back. "And Black Kings always rise."

I smiled at that. "Thanks, bro," I said.

"No doubt," he said. "You'll be in class next week, right?"

I didn't even have to think about it. "Yeah, I will," I said.

"Good," he said as he walked out of the room.

"Hey, Jonathan." Ms. DiCo now stood in front of my desk. We were alone. "You should think about joining the debate team. The whole reason I started this class was to get more kids interested in joining the team. We could use more people, especially freshmen and sophomores because we have a lot of seniors graduating this year. I can tell you're enjoying this class, and if you join the team, you can develop your speaking skills and have a chance to compete against other schools."

"So, it's like a sport?" I said.

Ms. DiCo laughed. "I'm not sure if I would classify debate as a sport, but it is definitely competitive, and you win trophies and compete for local, state, and national titles. Plus, we get to travel for some competitions."

I nodded my head as I thought about it. "I could try it out," I said, trying to imagine a competition where people argued for trophies.

"Great," Ms. DiCo said, smiling wide. "We meet here in this classroom after school. I look forward to seeing you next week!"

"Okay, Ms. DiCo," I said, returning her smile as I gathered my things and headed out of the room.

As I walked down the hallway, the smile stayed on my face. Those kids made me feel as though I had said something important, just by telling the truth. And they didn't laugh at me or make me feel stupid for being vulnerable. I didn't know the name for the feeling I had, but I liked it and definitely wanted to feel it again.

"Hold up, Mr. Conyers!" It was Dr. Hodge walking toward me like a man on a mission. I stood still, waiting to see what kind of trouble I might be in now.

When he caught up to me, he said. "It's been two weeks, and I'm still waiting for you to tell me what you're going to be doing after school," he said.

"I joined the debate team," I said, grinning in triumph.

Dr. Hodge narrowed his eyes for just a moment, like he was trying to decide if he should believe me. Then, he said, "If I recall, you do like to argue, Mr. Conyers, so debate sounds like the perfect activity for you." Then, it was his turn to smile. "Now, I can leave you alone," he said and turned and walked away.

Two weeks. It took me only two weeks at FDA to realize that the kids who had the most respect at school weren't the roughest or the toughest, they were the smartest. And they weren't just surviving, they were thriving. The kids with the highest GPAs had their pictures plastered on the walls in the hallways, along with successful school alumni who went on to graduate from college. These were the superstars at FDA, the ones who got the most attention and were praised and supported by the faculty and staff. Thanks to my naturally competitive nature and a lifetime of being told by my parents that I would go to college, I quickly fell under FDA's spell, and it felt like coming home to my true self. Back to where I belonged. I could stop hiding behind that manufactured mask of indifference, and I didn't have to dumb myself down for anyone. Yes, FDA had its fair share of students who were just there passing time, who didn't care about getting good grades. But the kids I was watching were serious about their academics and wanted to take advantage of every AP class and extracurricular activity the school had to offer. They had their eyes on the Ivy League. The only thing standing in my way was my fear that I might not be as smart as everyone else around me seemed to be. I wasn't sure if I could really keep up with the smart kids at FDA, but I was going to try.

The first day I went to debate team practice, two things became clear immediately. I understood why Ms. DiCo was teaching a debate class to recruit more students for the team. There were only seven other kids at practice that day, four underclassmen and three juniors. Most of the juniors and seniors who were technically on the team had stopped coming to practice consistently because of commitments to sports teams and things like SAT prep. The other thing I realized was that I had no idea what debate was all about. It was obviously about a lot more than discussing current events and sharing our feelings, like we did during the lunchtime class.

The core team was made up of three girls and six boys, including me. And even though we were only a few weeks into the school year, they were deep into their practice and preparation. I looked around the room and saw the word "resolved" on the board, followed by a statement about nuclear weapons being necessary for a peaceful democracy. The kids were talking about writing cases and doing research, and I was thoroughly confused.

"Don't worry, Jonathan." Ms. DiCo came right over to me when she saw the look on my face. "I'm sure this all seems overwhelming, but once you get caught up, it will all make sense." And then she told me about her favorite quote. "Do you know who Viktor Frankl was?" she started. I told her I didn't.

"He was a brilliant man who survived the Holocaust, but lost his entire family, yet he still managed to live a life of meaning. And he always quoted the philosopher Nietzsche, who said, 'He who has a why to live for can bear with almost any how.' When you find your *why* here in debate, Jonathan, that's when things really start to happen."

I gave her a look that, I'm sure, signaled I was still confused. But she just laughed. Then, she sat me down and gave me an overview of how high school debate worked.

Ms. DiCo explained that they were doing Lincoln-Douglas–style debates, which were styled after the seven debates between Abraham Lincoln and Stephen Douglas when they were running against each other in 1858 for the Illinois U.S. Senate seat. The focus of their debates was mainly slavery, so it became a highly publicized event at the time. Lincoln actually lost to Douglas, but it was those debates that brought him national attention and laid the groundwork for his run for president.

I had no idea who Stephen Douglas was, but Ms. DiCo seemed so excited about her explanation that I decided not to interrupt her flow.

"So, basically, when we debate in competitions," she continued, "we have a resolution, like the one you see on the board, and you will be arguing either in favor of the resolution or against it."

"Okay," I said. "That sounds doable."

Ms. DiCo laughed. "I mean, it is doable, but it takes a lot of work to win your argument, and there are specific ways you score points in competition."

"What do you do here during practice?" I asked.

"Good question," Ms. DiCo said. "So, what the kids are doing now is researching and writing their cases. Basically, a case is your argument for or against the resolution, supported by facts that you've researched. The thing is, you won't know if you are arguing for or against the resolution until you actually get to the competition. So, you have to be ready to go either way, which means you have to research both sides of the topic."

"Do you have to have it all memorized?" I asked, already beginning to doubt whether I really wanted to do what sounded like more homework.

Ms. DiCo threw up her hands and smiled. "Oh, no. Not at all. You don't have to memorize your speeches or your facts. You can totally use note cards, but you want to have a good grasp of the information so you can deploy it whenever and however you need it."

"Okay," I said, nodding my head, even though a million questions were running through my mind. And debate was now sounding less and less like something I really wanted to do.

"Don't worry, Jonathan," Ms. DiCo said. "It all feels really complicated when you get started, but once you get the hang of things, it's a whole lot of fun, and I think you'll really enjoy it. I can tell, just from how you participate in my class, you have a lot to say."

I smiled at that. That was the first time a teacher told me I talked a lot, but it wasn't an insult or a reprimand.

Ms. DiCo told me to sit with the two girls who were working on writing a case together so I could get a sense of what was required to prepare for a competition. She promised she would work one-on-one with me to explain things in detail a bit later.

After they said hi, the two girls, basically, ignored me. I listened to them talk about nuclear weapons policies and how to argue with the right contentions and values. I tried to keep up with what they were saying, but I had no interest in or knowledge of nuclear weapons, and the other stuff they were talking about went over my head. Pretty soon, I felt my eyes drooping, and I caught myself falling asleep more than once.

When practice was over that day, Ms. DiCo stopped me by the door. "What did you think?" she asked.

She seemed so excited, I didn't have the heart to tell her that I thought it was the most boring thing I'd ever done. Instead, I said it was fun.

This prompted a look. "I don't think you looked like you were having too much fun, Jonathan," she said. "But I promise, next practice I'll have time to help you out some more. Okay?"

"Okay," I said and headed out the door.

The next day that I went to practice, Ms. DiCo came right up to me when I came into the room. "I thought you might not come back after last practice." She grinned. "I know it's a lot at first. But listen, I'm going to sit with you today and go over exactly how everything works so you can get started on building your own cases."

After she got everyone settled, Ms. DiCo and I sat down side by side, and she broke down the whole concept of debate to me.

"The first thing you have to understand about debate," she started, "is that you have to find your voice. You have to believe in your right to command the attention of your audience. Because they have to listen to you."

Ms. DiCo explained that debate wasn't about the subject matter we were talking about, it was about understanding how to win an argument using the principles of logic and the fundamentals of philosophy and ethics.

"That's why I talk about philosophy and ethics so much in my class," she said.

And even though what she was saying still left me scratching my head, the fact that she was explaining it with so much passion made me try harder to pay attention.

In a debate competition, there are two people debating the resolution. The affirmative side argues for the resolution, the negative side argues against it. Each side gets six or seven minutes to make their argument, and then they get cross-examined by their opponent. After cross-examination (CX), each side gets to restate their argument at least one more time with closing arguments. To me, it sounded a lot like what I saw on TV, when lawyers fought each other in the courtroom. I loved *Law & Order*, and for a minute I saw myself in a courtroom arguing my case. But then Ms. DiCo brought up the whole ethics and philosophy thing again, and my mind wandered a bit. But, basically, I understood it didn't really matter what the resolution topic was, we had to base our arguments on bigger-picture ideas about life. Ms. DiCo called them "values." She said every argument came down to things like freedom, liberty, the pursuit of happiness, the greater good, and justice. These were principles of philosophy.

"So, let's say the resolution is, 'The right to bear arms in a democracy is morally justified,'" Ms. DiCo said. "Your job is to build a case for or against that idea, but you have to come up with a way to prove your point using one of the values. So, you could argue for the resolution with a case that said guns make people feel safe, and when people feel safe they participate more fully in society, therefore, the right to bear arms in a democracy is morally justified."

I made a face. "That sounds like you're just playing with words and meanings," I said.

"You're not wrong," Ms. DiCo said. "Writing a good debate case is almost like putting the pieces of a puzzle together, only the puzzle pieces are concepts and ideas. There's a process to put it all together. Once you understand it, you'll be able to put a case together on any topic. But be clear, we do a lot of this prep work together."

"You do?" I said, feeling relieved.

"Yeah, as a group we brainstorm ideas on how to argue for or against the resolution. Once we have the argument we're going to make, we look for facts, statistics, stories, and examples to prove our point. And then we're ready to write our case. And once you write your case, you can use it for every competition. Until the resolution changes, which happens every two months."

"So, we work together on doing all this writing and resolutions stuff?"

"Yeah," Ms. DiCo said. "When you're up there debating, you're all on your own. But everything else, we're doing it together. As a team."

I looked around the room and saw most kids working in pairs. Some were talking, others had their heads down writing furiously. It didn't look like any team I'd ever seen, but I decided to stick around. I didn't want to disappoint Ms. DiCo. I didn't want to deal with Dr. Hodge bothering me if I quit, and I didn't have anything or anyone else clamoring for my time.

"So, what should I do now?" I asked.

Ms. DiCo smiled and stood up. "I have some cases you can study to see how they're written. Let's just start you there."

Sometimes during practice, we would have prep debates during which we would take turns arguing for and against the resolution, so I slowly started to understand what a competition would be like. Ms. DiCo let me use prewritten cases to argue from. I still didn't have a whole lot of interest in nuclear weapons, but I liked the competitive nature of the process. I liked speaking and arguing. That part was fun. But the reading and researching and writing part, I still couldn't get excited about it, even though I liked to listen to the older kids spit fire with some of their speeches.

Malcolm, the kid in Ms. DiCo's elective class who told me we were Black Kings, was one of the kids I loved to listen to speak. He was that perfect mix of smart and cool, and he was always nice to me in class. We bonded over our love of football, and he was always giving me advice on which classes to take and what teachers to look out for at FDA.

"Hey, Jonathan, there's this summer program I think you should apply to." Malcolm stopped me one day after class. "It's called (MS)2. The 'M' and the 'S' stand for 'math and science.' It's at this boarding school called Phillips Andover in Massachusetts. They fly you out there, the food is amazing, and it's all free, bro. You don't gotta pay for anything. Of course, you gotta do all these math and science classes, but it's mad fun, I promise you. And it's for minority kids only who, you know, are really smart but come from poor communities. You should think about applying. I bet you'd get in."

This time, I knew what a boarding school was, but I had so many questions. Still, all I could fixate on was that Malcolm thought I was smart enough and cool enough to tell me about this program.

"Sounds good, bro," I managed to utter.

"Cool," Malcolm said. "I'll bring you the information about the program."

"Thanks, bro," I said. And we went our separate ways.

The next week, Malcolm had another idea for me.

"Yo, Jonathan, you said you wanted to play football, right?" he asked.

"Yeah," I said. "Why?"

"I just found out about this team called the Harlem Hellfighters. The coach played in the NFL, and he's supposed to be kinda famous. He's trying to bring football to Harlem. You wanna try out with me? As long as you're in high school in New York City, you can try out."

"For real?" I said as all of my dreams about playing football came flooding back.

"Yeah, man, I'm going to go try out this week. You should come with me," Malcolm said.

Two days later, Malcolm and I both made the Harlem Hellfighters team. It was a far cry from Justin's team at Western Branch High School. There was no official field, so we had to practice wherever we found space. That meant we didn't have a gym to practice in, either, and equipment was donated and secondhand. Coach was scrappy and used his connections to get us the basics, but it still felt like a sad imitation of a real high school football program. But at least I was in the game. Now I could, literally, follow in Justin's footsteps and make my way to college with good grades and four years of football. It occurred to me then that I might not even need to do debate anymore.

For a while, I tried to do both things, debate and football.

Both met after school, but I wasn't fully committed to either one. Coach was on my case about missing practice for debate. And DiCo could tell I wasn't totally committed to debate because I wasn't doing the research required to write a good case, and I had stopped coming to every practice. I blamed my absences from debate on football, but the truth was, everything besides the arguing in debate was boring to me. It was boring— and a lot of work. And even though I liked the kids on the team, and I liked Ms. DiCo's class, I just could not make myself care enough to try harder.

But football wasn't holding my focus, either. Three weeks into practice and we hadn't even played a single game, and there were no games on the schedule. I had a hard time believing that this version of high school football would bring any colleges looking for me. But if I quit, what would be my thing? I didn't know who to ask for help or advice, so I just stayed stuck in a holding pattern, hoping something or someone would help me decide.

"Mr. Conyers!"

Dr. Hodge caught me in the hallway during lunchtime. I was on my way to Ms. DiCo's class.

"Yes, sir," I said while doing a quick inventory of my uniform to make sure my shirt was pressed, my tie was tied, and I had on a belt. Dr. Hodge had caught me once or twice with uniform infractions, and I didn't want another confrontation.

"Ms. DiCo tells me you've been missing debate practice quite a bit lately. Is anything going on you need help with?"

"No, sir," I said.

"So, why are you missing practice?" Dr. Hodge demanded. "Is something happening at home? Do I need to call your mother?"

"No, sir," I said, hating the thought of having my mother show up at school. "I'm just having second thoughts about doing debate. I'm not sure I want to be on the team."

"Is that so?" Dr. Hodge said.

"Yeah, but I joined the Harlem Hellfighters football team," I quickly added, to make sure Dr. Hodge knew I wasn't hanging around in the Bronx.

"What is it that you don't like about debate?" Dr. Hodge asked.

I squirmed under his gaze and hesitated before telling the truth, but I didn't have a better excuse ready, so I said, "Debate is just kind of boring, and it's a lot of extra work. The teachers here already give us so much homework. Adding debate to everything is kind of a lot."

"Mr. Conyers, follow me," Dr. Hodge commanded as he started walking briskly down the hallway. I had no choice but to run after him.

Dr. Hodge stopped in front of a painting of Frederick Douglass. "Mr. Conyers, what does that say?" he said, gesturing to the words above Frederick's head.

"It says, 'If there is no struggle there is no progress,'" I read.

"Exactly," Dr. Hodge said, folding his hands in a prayer position. "And you, Mr. Conyers, seem allergic to struggle. And you need to get over that real fast. Everything isn't going to be easy. Discipline and hard work are going to have to be your best friends, or you won't get anywhere in life."

"I'm not allergic to struggle," I said defiantly. "I've been struggling my whole life! And I've worked harder at FDA than I have at any other school."

Dr. Hodge ignored my defense.

"Well, Mr. Conyers, you're a Black boy in America and that means you're going to have to work even harder. If you think what you're doing is good enough, you're mistaken. If you think quitting every time things aren't fun anymore is a winning strategy, you are not going to make it in this world."

"You don't know me," I said, trying to hold my tongue. What I really wanted to say was, *"Listen, white man, what do you know and where do you get off telling me how to be a Black boy in this world?"*

Dr. Hodge held up his hand as if to stop my thoughts. "Don't get mad at me for telling you the truth. I didn't make the rules that this world runs on, but I can help you follow them so you can be successful. The world isn't fair, especially to Black people. You gotta be smarter and better than all the white kids out there who can get away with being mediocre."

"But that's not fair," I practically shouted.

"I didn't say it was fair, Mr. Conyers," Dr. Hodge said. "But it is the way it is, and you are never going to beat the system by being lazy or quitting or looking for a shortcut. So, I suggest you think very hard before you quit the debate team."

My shoulders dropped, and I let out a heavy sigh. "Yes, sir," I said, and I walked back to Ms. DiCo's classroom.

After my "talk" with Dr. Hodge, I tried to see the positive side of debate. I tried to remind myself that debate was what the smart kids were doing, and if I applied myself, I might actually be good at it. I kept telling myself not to be a quitter, but I kept football in my back pocket. I was just hoping it would become clear to me which activity I should truly focus on. Which one would, as Dr. Hodge had said, help me rise higher.

I got my answer after I went to my first debate competition.

We took the subway down to Regis High School on the Upper East Side of Manhattan. Regis is a private Catholic boys' school with a reputation for being one of the best Catholic schools in the country. On Fridays, they hosted local debate competitions to give novice debaters the chance to practice competing and to have a chance to qualify for bigger tournaments at other schools. Ms. DiCo wanted us to participate so we could have the opportunity to debate against people other than our FDA teammates.

We would be competing against students from other private or special admittance schools, like Stuyvesant, and Ms. DiCo wanted us to be prepared. She warned us, "In debate, you guys are always going to find yourself in rooms with a lot of white people and a lot of wealth, and I don't want that to throw you off your game. You have to go into these competitions without feeling intimidated. So, the more practice you can get, the better," she told us.

Ms. DiCo was a white woman who had gone to Stuyvesant,

and then on to Yale. She didn't strike me as the type of white person who knew a lot of Black people in real life, except her students, but sometimes I felt like she was more offended by racism and bigotry than any of us. She was always talking about the "inequities in the system" and "fighting against oppression." She didn't like to use words like "minorities"; she preferred to refer to Black people and gay people and immigrants as "people from marginalized communities." And according to Ms. DiCo, we all deserved to be heard. We all deserved to be present in the rooms where decisions were made, and that's why she was so passionate about teaching debate. She was trying to pave the way for us to stand up and speak truth to power.

I respected Ms. DiCo's passion for debate, but I still thought she was a little bit corny sometimes and over the top. And I was always suspicious of white people who tried too hard to be down with Black people. But I could tell her heart was in the right place, and she obviously knew what she was talking about when it came to debate. That's why I agreed to go to the Regis school tournament, even though I didn't think I was ready to actually compete. But Ms. DiCo said I'd never get the hang of debating unless I threw myself into the action, so I pushed my anxieties aside and tried to prepare myself for something I still didn't understand fully. Up until this point, debate was relegated to what went on in Ms. DiCo's classroom. It was seven of us kids working together, debating against each other and listening to Ms. DiCo tell us how to make more cohesive arguments. Sometimes, it was an hour talking about some boring philosophical concept that was supposed to make us think deeper about the issues we were debating. Sometimes, it was an hour talking about the difference between two words that sounded the same to me, like freedom and liberty.

I kind of assumed a competition would feel like the same thing, just at a different school.

I was so wrong.

When I walked into Regis High School with my team members, I immediately felt the discomfort of being in a place I didn't belong. For starters, the building looked more like a fancy hotel than any school I had ever been in. There was no security desk and no metal detectors. Instead, we walked into a lobby flanked with marble pillars, where oil paintings of important white men stood watch from the walls. The kids we passed in the hallways were mostly white. All of them boys wearing crisp khaki pants with navy blue blazers. We stared at them, and they stared right back at us, the kids who didn't belong in their school. Ms. DiCo hustled us down a hallway to a large room where all the debaters were gathered. Ms. DiCo had been right—the room was filled mostly with white kids and us. But it wasn't just our melanin that made us stand out in that room; it was what we lacked as well. While we carried our spiral notebooks and index cards in our regular backpacks, many of the other kids came with leather briefcases, meticulously organized with all their materials. It was obvious to me, and probably to most of them, that our team wasn't in the same league as the rest of them. Yes, everyone was there to debate, but I couldn't help but feel like the hired help at the party.

I took that attitude with me when it was my turn to debate my first opponent. Each debate took place in a classroom. When I came into the room, I saw my opponent—a white boy with blond hair and green eyes that reminded me of the marbles we used to have in my kindergarten classroom. The only other person in the room was the judge. Since these were just practice tournaments, the judge was a volunteer from the school. He was also white. He told me to get set up so we could begin.

I assumed setting up meant taking my spiral notebook, my case that was printed out on three sheets of paper, my timer, and my two different-colored pens out of my backpack, so that's what I did. Meanwhile, my opponent was taking color-coded note cards and a stack of bulging folders out of his briefcase and arranging them meticulously on his desk. When he was done, he turned to me and shook my hand and introduced himself. I was shocked to find out he was only a ninth grader, like me. He just seemed so confident in this environment—I could tell right then and there he was going to win, and I was going to lose.

My opponent got to argue the affirmative, so he went first and made his case for why nuclear weapons are necessary to maintain a peaceful democracy. I was so busy worrying about how I was going to compete against someone who was so much better than me, I forgot to take notes during his speech to prepare for my CX. But, as soon as he finished, I was expected to stand up and ask him questions that would demonstrate that his argument wasn't that strong, or trap him into agreeing with a statement I was going to make in my own case. I stood up, holding my notebook in my hand even though it was blank, and at that moment my mind was, too. But I knew I had to say something, so I asked the kid basic questions from How to Debate 101 like, "What are the values in your argument?" and "What is your contention?" It was obvious to the judge and my opponent that I hadn't taken notes and that I was fumbling my way through the process. When I was done, my opponent looked smug, like he knew he was going to win. At that point, we all knew.

I went through the rest of the round, doing my part by reading the case Ms. DiCo had helped me prepare. I gave my rebuttal, and we went through another round of CX. I didn't think about enunciating properly. I didn't make eye contact with the judge. When my opponent stood up to question me for his CX, it took all within me not to just shout, "You already won. You don't have to show off and make me look stupid." Instead, I tried to answer his questions the way Ms. DiCo taught me, but I couldn't put my hands on my notes fast enough, so my responses were vague and imprecise. When it was finally over and my opponent gave his last speech and his voting issues, the judge announced he was voting for the affirmative. I wasn't surprised. I was just glad it was over. The whole process was embarrassing and infuriating. I was mad at my opponent for being better than me. I was mad at Ms. DiCo for making me come. I was mad because I hated looking stupid in front of other people. Especially rich white people. And I was mad that when it was over, my opponent looked at me like I had been a waste of his time.

"Hey, Jonathan." Ms. DiCo came up to me right after I finished. "How'd it go?"

"I was terrible," I said. "That kid made me look like a fool." I couldn't even meet her gaze.

"Don't be so hard on yourself. This was your first competition. And you're still alive. You finished. You didn't give up. That's a win for your first time."

"Whatever," I said.

"No, really, I've seen kids give up in the middle of the debate and just forfeit their turn because they get so frustrated or embarrassed. You didn't give up. You hung in there."

I looked Ms. DiCo square in the face now. She didn't seem to be playing me, but it was hard to accept what she was saying. What did she know about feeling less than in front of all these white people? She didn't understand that me losing wasn't just about debate; it was also about being a stereotype. I gave these white people exactly what they expected from a Black kid from a public school in Harlem. I looked stupid and uneducated and pathetic. I assumed Ms. DiCo had never been in that situation, so how could she tell me it wasn't so bad?

But she was fixated on the competition and nothing else.

"Were you able to read your entire case in the time allotted?" she asked me.

"Yeah," I said. "I finished reading it before the judge yelled 'time.'"

"Well, that's something to be proud of," Ms. DiCo said. "Just being able to get your whole argument out means you have good pacing, and you know how to use your time. You weren't so nervous that you lost track of the time. That's all good."

"Whatever," I said, shrugging my shoulders.

"No, it's not whatever. It's something," Ms. DiCo said as her cheeks turned pink as she grew more desperate to make me see that I wasn't a failure. "Jonathan, as soon as you commit to debate and really start trying, you're going to see some real improvement. You'll even start winning, but you gotta come to practice regularly and really do the work."

"You really think I could win a competition?"

"If you start coming to practice more consistently and commit to the team, there's no doubt in my mind you could start winning."

Despite my painful loss at Regis High School, something about debate kept me going back. It was a combination of Ms. DiCo's supportive attitude and the fact that I actually did like arguing and talking. These things came easy to me. I always joked that if debate were based solely on a person's ability to talk a lot and tell good stories, I would be a world champion. But the writing, researching, and practicing part was the necessary evil I still hadn't made peace with. But I was getting better at it.

Sometimes, just for practice, Ms. DiCo would have us argue about something silly or from the day's headlines, just to get us to practice technique, and I always killed it in those scenarios. I could almost always come up with a point to argue, and I was able to connect it to the values embedded in debate culture. In class and during practice, we might end up having these incredibly deep discussions about the drug wars, or trickle-down economics and how they affected society. I was learning so much, and I was able to articulate my ideas into coherent arguments. My classmates often clapped when I was done making an argument. And then Ms. DiCo would say, "See, Jonathan. That's the kind of attitude and precision you need to use during competitions!"

I finally made the decision that if I was going to win at debate, I was going to have to do more than show up for practice. Writing a really good case and doing all the research to be ready for a vicious CX meant I had to do the work outside of class, too. So, I quit the football team and decided, once and for all, that debate was going to be my thing. Once I made that decision, I finally stopped resisting doing the actual work. I took the time to study the resolution and write a case I actually believed in, rather than trying to memorize something someone else had written. I practiced my opening speech in front of the mirror at home, and I organized my cards with all of my facts so I could easily put my hands on them when being questioned for CX. Being in debate also helped me in other ways. To synthesize so much information to write a case, Ms. DiCo taught us how to read with emphasis and capture the most important information out of a story or article, quickly and efficiently. I ended up using those techniques in my other classes at FDA and I found myself able to keep up, even excel, in my classes that required a lot of reading, like history and English.

I kept going to the Friday Regis tournaments, and little by little, I was able to hold my own. When I entered a room, it wasn't so obvious anymore who was going to walk out the winner. But now, after every loss, I grew more and more determined to win. I wanted to win for Ms. DiCo. I wanted to win because I was working hard during practice and wanted the reward for the hard work. But deep down, I really wanted to win so I could say I was better than all the privileged white kids who had so much more than me. I wanted to win so I could say, "Yo, you guys, getting picked up in your Mercedes-Benzes and Lincoln Town Cars, I can still beat you, and I come from nothing. I don't have your private school education and your tutors and your money, and I can still beat you. Not on the basketball court, not in a street fight, but here in your house, in a battle of intelligence, and wit, and oratory style." Just like Frederick Douglass.

Dr. Hodge was right about two things: Discipline and hard work were paying off for me in debate, and I knew I could beat my opponents, if I just put my mind to it and didn't give up. Dr. Hodge's insistent voice was always in the back of my mind, reminding me to try harder if I wanted to see results, and not to give up or wait for the world to change its rules for me. I always thought Dr. Hodge was picking on me and that he was out of line telling me how I should behave as a Black boy in America, but his tough talk and high expectations were exactly what I needed at that stage in my life. I would have quit debate. And lost out on a life-changing opportunity if it weren't for Dr. Hodge holding up a mirror to my faults. I was looking for an easier path because my life was difficult enough, but Dr. Hodge refused to let me feel sorry for myself or make excuses for not doing my best. He was the toughest member of my village, but the lessons he taught me prepared me well for a future filled with challenges.

Four years after moving back to New York, my parents finally found a tiny one-bedroom apartment they could afford with the help of a government subsidy. The apartment was in the Castle Hill area of the Bronx, which suited my parents just fine, but it was farther north and farther west in the Bronx than our last shelter apartment, so that meant an even longer commute for me to school in Harlem. Even though I was grateful that we were out of the shelter system and all of the shame and uncertainty that came with it, our family dysfunction didn't disappear with a lease and a set of keys. My parents were still smoking crack, and my mother's MS was really causing her problems. She'd wake up in the middle of the night, screaming in pain, and we didn't know what to do to help her. Since Helena had given birth to her baby girl, she'd moved out to live with her boyfriend, so it was just me at home with my parents. By this point in my life, I was used to feeling like I was on my own. My parents' addiction kept them from being the type of parents who paid attention to what I was doing on a daily basis, or how I was doing it. My mother tried to act like she was aware of what was going on in my life, but her attention span was never consistent. Basically, my mother would spring into action if the school called, but otherwise she assumed I was doing okay and that she didn't have to worry about me. For his part, my father went to work consistently and, occasionally, would offer his advice or opinion when asked. Sometimes, there would be food in the house. Sometimes, there wouldn't. Sometimes, my mother would be overcome by guilt and so she would buy me an expensive gift, like a pair of two-hundred-dollar sneakers or a new phone, and sometimes I would have to go to school with dirty clothes because there wasn't enough money to run a load of laundry at the laundromat. Luckily, I knew my grandmother was always there for me if I needed a meal or a quiet place to study. My father had stopped beating my mother, but they still argued and fought a lot, and I hated to be around that as much as I hated to see my parents high. So, I stayed away from home as much as possible.

In middle school, Marquise, Dwayne, and Melvin had been my stand-in family. At FDA, the kids in Ms. DiCo's debate class and the members of the debate team became the people I felt I could really depend on and share my feelings with. I didn't know whether any of them had parents who had drug problems or if they had lived in homeless shelters, but everybody had family drama. Even Malcolm, whose mother was an English professor in the Bronx, didn't have a father in his life. We all came with imperfections, and debate gave us the perfect opportunity to talk through some of our deepest issues and concerns.

All of the emotions and secrets I had been silencing for years now had a forum for release. Going to debate practice almost felt like therapy to me. I cried during debate practice more times than I can remember.

And Ms. DiCo was always there to help and support us. And not just with debate-related work. She was always helping her seniors with their college applications and recommendation letters. She told us about scholarships and summer opportunities she thought we should apply for. We always joked that Ms. DiCo gave one hundred percent on her slow days and one hundred and fifty percent on her regular days. She would even buy us dinner sometimes after practice because she knew some of us wouldn't have a meal waiting when we got home. And it was because of her enthusiasm and her dedication to us we wanted to do well for her. At least I know I did.

Ms. DiCo probably had no idea that every time she encouraged me or pushed me to do better or told me I deserved to have people listen to me because I had important things to say, she was, literally, breathing life into me. She made me feel like I was really capable of doing great things. Just being myself. "You're enough just as you are," she would tell us. "Don't let anybody tell you that you need to change."

By the second semester of my freshman year, I started getting noticeably better at debate. Ms. DiCo was relentless in her training. On top of all the research we had to do to be prepared to meet our opponents, she made us go home and practice our speeches with pencils in our mouths, which would force us to enunciate properly. I felt ridiculous doing it, but I did it anyway.

I was now writing my own cases and holding my own when we went to Regis. It became common for me to win at least one round out of three. If the resolution was something I genuinely cared about, like prison reform, drug sentencing laws, or funding public school education, I was unstoppable. With each round I won, I felt my confidence growing, and I knew it was only a matter of time before I would place in the top-ten finishers. Luckily, debate is a yearlong activity, so I still had five months to hit that goal.

In the meantime, I continued to do well in school, and I had established myself as one of the "serious smart kids" at FDA who were trying to be about something. Both my history teacher and my science teacher had already hinted that I should be taking AP History and AP Biology my sophomore year. And AP Biology was usually a class for upperclassmen only. Dr. Hodge even stopped me on the way into school one morning to tell me he was proud of the progress I was making. "Keep up the good work, Jonathan," he said. "That's how we rise." With the exception of my home life, I could actually say I was happy with the way my life was going. My brothers would be proud that I was finally hitting my stride.

"Have you heard anything back from (MS)2?" Malcolm caught me in the hallway at school on a cold day late in February.

"No, bro, not yet," I said. "Should I have?"

"Did you get your application in on time?"

"Yeah. Mr. Murphy wrote my recommendation letter," I said.

Malcom patted me on the shoulder. "Don't worry about it, Black King. I'm sure you'll hear from them soon. I know you're going to get in."

I know my face looked worried, but I still said, "No doubt," to Malcolm.

"You're going to get in. Relax," Malcolm promised. And then he ran off to class.

I didn't want to get my hopes up too high because I wasn't used to getting what I wanted in life. But I really hoped and prayed Malcolm was right. Not only because I wanted to see what it was like to go to a fancy boarding school and learn high-level math and chemistry, but also because I dreaded the idea of having to sit home all summer watching my parents smoke crack in our tiny apartment.

A week later, I received word that I had been granted an interview for the (MS)2 program. Malcolm told me if I passed the interview, I was practically guaranteed a place. The door to possibility was now opening a little wider, and I allowed myself to dream a little bigger.

The interview was scheduled for a Saturday at a random office building in Midtown Manhattan. The program director was coming to New York and other cities around the country to interview the program applicants. We had to bring a parent to the interview with us, which left me in a panic. My mother couldn't take me because her MS was flaring up, which meant my father would have to be the one.

But my father wasn't like my mother. He didn't like being in social situations, and he didn't do small talk. I worried about the impression he would make on these boarding school people. On top of that, I didn't think my father hid his addiction as well as my mother did. When my mother did her hair and smeared on a bit of lipstick, you would never know she smoked crack on a regular basis. But, with my father, depending on the day of the week, there were things that gave it away if you knew what to look for. The bloodshot eyes. The cracked lips. The twitchy, itchy inability to be still. And it didn't help that the clothes he wore usually bore the stains and sweat from work. But my father was my only option, and he was willing to go, so he was the one by my side on Saturday morning.

The whole way into Manhattan on the subway, my father and I didn't exchange a single word. He didn't seem to notice that I was worried, or he didn't care. Meanwhile, I sat and tried to anticipate the types of questions I would be asked and wondered what, if anything, my father would be expected to do or say. I prayed he wouldn't embarrass me, or worse, say something that would ruin my chances of getting in.

Malcolm kept telling me I was going to get in, and he promised to show me around when I was there. He reminded me that going to the (MS)2 program was practically a guarantee that I'd get into a good college. Like Ivy League good. And after being at FDA for six months, I now understood that there was a hierarchy of colleges. Even though my brothers were all at different colleges in the South, I never understood what made one college better than another. I had since learned that schools had rankings that made one more prestigious than another. The debate kids were talking about going to schools like Harvard, Yale, and MIT. Those were the types of colleges, they assured me, that would open doors in corporate America and guarantee getting into the best medical schools in the country.

As the subway rumbled into Manhattan, I tried to review the points I made in my essay, but I kept sneaking glances at my father and worrying that, no matter what I did, my success would be derailed because of my father's addiction. Would my parents ruin another opportunity for me? I felt that familiar cocktail of frustration and anger flare inside. Why couldn't I have been born into a family with two normal parents, with a father who would help me prepare for the interview, rather than doze off and ignore me?

I told myself it didn't matter. I'd gotten this far by myself, I could finish the process by myself, too. All my father had to do was stay quiet, and I knew he was good at that.

When we made it to the building where the interview would take place, we rode up in the elevator in silence. We found the office and were met by a well-dressed, clean-shaven, bald-headed Black man.

He reached out to shake our hands. "My name is Dr. Ubinto, and I'm the interim director of the (MS)2 program," he said. He then turned to his colleague seated behind a table and introduced him. "This is Mr. Anderson. He sits on the admissions committee as well."

Once we were all seated, my father and I in two chairs in front of the desk where Dr. Ubinto and Mr. Anderson held court, the interview began.

Dr. Ubinto had a stack of folders in front of him, and he opened the one on top. "So, Jonathan, I want to start by saying your essay was very impressive. I think it's what made me want to meet you."

"Thank you," I said, feeling a swell of pride.

For the rest of our interview, I answered Dr. Ubinto and Mr. Anderson's questions to the best of my ability. It felt like they were trying to get to know me as a person rather than a checklist of my academic skills. They asked me about my hobbies and what I liked to do in my free time. They asked what my favorite class was at school, and they also asked what I thought my best qualities were. I was afraid my answers might not be good enough. And the fact that my dad was sitting in his chair looking like he was trying not to fall asleep made me nervous. A couple of times, I tried to make eye contact with my father, to signal to him to sit up and look like he cared, but that was hard to do with two sets of eyes on me.

"Well, okay, that's all we have to ask you, Jonathan," Dr. Ubinto said, closing his folders as the interview came to an end. And then he turned to my father. "Do you have any questions for us, Mr. Conyers?"

"Nah, I don't have any questions," my father said.

I let out an irritated sigh. Ms. DiCo always told us that asking questions meant you were paying attention. I felt my chances of getting into (MS)2 start to fizzle away.

Then, Dr. Ubinto turned to Mr. Anderson and whispered something. Mr. Anderson stood up then and said to my dad, "Mr. Conyers, can I show you out? Dr. Ubinto wants to ask Jonathan a few additional questions."

My father gave a grunt of assent, and he and Mr. Anderson left the office.

When the door closed behind them, Dr. Ubinto fixed his eyes at me and said, "Jonathan, whatever you got going on with your dad, you need to fix it. You're not very good at hiding your emotions, and the negative energy you're throwing at your dad isn't acceptable."

My instinct was to defend myself. "I wasn't trying to be disrespectful, sir, but there are just some issues at home and..."

Dr. Ubinto stopped me by holding up his hand. "I don't care what the problem is with your dad, and I'm not saying he's perfect, but what I saw was a father who showed up with his son today, and a son who had an attitude that presented itself as disrespect."

I hung my head but, inside, I was seething. This man didn't know anything about my dad and what he put me through, or what he put my mother through on a daily basis. And now, it was going to cost me this amazing opportunity? I couldn't let that happen.

"Sir," I started. "I'm sorry for being disrespectful to my father. We just have some issues that we have to work on, but I shouldn't have brought that here today."

Dr. Ubinto took off his glasses and studied me carefully before saying anything. He wiped his lenses and then slid the glasses back on and said, "Jonathan, I've interviewed six Black boys here today. And do you know how many of them came with their father?"

I shook my head no.

"One," he said. "You! *Your* father is the only one who showed up."

I sighed because I just didn't think I had to be grateful for something so small, when everything else my father did carried so much negative weight in my life. It didn't seem fair.

Dr. Ubinto sensed my reluctance. "I'm not here to say your dad should be awarded the Father of the Year Award. And I'm certainly not suggesting you don't have the right to be angry. What I am saying is that whatever wrongs your father has committed, he was here with you today, and he didn't have to be. He obviously cares about you and your future enough that he showed up and did his part. For you! I can't tell you how many young men would gladly trade places with you just for that. Just to have a father who would be there for them when they needed him."

This time when I hung my head, it was to re-examine my feelings. I was so mad at my dad all the time that I hardly ever stopped to think that just having my father in my life, who was available to show up for me, was something I should be grateful for. Marquise didn't even know who his father was.

"Jonathan," Dr. Ubinto said, "I'm going to accept you into the program because I can tell you have what it takes to be successful, but you must promise me that you're going to take advantage of every opportunity on the Andover campus while you're there. And that you'll bring the right attitude."

"Yes, sir, I will," I said. I paused before I asked, "So, that's it? I'm in? I get to come to (MS)2?"

Now, he smiled. "Yes, you do. Congratulations, Jonathan." He stood up then and walked toward the door. "You'll receive all the information you need in the mail, including your plane ticket."

I was grinning like a fool as I stood up. "Thank you so much." I ran out of the office and found my father standing by the elevator. I waited until the elevator doors closed behind us before I told him the good news.

"I got in!" I shouted.

"Good for you," my father said with a smile and that was that.

But it was enough for me.

When I went back to school, after I told Mr. Murphy, I told Ms. DiCo the good news that I'd been accepted into (MS)2.

"I'm so proud of you, Jonathan," she said, after I explained what (MS)2 was all about. "It sounds like an amazing program, and I'm sure you're going to do great!"

Just one month later, Ms. DiCo congratulated me again. I came in third place at one of the Regis competitions! That meant out of all the students competing that day, I had the third highest score of everyone. I couldn't believe it. Yes, it was just a novice tournament, but I was competing against private school kids and the kids who were smart enough to get into Stuyvesant. When my name was called and I went up to accept my trophy, you couldn't tell me anything. I had to hold myself back from doing a victory dance. I was a winner! I wanted to shout, "In your face, minions! I beat all y'all at a game that wasn't made for me to win." But, of course, I didn't, because I didn't want to embarrass Ms. DiCo, who was sitting in the audience grinning from ear to ear.

Once I went back to my seat with my shiny silver trophy in hand, Ms. DiCo leaned over to me and said, "When you come back from Andover next year, Jonathan, you gotta give me all you got for debate. This is just the beginning for you!"

The weekend after that tournament, I found out Marquise had been arrested and was being sent to a juvenile detention center. I felt guilty because, all year, I'd been so focused on my success at FDA that I hadn't been a very good friend to Marquise. I hadn't been around much, and we hadn't hung out in a while. As I sat in my bed on Saturday night, I thought about Mr. Marshall and what he had constantly been telling me about Marquise's journey in the world and mine. I wasn't sure I wouldn't be with Marquise on my way to juvie if I had gone to school in the Bronx with my friends. I certainly wouldn't be on my way to spending my summer at one of the most prestigious boarding schools in the entire United States.

Before I could change my mind, I called my friend Sherida, who was in eighth grade at M.S. 219.

"Can you give me Mr. Marshall's cell number? I know he always gives it out to kids at the beginning of the year."

"Jon, didn't you hear?" Sherida said, her voice low. "Mr. Marshall died a few weeks ago."

"What do you mean, he died?"

Sherida said that she thought it was a heart attack, they weren't sure. I didn't know what to say. Mr. Marshall wasn't old. He wasn't supposed to die. I never got to say thank you. The last thing he heard from me was me running my mouth, angry with him about going go to FDA.

"You okay, Jonathan?" Sherida asked over the phone.

"No," I said. And then I hung up.

I flopped down on my back on my bed and let the tears run in warm rivers down my cheeks as I thought about all that Mr. Marshall had poured into me. He put in a good word for me with that cop when Marquise and I got in trouble, and with Dr. Hodge. He never asked for a thank-you, never reprimanded me for being ungrateful. He went above and beyond whatever his job description was, always to show me that I was great and destined for great things. And now, he was dead. And he'd never know how much I loved and appreciated him. I never thanked him, and that felt like an agonizing sorrow in my gut. The guilt was overwhelming.

I promised myself that, from then on, I would always tell the people in my life who meant something to me that I appreciated them, and thank them for helping me. At fourteen years old, that would be easier than in adulthood when life gets so busy you simply don't have time to thank people in the moment, or because there's no time to reflect. But room must be made to acknowledge and thank the village that makes you. I learned from Mr. Marshall to make it a daily practice, before it's too late or the opportunity is taken away from you.

6

I Wasn't Supposed to Be
at an Elite Private Boarding School

I had never been on an airplane. And now, here I was, sitting on the tarmac at LaGuardia Airport waiting for our turn to take off on a flight to Boston. My stomach was full of nervous energy, and my leg bounced up and down of its own accord. I kept staring out the window looking at the other planes lined up in front of us. I didn't know if the fear I felt was about flying or about entering a world I'd never been in before, without my family or friends, and I just prayed I would fit in.

I did more research on the school once I knew I was going for sure and found out how expensive and exclusive Andover was. I didn't have to pay a cent for my summer program, but the regular tuition at the school was something like fifty thousand dollars per year. When I thought about how much money was being spent on me, I couldn't help but worry about what I had to do to earn that level of investment. As an adult, looking back, I know what I was feeling then was impostor syndrome, worrying I wasn't "good enough" to attend the same school that John F. Kennedy Jr., George H. W. Bush, and George W. Bush had attended. As I sat there on the plane, my mind jumped to the cheap clothes I had in my suitcase, the few dollars I had in my wallet to last all summer, and my public school education. Before I left, my grandma gave me a roll of quarters for the laundry machines and a lesson on how to wash my clothes so I didn't look dirty and disheveled "in front of all them white

people," she said. "You better not go there and embarrass yourself at that fancy school" is the last thing she told me. I promised
her I wouldn't, but now I worried that I would.

The engines on the plane started to rumble, and my hands
gripped the armrests on either side of me. I closed my eyes as I
felt the plane start to accelerate down the runway and, in what
felt like an instant, we were up in the air. I peeled open my
eyes, one at a time, and looked out the window at the world
below, and my whole face fell into a smile at the wonder of it
all. I saw the ocean, the city in geometric shapes, and the clouds
above me. Everything looked so beautiful and peaceful from this
vantage point. I felt myself relax, and I forgot about my worries
and paid attention only to the world outside my window. Maybe
it would all turn out just fine, I told myself. And I let myself
hold on to that thought for the rest of the flight.

"Jesus! Jesus! Jesus!" were the first words that came to mind
when the shuttle bus dropped us off on the Andover campus. My
jaw fell open, and I didn't even bother trying to pull it closed.
Everywhere I looked, I was met with opulence and grandeur.
The tall, dignified trees. The beautiful red-brick buildings. The
grass looked impossibly green. And the campus stretched far
beyond what I could see. I couldn't believe this was really just a
high school. Of course, I had seen pictures, but nothing could
have prepared me for Andover in real life.

"What world am I in?" I mumbled to myself as a counselor
walked us through the expansive campus to get to the dorms
where we would be staying. It took us about ten minutes to
get there, and I just drank up the view en route. I saw more
buildings, more trees, and a handful of students, most of them
white, milling around. When we made it to the building that
the counselor said would "be our home away from home for
the next six weeks," my first thought was that this building was
nicer than any place I had ever lived for my whole life.

Having gone to Regis High School for debate tournaments,
I knew there was a different world out there where money
wasn't a scarce commodity, but this was like a different world

on steroids. As we traipsed through the dormitory hallways, my anxiety returned. I was certain I wouldn't be able to fit in at a place like this. I was completely out of my league. This was far beyond being the new kid at a public school in the city. This wasn't going to be over in two hours like a debate at Regis High School. I didn't get to go home afterward. This was going to be my home for the next six weeks, and I cursed myself for thinking I could handle this. It was now crystal clear that I wasn't supposed to be at Phillips Academy Andover.

"Jonathan Conyers," the counselor lady called out.

I raised my hand. "Here," I said.

She double-checked her clipboard and then said, "This is your room."

Everybody else continued on down the hall and left me standing in front of a door that had my name, and the name of a kid named Jackson Mayes, taped on the front.

I opened the door and saw a neat, tidy room with two twin beds and two desks with matching chairs. The bare walls were painted a pale yellow, and the floors were covered with dark blue carpet.

Seated at one of the desks was a chubby, light-skinned dude who was now staring at me as I stood in the doorway. "Hey, Jonathan, right?" he said with what sounded like a southern accent to me.

"Yeah," I said. "You Jackson?"

"That's me," he said.

"Where you from with that accent?" I asked.

"Chicago," he said.

"For real? I thought you were from down South," I said.

"Nah, bro, unless you count the South Side of Chicago, South." We both laughed then, and the tension was broken.

"Is this your first year, too?" I asked as I pulled my suitcase into the room.

"No, this is my second year," Jackson said. "You're the new guy. They always put first-years with a second-year so you have someone to show you around and stuff." Jackson got up from his desk then and showed me which bed I could have and which dresser I could use. He told me how far down the hallway the bathrooms were and what time I had to be back in the dorms at the end of the night. I tried to act like I was cool with everything, but inside I was still holding on to the belief that I was going to mess up everything. I began to unpack my suitcase and tried to tell myself to calm down.

Just then, someone knocked on our door and Jackson yelled, "Enter." A brown-skinned kid with long, straight, black hair wearing, what I assumed was, some sort of Indigenous American headdress, complete with a feather, popped his head in and said to my roommate, "Yo, Jackson, have you seen Parker yet? Is he here, man?"

Jackson said he hadn't but would let him know if he did. After the kid left, I turned to my roommate and said, "Are there, like, real Native Americans here?"

Jackson smiled. "Yeah, dude. This program is for Black kids, Latinos, and Native Americans."

"Yo, ain't we all part Native American," I joked. "My mother always said we're part Cherokee."

"Nah, man, for real," Jackson said, getting serious. "These kids are coming from reservations in Arizona and places like that. Their life is crazy. I mean, I'm from the South Side of Chicago, and I've seen shit you wouldn't believe, but wait till you hear what life is like on the reservation. You'll hear about it when we do cultural sharing."

"What's cultural sharing?" I asked. But before Jackson could answer my question, a Black kid wearing a "Tupac Lives" T-shirt opened our door. "Yo, what's poppin in here?" he said.

"Yo, Ricky, what up, man?" Jackson went over to hug his friend.

Ricky turned to me and asked where I was from. We kept talking, and I felt myself slowly start to relax. People were coming here from all over, and everyone seemed to be cool. Nobody seemed too arrogant or bourgie, but, of course, I hadn't met any white people yet. I turned back to my suitcase trying to keep an open mind about everything when I heard a familiar voice.

"Yo, Jonathan, you made it! The Bronx is in da house!"

It was Malcolm. By now, there was a small crowd of students outside our door and spilling into our room. Malcolm took the opportunity to introduce me to the group and claim me. He pounded me up and put his arm around my shoulders. "Yo, everybody, this my brother from another mother. We family, so treat him accordingly. Nobody mess with him."

The guys and a few girls who were now all standing around said hello to me, and I fed off Malcolm's exuberant energy. My feelings of not belonging from just a few minutes ago were replaced with the familiar vibe of Black and brown kids coming together and holding each other up. It was intoxicating, and I was there for all of it.

I finished unpacking, and then Malcolm announced we were all going down to main campus to wait for everyone else to arrive. People started talking all at once about who they were excited to see, what they had to run back to their room to get, and begging others to wait for them at a certain spot. "Come on, Jonathan, let's just go," Malcolm shouted over the noise. With me at his side, Malcolm led the way across the campus, with a bunch of other kids from the dorm right behind us.

As we walked, Malcolm took the opportunity to point out different buildings and what we would be doing in each one. He stopped in front of a building that looked like a fancy version of City Hall and told me that this was where we were going to have our first official (MS)2 meeting in about an hour. "This is where everybody is going to come once they get settled in. Just stick with me," he said. As we stepped inside, I felt like I was in a rerun of Regis High School. Marble pillars, oil paintings on the wall, rich white kids, both boys and girls, everywhere I looked.

My anxiety crept back into my consciousness and tried to ruin my mood, but Malcolm interrupted my negative self-talk.

"See that girl," Malcolm whispered and pointed at a blond girl wearing a pale pink jumpsuit. "Her grandfather is some famous investment banker, and she, supposedly, has a trust fund

At my godmother's house, taking a picture on my thirteenth birthday

In reading recovery with my first-grade teacher on my seventh birthday

Chilling in bed, happy, with my new ponytail

My parents on their wedding day in 1988

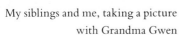

My siblings and me, taking a picture with Grandma Gwen

Hanging with my mother when we first moved to Virginia

With my siblings in New York City

Hanging out with my friend at our end-of-the-year debate celebration, 2009

My debate team, with DiCo, at Frederick Douglass Academy

On the Red Line, taking the train to Harvard University to compete at the Harvard Invitational Debate tournament, 2010

At my Stony Brook University EOP graduation ceremony with my mother and daughter

My Far Beyond the Expected poster hanging on Melville Library at Stony Brook University

My smiling daughter and me enjoying our time at a friend's wedding

At morning meeting during my second year at (MS)2 with my assigned big brother

Holding Emily
while watching TV

Nicky and Emily
taking a selfie

Emily, age 3, posing at our Stony Brook University campus apartment before going to day care

Emily, having a good time on the swings in a Brownsville park

Finding joy in my last days at (MS)2 before graduation with my best friend

Striking a pose at a debate tournament at Yale University

with more than a million dollars that she gets as soon as she turns eighteen."

"Are you serious?" I said, trying to imagine that kind of wealth.

"Like Dr. Hodge says, 'as a heart attack,'" Malcolm said, and then laughed at his own joke.

"That's bananas," I said in shock.

The girl walked by us then, and she waved at Malcolm.

"Hey, Malcolm, how's it going?" she said.

"Hey, Sarah." Malcolm gave her a nod. "It's all good."

"Cool. I'll see you around," she said, and walked away to join her friends.

Malcolm waited until she was out of earshot before turning to me to say, "Look, Jon, there's two groups of kids here every summer," he started. "It's us, the poor kids, and them, the rich kids. We come here for free and they pay the billion dollar tuition. Without them there would be no us, so be nice to them. You got it?"

"Wow, yeah, I got it," I said. It was just like how I always felt at Regis—we were the hired help at the fancy party.

"But don't worry," Malcolm rushed to assure me after seeing my look of concern. "We don't gotta interact with the rich kids except during the Friday night dances when they try to force us to 'integrate.' Otherwise, all the classes and all our activities are just with (MS)2 kids."

For the next hour, while we waited for Orientation to start, we hung around the lobby of the building where the furniture was so fancy I was afraid to sit on it. Malcolm told me to relax and enjoy everything, but it was hard for me. My mother, both of my grandmothers, and it seemed like every other Black person I knew of a certain age had always made me feel like we couldn't get caught being "messy" in front of the white people. Like somehow the white people would use our messiness to justify their racism and bad behavior. It was a terrible way of thinking, essentially blaming the victims of racism for racism, but at the time, I had those voices in my head and couldn't get past thinking I would get caught doing something wrong or embarrassing. I feared that I'd show my ass somehow and people, especially the white people, would know I didn't belong there among the civilized and privileged.

So, I stood there and tried not to take up too much space. And I watched Malcolm and my fellow (MS)2 classmates act completely unbothered by the fact that there were white people all around them. They just let their joy fly unbound as the other (MS)2 kids slowly trickled into the building. It felt as though I was at center court watching a family reunion. Girls were squealing and laughing. The guys were giving each other the types of full-body, soulful hugs that Black men invented. The faces I saw and the language I heard were all familiar, even though I was sitting among strangers. There was so much love flowing, it built a force field around us all that no amount of stares, snickers, or side-eyes from the white folks could penetrate. And the truth was, the white kids weren't even paying a whole lot of attention to what our group was doing. It seemed as though I might have been the only one worried about being messy.

By the time Orientation was over, I had let my guard down enough to bond with a bunch of other first-year students who were also trying to figure out how everything worked at (MS)2. I met a girl named Juanita and a guy named Mike, who I immediately fell in step with, and we were laughing and having a good time, making fun of our fears and concerns together. Juanita was from Chicago and Mike was from Atlanta, but we understood each other like play cousins from down the block.

When it was time to eat, I found Malcolm again and together we went to the Paresky Commons, where all the meals would be served. I stuck close to Malcolm because, once again, I was overwhelmed. I was expecting something like a school cafeteria, but the Paresky Commons was a two-story building that looked more like a fancy restaurant than any school cafeteria I had ever seen. There was a buffet set up that seemed endless, with so many different types of food offerings I could feel my mouth start to water right away. But just as quickly, I realized I probably couldn't afford half of what was on that buffet. There were fresh fruit and vegetables, a salad bar, pasta, three different meats, sandwiches, and what looked like lasagna. I also saw beverage machines and a dessert table.

"How much does this cost, bro?" I whispered to Malcolm as I tried to guess what the cheapest items on the buffet were. I was calculating what I might be able to eat and how long before my money ran out. "I have only one hundred dollars to last me the whole summer. That's all my Uncle Wayne could get me," I said, keeping my voice low.

Malcolm smiled and put his arm around me. "Bro, you can eat all of this. As much as you want, for free."

"For free?" I said. I didn't believe him. "Yo, they are just going to let us eat without paying. What do we have to do in exchange? Wash dishes or something?"

Malcolm shook his head and laughed. "Yo, Jon, it's all free. Just eat what you want, man. Don't make it a big deal."

I heard what Malcolm said, but I was still convinced someone was going to come up to me and hand me a bill after I ate, so I put only a few items on my tray. Just in case.

Malcolm told me I was acting weird, but at that point, everything felt weird to me. Andover was a whole new world.

That night, as I was lying in bed listening to Jackson snore softly on the other side of the room, my mind was racing. I was on system overload with all the new things and new people I had encountered. Nothing I read in a brochure or saw online could have prepared me for everything I had experienced just on my first day. But one thing I had happily discovered was that all the kids in the (MS)2 program were like me. Most of the Black kids were from big cities, like New York, Memphis, Detroit, and Cleveland, and they lived in poor neighborhoods and went to public schools, but they were all smart, and they all wanted something better. I found out I wasn't the only one who had only one hundred dollars for the whole summer, and I wasn't the only one with just a few items of clothing packed in their suitcase. I had found my people in less than twenty-four hours and that had become the best starting place for me. I just prayed I would be able to keep up with the academics and the hectic schedule that awaited.

"Breakfast starts at 7 a.m.," Malcolm reminded me before we said goodnight. "Whatever you do, don't be late."

Jackson woke me up at 6:45 the next morning. "Don't be late, means get there early," he told me. "Dr. Ubinto don't play."

I scrambled out of bed and headed to the bathroom to get ready, and soon enough, Jackson and I were eating pancakes for breakfast. By 7:58 a.m., we were in our seats waiting for Morning Meeting to start. And sure enough, at precisely 8 a.m., Dr. Ubinto, standing in the front of the room, looking stylish and sharp in light khaki pants and a black button-down shirt, brought the meeting to order.

"Good morning, everyone," he said. "For those of you who don't know me, my name is Dr. LeRoi Ubinto, and I am the interim director of the (MS)2 program. The fact that you are here, sitting in this room, means you are all the future. Congratulations to all one hundred of you." A bunch of kids started clapping and cheering, so I joined in the applause.

"That's right," Dr. Ubinto said. "Give yourself the applause. You deserve it for making it into this program. You are an elite group who stood out against the competition, and we know you will go far. But don't get it twisted, now comes the time for you to earn your place. It's time, ladies and gentlemen, to get to work."

I glanced at the kids around me, checking to see if anyone else looked as nervous as I felt. As Dr. Ubinto continued his speech, detailing the rigorous academic schedule and the high expectations, I wondered, again, if I had made a mistake in coming.

"Once it is determined which level of class you'll be in, A, B, or C," Dr. Ubinto continued, "you will get your official schedule, but, for the most part, Monday through Friday, you will start the day with Morning Meeting, and then you will be in class until lunchtime. Afternoons will be for English class and your chosen electives. You will have time in the evenings to do your homework, and on weekends, you will have activities available for you to participate in, but you will also need that time to complete your homework assignments. You must also make time to prepare for cultural sharing. But we leave that up to you all to figure out."

Somebody raised their hand and asked about the difference between A, B, and C classes.

"That simply refers to the level of difficulty per class. We know not everyone is at the same level, so we have you tracked by ability. Where you land is nothing to be proud of or ashamed of. Just by being here you should understand that you are a special group of students selected for your aptitude and potential. And you all have excellence running through your veins."

Jackson leaned over to whisper in my ear, "Yeah, but we all know that C track is where all the supersmart kids end up."

I just smiled and nodded my head at Jackson, but inside I was already wondering what level I would be in.

Dr. Ubinto finished his speech with a reminder that we were responsible for our own futures. "Take advantage of every opportunity while you're here," he said passionately. "We want you to succeed, but you have to want it, too."

When we were dismissed, I think every kid in that room felt a little better about themselves. I know I did. Malcolm said this was a program for minority kids, but I didn't realize how hard it was to get in. And here I was, among the chosen few.

And I was soon to discover that I was in the top tier of the chosen few. When we got to the academic building, I found out I had been tracked into the C classes, the highest level.

"How did I get into C classes?" I said to Malcolm, who was standing nearby.

"Because you go to FDA, motherfucker. We're the smartest kids here."

I must have looked doubtful because Malcolm reminded me. "Don't you remember that math packet they sent you in the mail that you had to fill out," he said. "Well, apparently, you did well enough to place in the highest classes here. You're smart, Jonathan. Just admit it, you're a math nerd." He laughed.

That made me feel good, until I found out that the new friends I had made the day before—Juanita and Mike—were in A classes, and first-years were only with other first-years, so there was no chance I'd be in a class with Malcolm or my roommate Jackson, either.

"You'll be fine," Malcolm counseled me. "Just think, if you can deal with Mr. Murphy, you can deal with any teacher here. They're all cool."

"Thanks, bro," I said and headed off to find my first class. Chemistry. I told myself that, so far, everyone I'd met at (MS)2 had been cool, so the kids in my classes would probably be cool, too.

When I found the room, the teacher wasn't there yet, but most of the kids were. Looking around, I got the feeling that I had definitely entered the nerd squad. Most of the kids wore glasses, and, as I settled in, I discovered most were from New York City like me. Interestingly, most of them were Latino. Everybody was friendly, though, and we started talking and laughing together right away. But when the teacher came into the room, we shut up and sat up a little straighter in our chairs.

The teacher was an older, bald-headed white man who also wore glasses. He looked like a chemistry teacher. He told us we were going to be learning everything this summer that we would be learning in our junior or senior year at our regular schools, beginning right away with converting units. That sounded cool to me until he handed out the first worksheets, and I realized I didn't know how to do any of the work that was on them. "That's the whole point," the teacher said when we all complained. "I'm going to teach you how to do it."

Very quickly, I fell into the academic rhythm of the summer, even though it was intense. The one class we didn't get too much homework in was English. My English teacher was a Black woman who ran her class like a therapy session. We would read books by authors of color, talk about our feelings, and write personal essays for our assignments. I always looked forward to that class and was grateful she didn't pile on homework because we got so much work in other classes. I had to use my study halls to get everything done. There was no time to waste, but also, everybody there was serious about their academics, so it didn't feel as though I was missing out on anything by using all my free time to study.

On weekends, we played sports or went to the mall, but usually we just hung out on campus, did our homework, rested, did our laundry, and got ready for the next week. We also used the weekends to prepare for cultural sharing, which I learned was when the students at (MS)2 put on a presentation in order to share something unique about their culture. It was usually a play, a musical performance, a dance number, or some combination of all three. The Black kids, the Latino kids, and the Indigenous kids had to write and produce their own piece that would teach the rest of us something about their community. The third-years were in charge of writing the scripts and organizing everything, and us first-years, basically, just had to do what we were told. Malcolm was one of the kids in charge of cultural sharing that summer, and it took a lot of work.

I depended a lot on Malcolm to explain how things worked, from the laundry machines to the way we were supposed to interact with the rich kids who were eager to "chill" with us whenever they had a chance. Even their interest in us made me uncomfortable. I couldn't figure out what they wanted from us, from me. I was always suspicious of their attention. Even the Black faculty and teachers, like Dr. Ubinto, were different from the Black people I interacted with back home. Dr. Ubinto carried himself like somebody's rich uncle, and he didn't hide the fact that he was gay, like a lot of the older Black men I knew back home who were still living on the down-low. He wasn't trying to be anybody's best friend, but he always made it known that he was rooting for us at every level. My English teacher was incredibly kind and nurturing, but she didn't eat meat and called herself a vegan. It was all new and different, and although I wasn't longing to *be* back home, I was longing to feel *at* home at Andover.

It was Malcolm who helped me see things in a different way. We were sitting on the couches in our dorm lobby on a Sunday, enjoying the opportunity to take time to do nothing.

"Can I ask you something?" I said to Malcolm.

"Sure, anything," Malcolm said. "What's up?"

"How do you get used to being around all this and just feel okay being yourself?" I said. "You talk to everybody. The teachers here all love you, and you just make everything look so easy."

Malcolm grinned. "Yeah, boy, I'm a Black King, don't forget it."

I laughed as Malcolm pretended to brush off some imaginary dust from his shoulders. But then he got serious. "Look, bro, you gotta stop giving white people so much power. You gotta stop thinking they're better than you. You a Black King, Jon. You don't have to be afraid. But also, you gotta realize that not every white person is your enemy. You're gonna meet a lot of people here who aren't Black but still got your back, and it's your job to take that assistance and fly with it."

"I hear you," I said, considering his words.

"And let me tell you something else, not every Black person has got your best interests at heart. My mother always be telling me that 'not all skin folks are kin folks.' You know who said that?"

I shook my head no.

"Zora Neale Hurston," Malcolm said. "Look her up."

I smiled at Malcolm. "Thanks, bro. I will."

After talking to Malcolm, I tried to walk around Andover with more confidence. I promised myself I would try to talk to everyone, not just the other Black kids. I reasoned if I could debate rich kids at Regis tournaments about nuclear policy and the principles of democracy, I could certainly manage a conversation with the faculty, staff, and other students around campus. Because the (MS)2 program brought in kids from all over the United States, I started talking to kids from Detroit and Cleveland, places I had never been and knew nothing about, and

I learned some Spanish from the Latino kids, and I bonded with a bunch of the Indigenous kids on the basketball court where we all loved to play together. Pretty soon, I found myself with friends from all over the country, and I realized that I had a lot in common with people I never would have thought of previously. That was a powerful lesson to learn at that point in my life, and it would help me in years to come.

But there was still something that wouldn't let me fully relax into the Andover experience. And it wasn't about feeling un-comfortable with all of the wealth around me, it was the guilt.

Every time I walked into the Commons for a meal, looking at the ridiculous amounts of food on display, morning, noon, and night, I wondered if Marquise had enough to eat wherever he was. And then I'd think about all my friends in the Bronx and about what they were doing this summer, trying to wait out the hours until school started up again so they'd have somewhere to go. Meanwhile, I was sitting on my ass surrounded by so much wealth it could choke a horse. And the teachers and administra-tors kept telling us we were the future with so much potential, and all I could think about was all the potential that was rotting back home in my neighborhood. Maybe I was feeling survivor's guilt, but I didn't have the words at the time to describe it. It was just uncomfortable. The feelings weren't always there, but when I had a moment to myself, or if I were struck by a particular sense of luxury or freedom, my brain would always remind me that so many people I knew, from my siblings to my friends, had to live with so much less. I knew I was lucky to be there, but I also questioned whether I deserved it. It was like trying to hold two truths in the same hand.

As the days passed, the survivor's guilt continued to linger, I just got good at pressing it down into my container of ignored emo-tions. And because there was always something new happening around campus, I was able to keep those emotions out of my way.

Every Friday night, there was a party for all the kids on campus. Both the (MS)2 kids and the rich kids. The hall of one of the main buildings was decorated, and there were snacks and music, just like at a school dance. The first time I walked into one of these parties, I felt like I had stepped into a movie scene where the kids have a perfect prom or homecoming dance. It was how I imagined high school was supposed to be.

During the parties, the (MS)2 kids would always sneak off and have their own gatherings, unbeknownst to the Andover staff. Our parties were totally bare bones, no frills, but we got to play our own music, act wild, and not have to worry about the rich kids wanting to up their cool points by slumming it with us poor kids. That's what Malcolm told me at least. He was adamant that none of the rich kids could know about our secret gatherings on Friday nights, and those were the rules. But he did make one exception for a kid named Elijah Smith. Malcolm said he felt sorry for Elijah because, even though he was rich, Elijah Smith was also Black, and he was one of the few Black kids in the regular summer program.

"That kid Elijah sure had a good time last night," I said to Malcolm on the Saturday after Elijah's first visit to one of our parties. We were sitting in Malcolm's room just chilling and waiting for our laundry to finish drying.

"Yeah, he's cool," Malcolm said. "For a rich kid."

"How do you know he's got money like that?" I asked.

Malcolm looked at me like I was crazy. "One, because he's in the regular summer program not in (MS)2 with us, but two, look him up on Google."

I made a face. "What do you mean?"

"Go ahead, use my phone," Malcolm said, handing me his phone. "Look him up and tell me what you find."

I keyed in Elijah's name, and the first thing Google showed me was an article about Elijah's father—who had the same name as his son—standing in a room with some of the top Black talent in Hollywood because he was some big-time movie executive. He looked very comfortable in his Armani tuxedo, arms draped around someone whose face I recognized but whose name I didn't know.

"Holy shit," I said. "He *is* rich."

"I told you, homie," Malcolm said, laughing. "I'm telling you, pay attention to who you hang with around here, you might meet someone who could change your life. We're getting front-row seats to how the other half lives. And I'm telling you, that's worth as much as the math and science they're teaching us."

I nodded to show I was listening, so he continued, "You gotta watch what these rich kids are doing. Have you noticed that they read the newspaper every day in the mornings and on their breaks? They got habits we should be copying if we want to succeed in their world."

"Do you want to be like them?" I asked Malcolm.

"Look, bro, I'm not saying that. I just want to be able to compete so I can get mine. Okay?"

Malcolm was right. I needed to pay attention. The other kids on campus—even those I didn't talk to—could teach me things so I would leave this experience smarter, with lessons learned beyond academics. Regardless of their racial or economic background, I had to learn to look for the people with the lessons I needed to learn, and not just wait for them to come to me.

After a month at Andover, I was beginning to see a vision for my future, and it was going to be bright. Between Dr. Ubinto's motivational speeches every morning and learning about the college visits we got to go on during our third summer, I now had real, tangible ideas about what was possible for me. Success was no longer just this vague notion of escaping the South Bronx or "having a better life." There were names and places I could now attach to my intentions and goals. I now had a new, more specific, blueprint for my future. Rather than just going to college, I was now planning to go to an Ivy League university. And I wasn't just going to escape the South Bronx, I was going to learn all I could, be successful, and come back to help the people in my community.

One day after lunch, I walked into my dorm room and heard someone wailing like a wounded animal, but no one was there. I walked back out into the hallway to figure out where the sound was coming from, but there was no one there, either. When I went back into my room, I realized the crying and moaning was coming from under Jackson's bed. So, I got down on all fours and found Jackson curled up in a ball. I asked him what happened, but he didn't even acknowledge that I was there. He was so caught up in his grief, it was like he didn't hear me.

I ran down the hall and got Malcolm to try to help, but Jackson continued to wail uncontrollably. He wouldn't tell us what happened. He couldn't stop crying, so Malcolm dashed off to find us a teacher to help.

Standing in the middle of the room, with Jackson's cries filling the space, I slid back down on the floor next to him. I didn't know why he was hurting, but I didn't want him to feel alone. "I'm just gonna lay on the floor with you, bro," I said. "I don't know what's going on, but I'm here for you."

Jackson kept sobbing as I laid there, but then suddenly I saw him start to unfurl himself from the ball he had been in and begin to crawl from under the bed. I quickly grabbed him a chair, and he fell into it and started sobbing again, and he didn't look up at me.

But then he started talking. "They killed my brother, man. They killed my brother."

Since we'd been roommates, Jackson and I had shared a lot about our family stories. I knew his brother was a big-time gang member in Chicago. Jackson and his brother sounded a lot like Marquise and me. Jackson was the smart one and, even though his brother had pledged his loyalty to the streets, he always protected Jackson. "Mama's gotta have one good kid," he'd tell Jackson. They were two brothers who'd grown up in the same home but led completely different lives. His brother was a gang banger with a four-year-old child, and Jackson was at Andover and doing college tours at Dartmouth.

Jackson finally looked up and met my gaze. There was so much pain in his eyes, I wanted to look away.

"Jon, they tied up my little nephew and killed my brother in front of him. They cut off all of his tattoos one by one and skinned him alive. In front of his child!" Jackson started moaning again. "Who the fuck does that? Who does that?"

With that, he slid off the chair and back onto the floor and cried harder, his body shaking. I started crying, too. Malcolm found us like this when he returned to our room with the house counselors. When I told him what happened, he slid to the floor in disbelief. "What the fuuuuck?" he said. The counselors managed to circle the three of us, and eventually got Jackson to agree to go with them. I didn't know where one took a person that had just heard his brother had been massacred. I didn't understand how they could heal that.

When Jackson came back to the room that evening, his eyes were still bloodshot red. He looked like he was operating in a different dimension. Malcolm and Ricky were in the room with me. Jackson went directly to his bed and laid down. He looked at the three of us and told us that he was okay. We were all quiet; the four of us enveloped in a room, dealing with the reality that, although we were at Andover and planned to take over the world, the world was still the world—and it was a cruel place for people like us, in the environments and circumstances we were forced to occupy.

"Thanks for listening to me, Jon," Jackson finally said. "I know that was a lot. I just can't believe it. I talked to my brother two days ago."

"You don't gotta thank me, bro," I said. "We're Black Kings," I said, looking at Malcolm. "And Black Kings always look out for each other."

Malcolm gave a wistful smile at that, and then announced he was going to go grab his blanket and pillow so he could sleep in our room tonight. Ricky did the same.

When Malcolm and Ricky came back and we were all lying in our beds, Jackson gave voice to all of his worries.

"If I go to my brother's funeral," he said, "I'll miss the final week and a half of (MS)2. I won't pass my classes. And then I won't be able to come back for my final summer." He started to cry again, and I just took it in. Because it wasn't fair. We were free for six weeks to just be kids, without worrying about the violence and the drama that hovered over our lives, but somehow the shit could always find a way to catch up with us.

"Man, it's like no matter how hard we work, no matter what we try to do to better our situation, we're always fucked, you know what I'm saying?" I said. "It's like we're trapped by circumstances we didn't ask to be born into."

"That's why we gotta do what we gotta do," Malcolm said, his voice laced with emotion. "We gotta be great, we gotta be excellent, we gotta pull ourselves out of this mess. And end this bullshit." Tears gathered in his eyes and mine. Throughout the night we took turns crying, then lifting each other up, and then wondering aloud why we had been chosen to carry this load.

The next day, Jackson went home for his brother's funeral. We went to our classes.

After Morning Meeting, Dr. Ubinto pulled me aside to make sure I was okay, since Jackson was my roommate. "I feel really badly for Jackson," I said quietly, "but I'm okay."

"Come and talk to me if you feel the need to," Dr. Ubinto said. "There's no prize for holding in all of your emotions and pretending you can't feel pain." I thought about all the times I pushed my feelings down and about Jackson under the bed last night, but I had no interest in examining those emotions. So, I just said, "Yes, sir" to be polite.

"You know, all of your teachers have only good things to say about you," Dr. Ubinto said, switching subjects. I thought about our interaction when we first met, the fact that he knew my dad and could see more about me than I had ever verbalized.

"Thanks, sir, I have been working hard," I started, and then I knew what I needed to say. "But I also just want to thank you for giving me this opportunity. It's because of you that I'm here. I have a really good chance to go to college now."

Dr. Ubinto leaned in close. "Mr. Conyers, you will definitely make it to college, but don't ever take your foot off the gas. Remember, you are a Black male in America and so every hurdle you have to jump over is going to be twice as high as the one for the white kid. So, coming here is important, but you also have to do exceptional work the entire way. Not giving up is part of the journey. But I'm sure you're up to it, Mr. Conyers."

Later that afternoon, I told Malcolm about my conversation with Dr. Ubinto, still buzzing from his positive energy. "He obviously cares about us," I said, but Malcolm looked confused.

"Dr. Hodge has said that exact same thing more than once, but you never got this excited."

"Yeah, but Dr. Ubinto really gets it because he's Black. And I trust him more."

"Jonathan, Hodge may be white, but he's one of the best advocates for Black boys in Harlem. He's the one who told me about (MS)2, and he's always looking out for us and bringing in resources other public schools in Harlem will never have. You gotta stop blocking your blessings, bro. Remember, you gotta understand that everybody who can help you isn't going to look like you."

I started to mentally rewind some of my interactions with Dr. Hodge and how he was always pushing me to be better. I thought about Ms. DiCo, Mr. Murphy, and even my reading teacher back in Virginia, Mrs. Causey. These people were all white, but they had all been helpful along my education journey. Certainly, I couldn't discount their impact in helping me get to where I was at that moment, pending my summer vacation at Phillips Academy with some of the smartest kids in the country. Malcolm was a good friend for making me think more expansively about who I invited into my village and who I could look to for advice and resources. It was true that I could never have enough mentors in my village. Being at Andover was making it abundantly clear that the real world wasn't going to make exceptions for me, so it would make sense for me to find all the help I could get.

The last ten days of the (MS)2 program passed in a blur. Jackson made it back for graduation. Graduation signaled the end of our magical parentheses from reality. The ceremony was full of us bawling about our forever bond, making plans for the next year, and relishing in all we'd accomplished, including some really good parties.

When the ceremony was over, and we were all mingling on the lawn eating fancy finger foods and taking pictures, Malcolm introduced me to his mom, Lynette. She had smooth, dark skin, long dreadlocks, and she was wearing a sleeveless sundress made out of some African print fabric. She looked exactly how I imagined the woman who birthed Malcolm to be. Like royalty.

Watching Malcolm and his mom, I thought about what I was going back to in New York. Life with my parents for another three years, before I could escape to college. I didn't want to say good-bye to this charmed life at Andover, all the new friends I had made, the fresh, healthy foods, the clean, unpolluted air, and the peace and quiet that settled over the campus every evening after dark. Once again, I felt the pang of frustration and anger that I couldn't have a "normal" life.

"Yo, Black King," Malcolm said. "What's the matter?"

I shook my head, trying to muster up a smile. "I'm just thinking about the fact that in twenty-four hours I'll be back in the Bronx with my parents."

Malcolm knew everything that entailed. "Listen, I'm not going to tell you that your life is going to be perfect when you get back. In fact, it's going to feel worse than ever after being here for six weeks. But you gotta remember that even though your parents aren't in the best of shape, you're still a Black King. You feel me?"

I gave him a dap. "If it wasn't for you, bro, I don't know where I'd be right now."

Malcolm smiled. "Black Kings always look out for one another, Jon. Remember that."

7

I Wasn't Supposed to Have a Happy Ending

I spent the three weeks before school started huddled in my room. Coming back to the Bronx from Andover felt like having a taste of heaven and then being cast back down to hell. I had to fight hard against the depression that wanted to smother my spirit, but it was impossible not to compare the gritty view outside my bedroom window in Castle Hill with what I had left behind in Massachusetts. On my second day home, I pulled up the calendar on my phone and counted the actual number of days before I would be on an airplane heading back to Andover. I had 347 days to go.

There was no use trying to talk about it with Omari, Melvin, Dwayne, or Marquise. Not only had they'd never been in an environment like that, but they also had no sympathy for a kid wishing he were back at nerd camp. Rather than expecting something that was impossible for them to give, I simply stayed away. It was easier.

I felt like I had changed so much at Andover. My whole view of the world was like one hundred times bigger and brighter. I saw what reality looks like on the other side of poverty. I enjoyed every minute of having a clean, safe place to sleep, tons of healthy food to eat, and unlimited resources for anything and everything a person could dream of. I had a real vision now. I had seen it, tasted it, and lived it, so I was more motivated than ever to get out of the Bronx, away from my parents, and live a life where my own imagination and intelligence could take me as far as I wanted to go.

Getting into one of the top colleges in the country was my biggest priority, a college that would guarantee the kind of success that wouldn't leave me teetering on the edge of respectability. My brothers were still struggling financially after college and trying to find their way, which also made me realize that college in and of itself wasn't enough. I needed to distinguish myself among the elite, claim my seat at the table of the real powerbrokers and powerful—people like the parents who sent their kids to Andover.

I felt ready to take on the world. But once school started, I quickly realized that tenth grade wasn't going to be a walk in the park. Mr. Murphy's homework assignments for his AP European History class took hours to complete, and AP Biology was a lot less math and a lot more reading than I was used to for a science class. But since I was the only sophomore in that class, I didn't want to admit I was struggling and have the teacher think she'd made a mistake letting me take the class. I just kept my head down and forced myself to keep reading until the information stuck in my head.

Despite my overwhelm, when Mr. Murphy told me about an opportunity where I could take college courses at City College on weekends, I jumped at the chance because it sounded like the perfect thing to add to my résumé. Dr. Ubinto had drilled into us that we needed extracurricular activities to look attractive to the top schools. "You can't be complacent and just think a good GPA is going to get you anywhere," he told us.

That's also why when my biology teacher told me about a program called Mentoring in Medicine that paired Black students interested in a career in medicine with Black medical professionals, I signed up for that, too, because it would show colleges I was serious about pursuing a career as a doctor.

I returned to debate with a new focus, too. I fed off Ms. DiCo's enthusiasm that I was going to kill at debate this year. I was eager and ready to test my skills against these rich white kids and prove I could beat them at their own game. I now saw debate as warm-up practice for what I was going to face in real life. I figured if I could hold my own in debate, I would be well on my way to a successful future.

We wasted no time at practice. There were three new freshmen on the team who had to learn everything from scratch, but those of us returning jumped right into researching and writing our cases. Ms. DiCo said I was definitely ready to start going to the bigger tournaments beyond Regis. That got me motivated to research and write really good cases for the first resolution of the season. No more slacking off. I was excited to see how I would do at the competitions beyond Regis, and I really wanted to make it to the Harvard tournament that year. The Harvard tournament was considered the Olympics of the high school speech and debate competition circuit. Every year, it was held over Presidents' Day Weekend, and students came from all across the country to compete. But Ms. DiCo refused to take anyone to Harvard who wasn't ready, so I promised myself I was going to be ready.

Many nights, I'd be at school practicing for debate until 8 p.m., and I would still sometimes have to stay up until two in the morning doing homework. Mr. Murphy forced all of his students to learn and use the Cornell Notes system in class, which was a system created by a professor at Cornell University that helped students synthesize and streamline their note taking practice. Even though, at first, I resented being told how to take notes, the system helped me study and retain information more efficiently. And I ended up using that system to get me all the way through college.

I was doing a lot, and it was stressful, but whenever I was in doubt and wanted to quit or take a break, I would find my inspiration to keep going when I came home to our tiny apartment, looked into an empty refrigerator, and found my parents clocked out on their air mattress on the floor. If I didn't work hard enough to get out of this place, this would be all I had to look forward to. I couldn't bear the thought that this would be my future. I was willing to do whatever it took to move the course of my future far away from my present circumstances. I'd think about Dr. Hodge's constant messaging. It was the struggle that I had to endure to see the progress.

Doing my schoolwork, debate, and going to college classes on Saturdays was exhausting, but staying exhausted left me less time to focus on the things I couldn't change. Staying busy was my coping strategy. And it worked. As long as I remained cocooned in my academics, I could survive the next three years.

But then things started to change.

Malcolm and I were sitting on a bench near FDA, eating french fries after school one day, when he broke the news to me. "Dr. Hodge is retiring. He asked me and a couple other students to be on the search committee for his replacement."

"For real?" I said as I licked barbecue sauce off my fingers.

Malcolm nodded. "This isn't going to be good, Jon," he said.

"What do you mean?" I asked.

"Things aren't going to be the same at FDA," Malcolm explained. "Dr. Hodge is the reason FDA runs the way it does. It's the reason we have so many AP classes and a robotics club and why I got to go to Japan my sophomore year. Without Hodge..." Malcolm shrugged his shoulders. "I don't know what's going to happen, but things just aren't going to be the same."

Malcolm's words sent a slow panic through my veins. Dr. Hodge was part of my village now; plus, he was the captain of the FDA ship. The thought of him disappearing from my life left me feeling unsettled, like I was standing on a fault line and waiting for the earth to start to shake.

"When's he leaving?" I asked.

"He's going to stay until the end of the year," Malcolm said. "And he's pushing hard to find a Black principal to replace him who will keep the school the same, but Dr. Hodge is irreplaceable if you ask me. I'm just glad this is my last year."

I threw my fries, which were now cold and soggy, into a trash bin. "Well, I still have three years to go at FDA, so what does it mean for me?"

Malcolm turned to me. "I don't want you to freak out or anything, Jon. I just wanted you to be prepared."

It didn't take long for everyone to find out that Dr. Hodge was retiring after fourteen years leading FDA. He said he wasn't going to another school, he was retiring for good. He said it was time for him to rest. Thanks to Malcolm, I wasn't surprised by the announcement, but I was surprised by how quickly things started to change at the school. It felt like the minute word got out that Dr. Hodge was leaving, the wind went out of FDA's sails. Everything that had made the school special melted like sugar in hot water. For starters, Dr. Hodge stopped standing outside the school every morning to greet the students and ensure we were all in uniform and looking sharp. He was no longer seen roaming the hallways keeping track of everyone and everything between classes, either. Fights started breaking out in the hallways, and kids were becoming rowdy in the classroom with no fear of being sent to the principal. Luckily, all of my teachers maintained their high standards in their classes, and I didn't feel a shift in my academics, but there were other ways I felt the changes in the school.

"Before we start practice today, I have to catch you up on some things," Ms. DiCo called us to attention.

She stood in front of her desk and leaned against the edge. She was wearing her new favorite outfit, a pair of khaki pants and a polo shirt. The other nine members of the debate team and I grabbed chairs in the front of the room and waited for Ms. DiCo to speak. I could already tell that whatever she was going to say wasn't going to be good news. Her face told us everything.

"Okay, so you guys know Dr. Hodge is retiring, right?" Ms. DiCo began. "Well, because he's been really busy wrapping things up on his end, he hasn't been able to offer any suggestions for finding funding for the debate team."

Everybody started talking at once, but Ms. DiCo held up her hand to quiet us. "No, don't blame Dr. Hodge because we have never had a lot of money for our scrappy little team, but if you guys want to travel to some of the bigger tournaments this year, you're going to have to do more fundraising."

"What kind of fundraising?" one of the new freshmen asked.

Ms. DiCo put on a hopeful grin. "We're going to sell candy bars."

Everybody in the room groaned. "Seriously, Ms. DiCo?" Keisha, our new team captain, said.

"How much does it cost to go to these tournaments?" I asked.

"To compete, it costs anywhere from twenty to ninety dollars per student. And then if we have to spend the night, there's hotel, and food, and transportation costs we have to cover, too. That's why schools that don't have a lot of funding, like ours, don't have debate teams."

"That's so unfair," Keisha said.

"I know it is, which is why I work so hard for our team," Ms. DiCo said. "And it's why you guys have to get out there and sell candy bars to get the money so we can compete."

"That means we gotta sell a lot of chocolate," Demetrius, one of the other sophomores on the team, said.

"Well, it's not just chocolate bars you can sell," Ms. DiCo said as she walked over to the supply closet behind her desk. "I've taken the liberty of going to Costco to get you some other things to sell in addition to candy bars." With that, she opened the closet and showed us stacks of Gatorade, juice boxes, and bagged snacks, along with the generic fundraiser candy bars. "You guys can come in here and grab this stuff and sell it during lunch hour, and you can sell the candy bars to your family members or friends," she said. "This is the only way we're going to be able to raise the money to go to the tournaments, so everybody needs to pitch in and do their part."

Everybody started talking then, scheming and planning who would sell what during which lunch periods, trying to maximize our profits. But I didn't jump into the conversation. Just thinking about trying to sell chocolate to the people who lived in my neighborhood made me want to tell Ms. DiCo her plan was a joke. Nobody was going to buy those waxy, crayon-tasting chocolate bars from me. And quite frankly, I didn't have time to sell candy with everything I had going on. But I didn't say anything to Ms. DiCo, or any of my team members, because I didn't want to seem like I didn't care about the team. And it wasn't Ms. DiCo's fault that the school had no money. She already spent her own money buying us pizzas if practice ran late, or sometimes pay for a taxi to take us home if it was really late at night. And she never complained or made us feel bad that she had to dip into her own pockets to make sure we had what we needed to pay for the tournaments. I couldn't blame her for something that wasn't her fault.

When I walked home that night, I realized the anger I was harboring was for Dr. Hodge. He was the one who convinced me to come to FDA. He was the one who told me to stay on the debate team. "Don't quit," he told me. And now he was quitting, leaving FDA. "I'm your daddy now," he'd said to me. But unlike my real father, Dr. Hodge was abandoning us. I didn't want to feel sorry for myself, but I couldn't understand why I wasn't allowed to have one good thing in my life be permanent. Mr. Marshall died, and that wasn't his fault, but the end result was the same: me without people in my life who were committed to my success. It felt like every time I thought I was safe, people left me and the ground beneath me started to shake.

Ms. DiCo refused to let Dr. Hodge's retirement, or a lack of money, stop us from getting to our tournaments. She never gave up on us and was true to her word that, if we took debate seriously, she would take us seriously. Case in point: the Scarsdale Invitational Tournament. The tournament took place over the weekend, so we needed transportation to Westchester and accommodations for two nights—not to mention the fee to register our team to compete. Our snack sales covered only the tournament fees, but Ms. DiCo figured out the rest.

"Okay, you guys," she explained to us on the Monday before the tournament. "I reached out to my old debate coach at Stuyvesant, and she's taking her team to the tournament on a bus. Since there are only seven of us, she said we could ride with them for free."

"Wait, your high school debate coach is still alive?" Demetrius asked.

Ms. DiCo laughed. "Demetrius, how old do you think I am?"

Demetrius shrugged. "I dunno. It just seems crazy that your teachers are still teaching."

"I'll have you know, Demetrius, that my debate coach, Ms. Sheinman, is still teaching and coaching debate at Stuyvesant, and, in my opinion, she's still the best of the best. And I'm grateful she's willing to do us this favor, so I expect you all will be on your best behavior."

Of course, we were going to be on our best behavior, but somebody did holler out on the bus, "Oh, shit, we're in Beverly Hills," when we arrived at Scarsdale High School. It was hard not to be impressed and a bit overwhelmed by the wealth all around us. I just couldn't get over the fact that we were only ninety minutes away from the South Bronx and this level of abundance was possible. Scarsdale High School felt like a private school on the same level as Regis High School, but it was just a public school in a wealthy suburb.

Since we couldn't afford to stay in a hotel, Ms. DiCo worked with the Scarsdale debate coach to help find some people from the school community who would host our team. I ended up staying with Demetrius and two other kids on our team in somebody's basement. But the basement was nicer than any apartment I'd ever lived in. They had a baby grand piano down there! All four of us agreed that the best part of the competition was staying in that basement.

On the bus ride back home, I sat next to Ms. DiCo, and I thanked her again for finding us a place to stay so we could attend the tournament.

"You know, I've lived in the Bronx all this time, and I've never even heard of Scarsdale, even though it's, like, right on the other side of us," I confessed. "Even though I didn't do that well in the competition, I'm really glad I came."

"I'm glad you came, too, Jonathan," Ms. DiCo said. "Because I want you to see more of the world and get comfortable speaking up when you might be the only Black person in the room. This is the education you need, more than anything you read in a textbook. Participating in these bigger tournaments outside the city is going to provide you with everything you need to succeed in the real world. I'm telling you, debate is the great equalizer."

Ms. DiCo was always so passionate about debate. She really made it seem as though it was the answer to everything that was wrong in the world.

We were both silent for a moment as I turned my attention outside my window, watching the massive, single-family homes with manicured lawns go by. It was hard not to wish for a life like this, especially now that I knew how close it really was.

Ms. DiCo cleared her throat, and I turned back to her. "Jonathan, I know things are hard for you at home, so if you need to talk, you know I'm here for you. And I don't ever want you to worry about not having the money or selling enough candy bars to come to a weekend tournament. If you want to come, we'll make it happen."

I wanted to throw my arms around her and hug her and thank her for seeing my need, but I held back. As much as I appreciated Ms. DiCo's care and the positive energy she poured into me and all the other members of our scrappy little team, I was wary of sharing too much. I felt the need to maintain the myth that I could handle what was on my plate. I didn't know why, I just didn't think anybody truly wanted to know how much pain I was holding inside. So, I said plainly, "Thanks, Ms. DiCo."

By early December, Ms. DiCo confirmed she would be taking a group of students to the Harvard tournament in February, and I was one of them! Ms. DiCo said I was good enough to compete at Harvard at the junior varsity level.

"Yes!" I shouted and high-fived Demetrius when she told us. I knew Ms. DiCo didn't play favorites when it came to the Harvard tournament. She told us from day one that she would only take students she felt had a chance to actually perform well.

She didn't want anyone to embarrass themselves, either, because only the best of the best went to Harvard to compete.

Ms. DiCo gave us all a minute to settle down, and then she continued with her announcements about Harvard. "The resolution you'll be debating at Harvard is, 'Juvenile defenders should be tried as adults in the criminal justice system in the United States.' This is a really meaty topic that I think you'll all be able to come up with really good cases for. But remember, your cases have to be really well researched, and you're going to have to come up with some unique angles to argue so you can keep your opponents on their toes. Now, we have only about eight weeks to get ready, so from now on, you better come to practice to work. And for those of you who aren't going to Harvard, you can still work on cases and practice with the kids who are going. So, let's get started."

After everyone got settled into practice, Ms. DiCo came over to me and said, "Jonathan, I know this is a topic you care about because of what you've shared with me about your friend Marquise. And I know you always do your best when you have a personal connection to the issue, so I have a feeling Harvard is going to be a really good tournament for you."

I grinned from ear to ear because she was right. I cared about the juvenile justice system because I'd almost been a part of it, and it had stolen my best friend from me, and countless other kids from my neighborhood were victims of it as well. I was excited to write an amazing case against the resolution, and it would be a real challenge to write my case in support of the resolution. But I was up for it, not only because I wanted to do well at Harvard, but because I also dreamed about qualifying for the state competition where all of the best debaters from all over the state of New York competed at the end of the season.

So far, I still hadn't proven myself a winner at anything in life. I didn't have a championship ring or trophy from any sports I'd ever played like my brothers did. I was a good student at FDA, but I wasn't the number-one student in any class. I was eager and hungry for a win, and it felt like I was getting closer in debate. I felt like I could do it, and now Ms. DiCo was telling me she thought I could do it, too. I was ready and willing to do whatever Ms. DiCo told me to do to get ready for this tournament because I was ready to finally claim my spot on top and have my thing that made me special. My mother always told me the only thing I was really good at was running my mouth, so it was time to fully embrace that.

But just as I started to dive into the preparations for the Harvard tournament, more tremors started to rumble.

"How could you guys do this again?" I shouted at both of my parents. It was two days before Christmas, but this was hardly the present I wanted or needed.

"We've been here less than a year," I said, "how could you guys mess this up already?"

"You better watch your tone, Jon," my father warned me.

I ignored him. I was too mad. "Y'all can't keep nothing, can you?" I said, pacing around the tiny living room, my hands balled into fists.

"Boo Boo," my mother cooed. "It's not like that, it's not our fault."

I shook my head. It was never their fault for smoking up all the rent money. I was only sixteen, but I was so tired of my parents' lies and excuses.

"You have to believe us," my mother tried again. "The landlord called and said her son is coming home from jail, and he has to live in this apartment. It's her apartment, so we have no choice. We have to leave. But it's not our fault."

I didn't know whether I should believe my mother's story or not. My parents had gotten evicted so many times, and they lied so much. I had no reason to trust her. And whether I believed them or not wouldn't change the fact that we were going to be homeless. Again.

Just thinking about packing up and moving one more time loosened the cork from all of the pent-up anger and frustration I felt toward my parents. "I can't do this anymore," I yelled. "How am I supposed to be successful? How am I supposed to do well in school if we're homeless and moving around all the time? You're the ones who always said education is everything!"

I felt such an intense rage I wanted to break everything in the apartment, but there was nothing strong enough in our living room to take my blows.

My mother started to cry. "I'm so sorry, Boo Boo," she said. "We didn't want this to happen, but the landlord said we have to get out. But I swear, we didn't do nothing wrong this time."

"Yeah, whatever," I said over my shoulder as I headed out the door. I needed a wide-open space to release the anger from my body.

Once outside, I realized I had nowhere to go. I just started walking. I thought about calling my grandmother, but I knew that staying with my grandmother wasn't a long-term solution. Inevitably, we'd end up butting heads again over Jesus and drug addiction.

"Damn it," I cursed aloud. *Why couldn't I just have one thing in my life stay steady?* I wondered.

In my mind, I tried to count how many times we'd had to move because my parents didn't pay the rent or we got evicted because of their behavior, but I lost count after eleven. I couldn't even sort through all of my early childhood memories from before we moved to Virginia because it was such a shit show of confusion, shuffling from one apartment or shelter to the next all over New York City. I was pretty young at the time, but I could never shake the sense of fear and uncertainty that was seared into my DNA from those early years of my life. And now, it was happening again, and the anger I felt toward my parents was magnified because of all of their past mistakes.

I tried to call up some of the sympathy Ms. DiCo told me I should have for my parents.

She told me I needed to consider my parents in a different light. After she made us study the crack epidemic in the '80s so we could better understand the drug policies that the United States government employed, I understood what she meant. My parents, like many other Black and brown people in poor neighborhoods in the 1980s, saw their communities flooded with cocaine and crack, while the government turned a blind eye to how it destroyed people's lives and livelihoods. And then offered harsh prison sentences instead of addiction treatment to the people who got addicted. I never knew any of that, and when I was sitting in the classroom with my team members, I could see my parents as victims in the drug wars. And I actually came up with a grudging respect for both my mom and my dad. After all, my father always managed to hold down a job, and my mother never let us get taken away and put into the foster system. But that grudging respect wasn't enough to temper the anger and disappointment that was now roiling through my system at the mere thought of having to move back into the shelter system again.

Later that night, I called Justin to complain about our impending eviction. "Yo, I just can't keep doing this," I said. "How am I supposed to get good grades in two AP classes and take these Saturday college courses if we're moving every six months?"

"I know it's hard," Justin said, and I heard him sigh through the phone.

"It's not just hard," I said. "It's so damn aggravating. Why can't Mommy and Dad get their shit together?"

"You know, Jonathan, I asked myself that very same question every single day I lived in the house with them, and I never found an answer."

"Well, I got two and a half more years of this," I said. "What am I supposed to do?"

There was a moment of silence on the other end of the phone, and then Justin said, "You could come down to Virginia and live with me."

"Really?" I asked, trying to imagine going back to live in Chesapeake, where Justin now lived.

"I'm serious," he said. "I haven't been there for you since you all went to New York, and if anyone knows how hard it is living with Mom and Dad, it's me. If you want to get away from them and come down here, just let me know, Jon."

I didn't want to move to Virginia; I just wanted my life in New York to get better, but I was filled with a sense of gratitude knowing my big brother was willing and offering to take care of me. It was enough, as it often was, to just know there was someone in my corner, in my village, who would catch me if I fell.

When winter break was over, I wanted to talk to Ms. DiCo about our impending eviction. I wanted to hear her advice. I knew there wasn't anything she could do to change my situation, but Ms. DiCo was always good at helping me see things in a different way so I could deal with them better. She always reminded me to think about people such as Viktor Frankl, the Holocaust survivor who lost his entire family in the war, but then found a way to find meaning, even happiness, in his life. She helped me see my life as part of a bigger reality, not just the moment I was living in now.

The only problem was, Ms. DiCo had suddenly become difficult to locate at school. I could not find her during my lunch hour; she was coming late and leaving early from debate practice, and, overall, she just seemed distracted and not herself.

"Yo, what do you guys think is up with Ms. DiCo?" Keisha asked the group. "She's been acting really weird lately, don't you think?" It was yet another day that Ms. DiCo was late, and she'd asked Keisha to run practice until she got there.

"Yeah, I don't know what it is," Monique, one of the other leaders on the team, said, "but it must be pretty serious because she's running out the door all the time after class."

"Whatever it is, I hope she figures it out because we need her," I said. "With Hodge leaving and everything going crazy around here, if Ms. DiCo isn't okay, this team is screwed."

Before anyone could say anything else, Ms. DiCo walked into the room, apologizing for being late. But none of us was thinking about her tardiness anymore because we were all staring at how she looked.

Her hair, which she had been wearing progressively shorter, was now in a fresh cut, but it was cut in a man's style. She was also wearing a man's suit with a tie and black lace-up shoes. Nobody said anything as we all stared at her. And, for a moment, she just stared right back at us, standing in the front of the room, looking just as confused and at a loss for words as we felt. Then, she cleared her throat and apologized for being late. With her suit on and her short hair, Ms. DiCo looked like a teenage boy, like she was a student right alongside us. We all sat there waiting for an explanation—not for why she was late, but why she was dressed like a dude.

Ms. DiCo looked down at her shoes and then looked up at us and said, "This is who I am. I'm not a woman. I'm a man. And I hope you'll accept me. You don't have to call me Mr. DiCo, but I'd prefer that you don't call me Ms. DiCo anymore. Just call me DiCo."

All of us kids looked at each other and then back at DiCo, who had returned to studying her shoes. A million thoughts raced through my brain, but the most pressing one was that everything now made sense. DiCo's distracted behavior, why she'd been leaving school early and had taken to wearing only slacks and polo shirts. The fact that DiCo was "coming out" as a man didn't actually seem too crazy to me because all the pieces fit together. But still, it was a lot to take in on a Tuesday afternoon during debate practice. But when I saw the fear and worry on DiCo's face, I stopped thinking about what it all meant, and, instead, tried to assure my favorite teacher that as long as she wasn't going to change who she was, whether she was a woman or a man didn't matter.

Monique and Keisha walked up to DiCo right away and wrapped him in a hug, and that broke the tension that was hanging over all of us.

"Okay, DiCo," Monique said. "We love you. But can we talk about them shoes? You can do better. Much better."

And then everybody laughed. We all made some jokes, and DiCo gave us all a grateful smile, and we all pretended that it was just business as usual that our teacher transitioned from a woman to a man.

I didn't have time to sort through my feelings about DiCo's

transition because I was singularly obsessed with preparing for Harvard. At that point, as long as DiCo was still willing to coach us and get us ready for the competition, his gender identity didn't really matter to me. Plus, DiCo was one of the few steady figures in my life, so I didn't feel like I had the right or the reason to get hung up on his transition. He always supported me without making me feel ashamed of my background, so I figured I could do the same for him.

Every week, as the tournament grew closer and closer, I felt like Ahab getting ready to go in search of Moby Dick. I worked on my cases, adding more research and statistics to bolster my arguments. I also studied everything I possibly could about the juvenile justice system, so I could be ready for any argument an opponent threw out. All of this on top of all of my homework and my Saturday college classes. It was a lot on my plate, but I appreciated the mind-numbing pace because it kept me from worrying about where we were going to live next and when we'd have to vacate our current apartment.

Right after the holidays, we got word that we didn't have to leave our apartment right away because there had been some kind of delay on the landlord's son's release from prison. I was glad we didn't have to move during the coldest days of winter, but I hated being on hold, just waiting for the day we'd be kicked out onto the streets. The cracks in the foundation under my feet continued to rumble, but I ignored them and focused all my attention on debate.

One day during practice, DiCo forced me to debate him, which he never did. DiCo had debated all through high school and was still a passionate and aggressive opponent—and he really let me have it. He wasn't going easy on me or trying to nurture me into a win. On the contrary, every time I'd make a point he'd demolish it, and his CX was fire.

"I'll repeat my question," DiCo said, but he wasn't acting like my teacher or my coach. He was my opponent. "How will you ensure that juveniles who commit violent crimes don't commit more crimes if you don't prosecute them to the fullest extent of the law? Isn't that worse for society? Won't that cause more harm than good?"

"No, that's not true," I said, trying to find my source that negated that a child who commits a crime will do it again. But before I put my hands on my notes, DiCo threw out his next question.

"You say it's not true but, according to my sources, forty percent of juvenile offenders do return to commit crimes, even if they're put in juvenile facilities, so that would indicate they need harsher sentencing and longer sentencing," DiCo pushed on.

"How can you say that?" I cried. "You think putting a kid in a cell for twenty years with grown adults is going to make him less angry and less violent? All he's going to do in that jail cell is try to figure out how to get revenge, if he doesn't try to kill himself first."

DiCo put his cards down and became my coach again.

"Jonathan," he started, "you can't let your emotions get the best of you. You have to stick to the facts if you're going to win. I want you to use your story and your experiences to help make your case, but you can't let your opponent get you off your game. Or press your buttons."

Even though it was just practice, and I knew DiCo was just trying to help me, my heart was beating with righteous anger. This issue was too close to home for me, and DiCo just proved that I needed to do more work to be ready for the Harvard tournament.

After that day, I started coming to school early each day so DiCo and I could work on my speech together. DiCo gave me even more articles to read with more facts and statistics I could use in my cases. DiCo also helped me finesse the way I wove my personal experiences into my speech, so I could make a more persuasive argument without losing points for lack of evidence. "Remember, the judges prioritize facts over feelings, so you can't depend on your personal story, but you can use it to make your case more compelling," DiCo counseled me. "It's a delicate dance, but you can do it."

During our last practice before the tournament, DiCo listened to me present my case supporting the resolution to prosecute juvenile offenders as adults. I was arguing against everything I believed in, but I still nailed it. DiCo gave me a standing ovation. That's when I knew I was ready.

Although the Harvard tournament was going to be our most serious competition to date, we were still going to have fun along the way. It was so rare that any of us got to get away from our lives in the city and travel to someplace such as Cambridge, Massachusetts. Packing a suitcase, traveling without our parents, riding with friends, it felt like freedom—and we were going to take full advantage.

Just like for the Scarsdale tournament, DiCo asked his former coach if we could hitch a ride on the Stuyvesant bus to Harvard. Even though Demetrius and two of the other kids on the team were hustling hard selling candy bars on the subway and Gatorade in the FDA cafeteria, we still didn't have enough money to pay the five-hundred-dollar tournament fee, bus fare, lodging, and food. This time, DiCo contacted one of the Black student groups at Harvard and convinced them to host the six of us in the dorms, which also meant we could eat in the Harvard cafeteria. DiCo understood that, for so many of us, even a small amount of money to pay for food would have made the trip impossible, so he did whatever he could to make it possible. He was living proof that where there was a will, there was a way. He didn't let money or excuses keep him from keeping his promises to bring us to Harvard, and that meant a lot to me. Now, it was up to me to do my best in the competition.

It was still dark and freezing outside when we climbed aboard the bus on the Friday morning of Presidents' Day Weekend. The Stuyvesant kids had already claimed the front seats, so without saying anything aloud, we all just headed to the back. Monique and Keisha were focused and used the three-hour ride to study their notes, but the rest of us were just talking and having fun.

We made it to the Harvard campus in time for lunch. Arriving at Harvard provoked flashbacks of my first time at Regis, only there were so many more kids at this tournament. But the divide between them and us was still the same and amplified by the sheer number of competitors in attendance. Almost everyone there was white—and then there was us. And, once again, it was our poverty as much as our skin color that made us stand out. Most of the other kids were sharply dressed in pressed slacks, dress shirts, coats, and ties. The girls wore skirts and blouses and many were in heels. In addition to leather briefcases, some of these kids even had rolling suitcases to carry their notes. We couldn't compete on the fashion front. Most of my team-mates looked like me—sporting polyester pants, sneakers, and Family Dollar backpacks. And despite all of our preparations, I wondered if we could actually compete against these kids who had so many advantages over us in every single way.

Because Harvard was such a big tournament, the competition was spread over three days. I had my first round after lunch on the Friday we arrived. Before I left the cafeteria to find the room I would be debating in, DiCo wished all of us luck. Since he had signed up to be a judge, he wouldn't be able to watch all of our rounds.

"Just do everything we practiced," DiCo told me before he left. "Don't get flustered. Don't let anyone get in your head. And don't let your emotions get the best of you. Stay focused."

"I will," I said, nodding and feeling like Muhammad Ali right before he stepped into the ring. But instead of boxing gloves, I was using a box of note cards as my weapons.

When I found the classroom where I would be debating, I did a quick check of the room. My opponent, a white boy in a full blue suit and a red power tie, had already set up his note cards and folders at his desk. The judge was also already seated, so I took my place at my desk and started unpacking my cards, my notebook and pens, and my two cases—affirmative and negative—that were freshly printed before we left New York. I was tempted to stick a pencil in my mouth like DiCo taught us, to practice my enunciation, but I held off. When I got settled, the judge informed us who would be arguing for the resolution and who would be arguing against it. When she said I would be arguing against juveniles being tried as adults, I felt my heart flip in excitement. Even though I was prepared to argue either side, I knew my strengths.

Since my opponent was on the affirmative side, he got to present his argument first, and I got to question him right after. And it was there that I shined. CX was where I hit my stride and could form my questions in ways that almost made it impossible for my opponent to answer effectively.

"Do you know what it's like to grow up without a mom or a dad?" I began my line of questioning.

The kid answered no.

"Have you ever eaten potato chips for dinner because it was the only thing to eat in your house?" I pressed.

Again, the kid answered in the negative.

"Do you know anyone who has been entangled in the juvenile justice system?" I asked, already knowing the answer.

Once he said no, I said, "Then, maybe you're not the best person to make this argument about the juvenile justice system." I had to force myself not to smile, because, at that point, I knew I had gotten into my opponent's head. The judge wasn't going to hand me a win for my CX, though. That came down to who made the most compelling argument and who was able to defend said argument throughout the debate. She also had to assign speaking points. I tended to get high speaking points because I had finally learned—thanks to DiCo—how to deliver my points with flair and personality. I wasn't just up there spewing facts like a fire hydrant.

Because I won my first round, and the next round after that, I knew I was going to face higher-caliber opponents on Saturday because of Power Pairing. Power Pairing meant I would be debating against other kids who, like me, had gone undefeated on their first day of the tournament. Unlike the Regis tournaments, the Harvard tournament consisted of six rounds. To make it to the elimination rounds on Sunday, you had to win at least four out of six rounds on Friday and Satur-day. The elimination rounds on Sunday would, eventually, lead to quarterfinals, semifinals, and then the last two debaters in the junior varsity and varsity levels would compete on Monday for the first-place trophy.

That night in the dorms, my teammates and I huddled together to practice for the next day. We shared the statistics and facts we'd heard from our opponents, and reworked our cases to read even better. I think we all had dreams of making it, at least, to the elimination rounds. DiCo came by to check on us and to remind us not to stay up too late. "Tomorrow is going to be a long day, and I know you want to win," he said, "but you can't win if you're falling asleep at the table."

The next morning, I woke up nervous. I could barely eat anything at breakfast I was so worried about who I would be facing with the Power Pairing. I think I let the worry get to me because I lost my first two rounds of the day. I was so mad, I had to give myself a talking-to between rounds and get my head straight. I found a quiet corner and just told myself to focus. *"You can do this, Jonathan. You're not stupid!"* I could hear my mother's voice in my head saying the same thing.

The pep talk worked. I won my next round, and I was now back in the running. I had won three rounds and lost two. I needed only one more win to be in contention for the elimination rounds.

As I was packing up my stuff, the judge came over to me with a smile on his face. He was a pleasant-looking middle-aged white man with a graying mustache.

"Hey, Jonathan, I just wanted to tell you I thought you did a really good job. I was very impressed," he said.

"Thank you, sir," I said as I continued gathering my things.

"Can I give you a piece of advice, young man? About your technique and your style?" he said.

"Of course," I said.

"Okay, here it is," he started, bringing his hands to his chin. "You need to slow down when you're talking during your rebuttal and show a bit more sportsmanship. You don't have to make the other kids feel bad because they haven't had your experiences. Do you understand what I'm saying?"

I nodded my head. "Yes, sir." I knew I got cocky when I was doing my rebuttals and cross-examination, but that's just because I was confident in what I was saying.

"Hey, don't get me wrong, you obviously know what you're do- ing, and your case was really strong. In fact, I'd say if you don't win today—this tournament is rigged. Just try not to be so intense."

I didn't know what to say to that, but I stammered out another "thank you" and then grabbed my stuff and ran to find DiCo to tell him what the judge had just told me. Not the part about me being too intense, the part about me winning. That judge said I could win the whole tournament!

DiCo was in the cafeteria. "I knew you could do it, Jonathan," he said while clapping me on the back after I told him the good news. "I knew it." Then, he asked to see my scorecards, so I handed them over.

As DiCo read over my scores, his face started to change. The color rose in his cheeks, and he began to frown. "Jonathan," DiCo said, "did you notice that even though you've been win- ning, your speaker points are dropping each round? And all the judges are writing the same thing: 'Jonathan needs to stick to the facts. His life story gives him an unfair advantage.'"

DiCo handed back my cards in a huff. "This is ridiculous," he said. And then he told me he was going to come watch my next round.

"You don't have to come," I said, sensing his agitation. I didn't want to feel like I couldn't handle myself.

"No, I want to come to see what's going on," he said, making his voice sound calm and cool. "Besides," he added, "this could be your most important round. And I want to be here for it."

I shrugged. "Suit yourself."

Later, DiCo and I found the room I was debating in. He took a seat in the back of the classroom while I set up and scoped out my competition. Another boy, another set of khaki pants. Brown hair, blue eyes. Another minion in my estimation.

Once again, I got to argue against the resolution, so I was in my zone. Even though there was a lot riding on this round, I told myself to stay focused and try not to be too intense like the other judge said. But I also felt confident because he told me he thought I could win.

As I read my case, I thought about Marquise and tried to pour my feelings for him into the tone of my voice and the examples I offered during cross-ex. I wanted the judges to understand that this wasn't just a public policy decision—we were talking about the lives of innocent children who deserved to be nurtured and cared for, not locked up with convicted criminals. When I rested my case, I hoped, somehow, I had made amends to Marquise for what he had sacrificed for me to go free. I snuck a glance at DiCo behind me while we waited for the judge to announce the winner. DiCo threw a thumbs-up in my direction, and I held my breath in anticipation. But when the judge finally stood up, he gave the win to the minion, not me.

I lost. My Harvard experience was over.

DiCo came right over to me with a smile. He said he was so proud of me. For a moment I thought he was going to hug me, but he patted me on the back instead. "I know how much you wanted to win, but you did your best and, sometimes, there's just somebody better."

I sighed as I started to gather my things. "I know," I said. "Still, it would have been nice to win."

"I hear you," DiCo said. "But remember, you're just a sophomore, you still have two more years to win at Harvard."

"I guess," I said, then handed him my scorecard. "Here, you can keep this." He liked to keep the scorecards so we could use them in practice to work on whatever we got points taken off for. But when DiCo looked at the scorecard, he hissed, "What the hell?"

I looked over his shoulder and saw that it said, "Jonathan used his personal story too much."

DiCo marched right over to the table where the judge was still seated and smacked my card down on the table. "What is the meaning of this? This is the most ridiculous example of white privilege I've ever seen in my life."

I came over to the table and tried to calm DiCo down, but he was on a roll trying to teach the middle-aged white woman who had delivered her verdict about white supremacy. I just stood there.

"These white kids here have access to every single resource available. But you're penalizing Jonathan because he was born into poverty and has friends who actually have been in the juvenile justice system? He can't win because he's using the only advantage he has, which is experience with the subject matter? You have got to be kidding me."

"Um, sir, you need to calm down," the woman said to DiCo.

"I will not calm down because we're supposed to be the adults here teaching these children that, if they put in the work, they can be judged fairly on the merits of their arguments, and you're taking that away from him. You're showing him exactly how unfair our system is, right here and right now."

"Let's just go, DiCo," I said, pulling his arm. "It doesn't matter."

DiCo whipped his arm away. "It *does* matter, Jonathan. This isn't right, and it isn't fair." And then he pointed at the woman and said, "You should be ashamed of yourself."

I don't know why, but I laughed when he said that. It was probably a survival instinct, to laugh in the face of painful truths that are too much to bear, but DiCo thought I was laughing at him, and he stormed out of the room. I walked out after him, but he was too far down the hallway to catch up without running after him, and I didn't know what I would say if I did catch up. I wasn't used to people sticking up for me like DiCo just did. I wasn't used to white people calling other white people racist on my behalf. I also wasn't used to winning, so even though I had wanted the win so badly, I was used to losing. That's just how my life was.

Later that evening, I wasn't even thinking about debate or racism because I was enjoying myself too much at my first college party. DiCo had told us we were on our own in the evenings, so some of the Black students who were hosting us at the dorms took us to a party, but it was pretty lame. Lucky for us, one of DiCo's former students, a kid who had also been on FDA's debate team, but who now went to MIT, came to watch the debates and catch up with the seniors on the team. His name was Devon. Once we had all decided that the Harvard party wasn't happening, Devon invited all of us to come to a party at MIT. The girls stayed behind, but the four of us guys took Devon up on his offer, and we took the train over there.

The MIT party was lit, and we were amazed that the kids at the nerdiest school had such fun parties. And these were Black and brown kids who didn't look any different from the kids I met at (MS)2. I turned to Demetrius at one point and shouted over the pumping music, "I had no idea college could be this fun!" We didn't drink or do anything that would get us into trouble, but I took a good mental picture of myself in a place like MIT or Harvard. I had thought going to a prestigious college or university would mean just a lot of hard classes and endless studying, but these kids were having mad fun.

All this time, I thought college would be one more painful step to getting to the promised land, but now I realized college was the promised land. Whatever it was, after hanging with Devon and his friends, I was more determined than ever to get there.

We stayed at MIT for a couple of hours, but we made sure to get back to Harvard before curfew. None of us wanted to make DiCo regret bringing us.

The next morning when we were packing up to go home, DiCo came into my room and sat down on the chair to apologize for his outburst at the judges. "I was angry," he said. "But not at you. I was angry at them. I was angry at the system." He shrugged. "But I wasn't angry at you. And I probably shouldn't have yelled at that poor woman."

Now, it was my turn to shrug. "It's fine," I said. "I'm okay."

"Why aren't you more upset, Jonathan?" DiCo asked, getting agitated all over again. As if I had said something to insult him personally. "You worked so hard for this, and I know you wanted to win."

I plopped down on the edge of the bed. "DiCo, this is normal life for me. Disappointment and not getting what I want are what I'm used to. It doesn't make sense for me to care too much because, then, what do I do when I lose?"

"Well, you better start caring more," DiCo said, "or this is going to be your life forever." And with that, he left me alone to finish packing.

The whole ride home back to New York, I thought about what DiCo said. I asked myself if I should have been indignant, outraged, and annoyed that I had been penalized for being born poor and Black. Of course, I should have. But what would I do with that anger? Just thinking about it, I could feel the resentment heating me up from the inside. I hated being penalized for something I had no control over. I hated the fact that where I came from colored everything about me and kept me from being seen for my achievements. Of course, I wanted to win. But I was more practical than that. I didn't have the privilege of expressing my anger in a room full of white people. That was, literally, a privilege only white people enjoyed in America. For a Black man, getting angry in public could mean getting killed. And even if I did raise my voice and say that things were unfair, what would it get me? Not the win. I knew that the only thing that would change my circumstances was working hard until I could create my own new circumstances. Having DiCo stand up for me, though, was encouraging. I thought if more white people cared as much as DiCo did about equality and justice, we'd all be better off.

After the Harvard tournament, DiCo's focus on our team waned again. He had more pressing issues to deal with at FDA, mainly teaching the FDA community how to deal with an openly transgender man.

There were a lot of different opinions circulating about DiCo once he transitioned. The students made fun of him. Faculty members talked openly about their disapproval, like he was some sort of freak who didn't belong around children. And some members of the administration questioned his ability to teach now that he had "come out." At the time, I understood that the rumor mill was running wild, and I understood that being transgender was a lot for people to process. It was a lot for me to process, too, but it wasn't something that made me question my allegiance to DiCo. He was still my favorite teacher and the person at FDA who I felt understood me the best. Ever since I first walked into his classroom freshman year, and he made a space for me, DiCo had been there for me. So, I wanted to be there for him as the rest of the school community tried to wrap their heads around his identity.

For his part, DiCo tried to help everybody at FDA understand what transgender meant and what it didn't mean. He offered to set up an after-school program for LGBTQ kids, but the administration nixed that idea. And then a rumor started circulating that a kid had pushed DiCo down a flight of stairs.

DiCo refused to talk about it. But something in him changed after that. Every time I saw him, he looked sad. At debate practice, he sat in his chair staring out the window rather than interacting with the team. More often than not, he let the captains run practice. So, the tables were turned now. I witnessed all this negative attention swirling around DiCo and tried to do my best to let him know that not everyone had a problem with his transition. I told him I understood how it felt to have to hide who you really are, and that I was proud of him for taking off his mask and being his true self. He said he appreciated my kind words. He assured me that he was okay. But he wasn't acting okay. He was acting anything but okay.

And then, one day in April, DiCo came to the team with an announcement to make. He stood in the front of the room, but he wasn't looking anyone in the eye. His gaze was focused beyond us, like he was waiting for someone to come through the door and save him. Normally, DiCo was so good with eye contact, so we knew something was up. He started to speak, but he was stuttering. He looked like he was going to cry. Finally, I said, "Just say it, DiCo. It can't be that bad."

He cleared his throat then and said, "I'm leaving FDA. I won't be coming back after this year."

Everybody started to talk at once, but DiCo calmed everyone and said, "Don't worry, I've already found someone to coach the team, so debate will still be here for all of you."

Like he thought that was what we were worried about. The debate team. Or that he could be replaced so easily with just another body.

"What are you going to do?" Keisha asked.

"I'm going to teach at a different school," DiCo said. "I just can't keep working here because it..." he paused for a second and then finished his sentence, "it just doesn't feel safe for me to be here anymore."

I should have been moved by DiCo's emotions. I should have felt terrible for him, but once he said he was leaving, something inside of me just turned off. I shut down. It was like the last bit of disappointment I could stomach. The proverbial straw had broken the camel's back.

"So, you're just going to quit?" I said aloud. "Things are too hard for you, so you're just going to leave?" I shook my head in disgust. "You always tell us not to give up. To dig deep. Even when it's hard. Find our why. But you don't have to do the same thing?"

DiCo just stared at me like I'd stabbed him in his heart. But I didn't care. I couldn't feel sorry for him because my own heart was already bleeding. I stood up and left the room.

After DiCo's announcement, I, basically, stopped going to debate practice. Whenever he would catch me in the hallways to ask why I wasn't showing up, I'd make up some lame excuse. "Sorry, I'm just really busy," I'd say and keep on walking.

"Do you want to talk about it?" He'd try to start a conversation with me, and I would give a fake smile and tell him that there was nothing to talk about.

"I'm fine," I'd say. "You gotta do you, right? What else is there to say?"

And then he'd look at me with that pained expression, when the lines above his eyebrows would furrow and his eyes would darken. And I would think, good. Maybe he now knows how it feels to have someone you thought was your friend abandon you.

I knew I hurt DiCo by shutting him out, but I was too hurt to care. I thought he understood how much he mattered to the members of the debate team. How much he mattered to me. I thought he knew that he was the only person I trusted who understood how hard my circumstances were. I thought he knew that I needed him to remind me on a regular basis that I could handle two more years of the struggle before I could be free. I thought the fact that I was okay with his transition, that we accepted him for who he was, would be enough for him to stay. And fight. For himself. But also for me. But in the end, it wasn't enough, I realized. I wasn't enough. I never was enough for anyone to stick around for. Nobody was willing to put me first. Not my parents, nor my brothers. Dr. Hodge was leaving FDA and now DiCo. Even my grandmother, who would give me the last dollar from her pocketbook, wouldn't put my needs first and stand up to my mother about her addiction.

The rumbles in my foundation were now a full-fledged quake, and I scrambled to find a safe place.

Within a few weeks of DiCo's announcement, my life looked shockingly different from how it had just one month before. I stopped caring about the future I had been running toward. I stopped doing my homework. I started smoking weed again, and I started staying at my grandmother's apartment on weekends so I could hang out with Dwayne, Omari, Melvin, and Marquise. They were quick to accept my apology for ghosting them, and they acted as if they knew I'd come to my senses sooner or later.

"We never understood why you wanted to do all that geeky stuff anyway. Acting white will never get you anywhere, Jon," Dwayne said. "You gotta stay true to the game. And you know we're always going to have your back."

"You guys are my family," I said, feeling comfort in their willingness to welcome me back into the group, no questions asked.

I felt safe. I knew my way around this world, and I figured if I stopped trying to escape it, I'd stop being disappointed. I was ready to just give up on my promises—like DiCo. Quit like Dr. Hodge. Even Malcolm quit the debate team because he said it was too much to handle.

The thing is, every day I woke up, I still wanted to win. Lifelong dreams don't die that easily. I still wanted the dream life that came on the other side of a college degree. But I would tell myself to get used to less so I would stop being disappointed by my own expectations. I tried to force myself to forget with more weed and less time in school. I had to ignore the looks of disappointment and confusion on the faces of my teachers.

Then, I got an email informing me that Dr. Ubinto was leaving (MS)2. This would be his last summer serving as interim director. One more disappointment in my life, and I was devastated all over again. The spiral continued.

Because I could never truly depend on my own parents, I formed really strong attachments to these parental figures in my life, so when they "left me," it felt like a betrayal. I had held up my end of the bargain in our relationships. I had followed orders and worked as hard as they told me to. I took the AP classes and the college courses. I stayed up until all hours of the night studying. I went to Andover. I was following the rules that my mentors had set for me, and then, one by one, they were disappearing from my life.

The only positive thing to happen during this tumultuous time was that I met a nice girl named Nicolette. She was the friend of a girl Omari wanted to get with, but she wouldn't do anything without Nicolette being invited along. Omari begged me to come distract Nicolette so he could do his thing. When I hung out with Nicolette, I liked her right away. I tried to put the moves on her, but she wasn't impressed by my game. I actually liked that about her and decided to try to get her to change her mind about me, using less game and just being myself.

We started talking after that, and I discovered that Nicky was really nice and easy to talk to. She was her own person—

she wasn't trying to be like everyone else. Every time I saw Nicky, she had a flower in her hair. Even her style was unique. She changed her hair color all the time, she almost always wore dresses rather than jeans or sweats, and her favorite shoes were moccasins. I really liked getting to know this girl, and hanging out with her felt like the one good thing in my life while everything else was falling apart and coming undone.

I could feel myself sliding dangerously close to the edge of the wide-open crater that had opened beneath my feet. And I knew if I fell all the way in, I'd never be able to climb out.

At school, my teachers were hounding me about missing assignments. I was doing the minimum to pass my classes. Meanwhile, at home, the looming threat of going back to the shelter system added a layer of anxiety to my anger and disappointment with the world, and I started feeling trapped, and the need to escape was overwhelming. I was doing my part to blow up every good thing in my life, and there was nobody—not my parents, not DiCo, or even Dr. Hodge—willing or able to stop me. Or help me. And I needed help. I knew I did. Even as I intentionally made bad choices, it was a cry for help. I needed somebody to save me. I just wanted to have a decent life. I wanted to be taken care of instead of being responsible for every single thing myself. I wanted to know that someone was going to be there for me if I fell.

Which is why, on an evening toward the end of May, I picked up the phone and called my brother. "Justin, I'm ready," I said.

"Ready for what, Jon?" Justin said.

"I'm ready to come live with you. Can I still come?" I was going to have to save my own life, before I destroyed it.

8

I Wasn't Supposed to Be a Statistic

For my move down South to be legal, my mom and dad had to relinquish their parental rights. My mother didn't fight to keep me, and I felt ready to be free from my parents for good. I always knew that the day would come when I would leave them, I just didn't know it would come before I turned eighteen.

Once my parents signed the official paperwork, technically I became a foster child, and Justin, who was only twenty-two years old at the time, became my legal guardian. Since Justin had enlisted in the military to help pay for college, Jay decided to move in with Justin so he could cover parenting duties when Justin was away. We didn't have time to play family reunion when I first got to Virginia, though, because I had to be on an airplane back to (MS)2 within days of my arrival.

When I arrived at Andover, the physical beauty of the place had a calming effect on my psyche. I knew I almost blew up my life at the end of tenth grade, but being back among my friends and the supportive teaching staff and counselors reminded me of what was possible if I just stayed on track. Talking to my friends, I was reminded that my troubles weren't unique and that I was luckier than so many other kids who didn't have a chance to come to a place like (MS)2 for six weeks of liberation from their home life.

I'm sure on the outside, anybody who saw me that summer thought I was enjoying myself, and in many ways I was. I was a big brother to a new first-year. I participated in all the activities (MS)2 offered, and I was even voted, by the students and faculty, to be the head of cultural sharing the following year. So, I was obviously doing everything right. But there was always a voice in the back of my head reminding me that my life at Andover wasn't real, so don't get too comfortable. *Don't let your guard down and let anybody get too close. Protect your heart.* The impending departure of Dr. Ubinto served as a constant reminder that people didn't stick around. The only message truly coalescing in my mind that summer was that I couldn't depend on anybody but myself.

Six weeks later, it was time for me to return to Virginia and start over again as the new kid.

Again.

My brothers and I lived in the same complex in Wellington where we'd last lived as a family in Virginia, and I was registered to attend the same school all three of my brothers attended, Western Branch High School. I tried out and made the varsity football team, and I placed into mostly AP and honors classes. As a member of the football team, I automatically became "popular," and I'd sit with the other team members at lunchtime. On game days, I'd floss through the school's hallways in my football jersey. School kept me busy Monday through Friday, and, at home, Jay and I got into a routine. We ate lots of fish sticks, Chick-fil-A, and Panera sandwiches for dinner. Between the two of them, my brothers provided a nice, stable environment for me, leaving me wanting for nothing. I even signed up for driver's ed because Justin said he'd figure out how to buy me a car for senior year if I learned how to drive. But despite this picture-perfect life I now had, I was homesick.

In theory, I should have been ecstatic that I had escaped living in New York with my parents. I finally got what I said I always wanted. A normal life. Structure, stability, and parental supervision. But all I could think about, every day when I woke up and right before I fell asleep at night, was that I wasn't supposed to be living this life. This wasn't where I was supposed to be.

The life my brothers had crafted for me felt like an ill-fitting wool sweater. It was too tight. It made me itch. It made me feel uncomfortable in my own skin. And that is the most tragic thing about growing up in dysfunction. It distorts your concept of reality and your place in it so much that when normal is finally handed to you, you don't know what to do with it. I felt like I didn't deserve this life my brothers had given me. I didn't trust that it was real. I lived with a perpetual fear of it being taken away like everything else good in my life. The very idea of this new life felt like a trick, and I was determined not to fall for it.

What that looked like in real time was me in a constant state of agitation, anger, and confusion. I wanted to be prepared for the worst because I knew it would come. So, I was edgy and testy and withdrawn. I didn't smile as much as I usually did. Justin and Jay could tell something was wrong, but I brushed off their concern. "I'm cool," I'd say, even though I wasn't. But they left me alone. Meanwhile, I would spend hours on the phone with Nicky telling her that I wanted to be back in New York.

My brothers sent me back to New York for a long weekend hoping it would shake me out of my funk, but it had the opposite effect. After spending almost the entire time with Nicky, and feeling so comfortable in my familiar surroundings, I decided that the only way I could get back to feeling like myself again would be to move back to New York.

I waited until the semester was almost over to tell my brothers how I felt. They sat at the kitchen table while I stood and made my plea.

"I need to go back to New York," I said. "I can't stay here anymore."

They didn't say anything at first, so I kept going. "I appreciate everything you guys have done for me, but I just think I need to be back in New York. I don't think it's right that we all abandoned Mommy. She's got nobody looking out for her, and Dad might do something stupid. Somebody should be there for her. Her multiple sclerosis is acting up, too."

"So, this is about Mom?" Justin asked, like he was trying

to understand my logic. "You want to go back to New York because you think Mommy needs you?"

"Also, I just miss her," I said, which was true, but I missed Nicky more. I wasn't about to tell my brothers that, though.

Justin and Jay both looked at me like I was crazy, but they kept their arguments based on reason.

"What about football?" Jay asked.

"Got that figured out," I said. "My friend Demetrius told me the new principal they're bringing to FDA is going to start a football team," I said. "And you guys, we all know I'm never going to be a football star here in Virginia. I spend more time on the bench than on the field. But in Harlem, I could be on the starting line, no doubt."

"Where you gonna live?" Justin asked, leaning back in his chair and crossing his arms.

"I already talked to Mommy about it," I admitted. "She and Dad got a one-bedroom apartment in the Bronx now, and they said I could have the bedroom."

Jay scratched his head. "You sure this is what you want? You really sure? Because you really wanted to get out of New York not so long ago."

Honestly, I didn't know what I really wanted, except to feel as though I belonged somewhere, and that somewhere wasn't Virginia.

"Yeah," I said. "I want to go home." They both looked disappointed, and for a minute I wished I hadn't said anything.

"Look, Jon," Justin said, standing up from the table. "You gotta be responsible for the choices you make, you know what I'm saying? You wanna stay with us, you can stay. You wanna go back home, go back home. Just do what you need to do. You know what we expect of you. So, if you want to handle that on your own, that's on you."

I promised both Justin and Jay that I would make them proud. I reminded them that even though FDA was no Western Branch High School, it still had a solid reputation for getting kids into college.

"I'm not going to ruin my future just by going back to New York," I said. "You know I'm not going to let you down."

"You better not," Justin said. "Because it's all on you now."

I was back in New York before Christmas. Nicky was standing at the bus stop, waiting for me when I got there. As soon as I saw her waiting for me, I knew I had made the right decision to leave Virginia.

"Let's get you home and unpacked," Nicky whispered in my ear when I hugged her.

Home was now a new apartment on East 173rd Street in the Bronx. I was grateful my parents hadn't been forced to go back into the shelter system, but I was nervous to see where they had landed. As soon as we walked in the door of the new apartment, my mother hugged me hard and said hi to Nicky. And then she had to leave. "I'm going over to see my mother," she said. "Your father and I will probably just sleep over there tonight so you guys can have the apartment to yourselves," she said, winking at me, acting like a teenage friend, instead of a parent. And then she was gone.

Alone, Nicky and I walked around the apartment, poking around to see what it was like, and I instantly regretted having my girlfriend with me. Nicky had lied to her mother and told her she was staying over at her friend's house, so she could be with me on my first night back, but now I wish I had told her not to come. This was the first time Nicky was seeing where I lived and how we lived and, seeing it through her eyes, I just wanted to melt into the floor. The whole place was tiny, my parents' mattress covered the living room floor and took over part of the kitchen as well. There was no furniture anywhere, except for the crates full of pornography videos that lined the wall. In the one bedroom, the room where I would be sleeping, there were some blankets on the floor for my bed, along with a small television, and a box full of shredded newspaper where my mother's cat, Blackie, did his business. The room stank and it was cold because there was no heat.

"This is disgusting," I said, my body radiating with

embarrassment. "I'm sorry, Nicky," I said, not even knowing what I was apologizing for. The apartment. My parents. Or the fact that I couldn't pretend to be the perfect boyfriend now that Nicky knew we lived like animals.

"You don't have to apologize," Nicky said. "This isn't your fault or your responsibility. I'm just glad you're back for good." And she reached for my hand.

My heart warmed with joy at that moment. Nicky didn't judge me. She didn't run away and make excuses. She sat down with me in that cold stinky room, and we talked until we fell asleep, huddled together in the nest of blankets on the floor. And as uncomfortable and tragic as the situation was, I finally felt like I was right where I belonged.

The next morning, Nicky and I stumbled into the kitchen looking for something to eat. My parents were still gone and the apartment was cold and quiet.

"What's this?" Nicky asked.

I turned away from the empty refrigerator and saw her pointing to an old pill bottle on the counter, with a blackened hole melted into the sides. For a moment I froze, like when you get caught doing something you know is wrong, and you're desperately scrambling for an excuse that will get you out of the situation.

Nicky stood there waiting for an answer.

I decided to tell her the truth. A truth I'd been hiding from Nicky all this time. A truth I instinctively hid from everybody.

I scratched the back of my neck and then said matter-of-factly, "That's how my parents smoke crack. They burn it in the bottle and then smoke it."

I watched Nicky's face go from shock to what looked like pity. "I'm so sorry, Jonathan," Nicky said. "But now everything makes sense," she added quietly.

I shrugged. "I guess, if having parents who've been doing crack for your whole life makes sense."

"Why didn't you tell me before?"

"I don't know," I said. "I mean, who wants to tell their girl that their parents do drugs?"

I wanted Nicky to see me as this smart kid who was going places. Someone who was going to college and was going to be a doctor. She loved that persona I played, and I loved being that person in her eyes. Nicky even told me that it was only after we started dating that she actually started thinking seriously about going to college herself. "You inspire me, Jon," she told me a few weeks after we started hanging out. But now Nicky was seeing the truth of who I really was and where I came from, and so I waited for the rejection. I waited for the look in her eyes to go from admiration to disgust. I waited for her to make an excuse for why she had to hurry up and leave.

"I get it," Nicky said. "And I don't blame you, but I think it's harder to keep secrets than it is to be honest."

"Not really," I said cautiously. "I got so many secrets, you're going to have to stay with me forever to uncover them all."

Nicky laughed. "Oh, really, well, maybe I have some secrets of my own, too," she said.

I walked over to her and wrapped her in a hug. "You want to tell me some of your secrets?"

Nicky laughed again, and we went back to my bedroom, forgetting all about finding something to eat. But that moment sticks with me in my mind as the moment when I understood what it meant to accept somebody fully, without judgment. Nicky gave me that gift, and with it, she made me realize that I was not a product of my environment or my parents' mistakes. I could be whoever I said I was going to be and truly be judged on my own merits. That was a freeing thought that I would need reminding of over the years, but Nicky gave it to me first.

After the Christmas holidays, my mother went with me to FDA to get me registered again into their system. And my grandma gave my mother some money to buy me an actual bed and a dresser for my bedroom. Blackie's litter box also got moved out of my room. During those two weeks before school started,

I spent most of my time with Nicky and tried to get myself mentally ready to go back to FDA. I heard that a new principal had been hired, but I didn't know much about him. Because we went to register during winter break, I wasn't able to see what the school was like in its first year without Dr. Hodge. Had I seen it, I might have hopped on the first bus and headed back down South.

Going back to FDA and finding it transformed from the school it once was into a school that now operated like a high school version of M.S. 219 was devastating. Without Dr. Hodge, FDA was a shell of its former self. The ethos of excellence that used to flow through the hallways was a thing of the past. Thankfully, the school guidance counselors were still pushing to get as many kids into college as possible. And, at the end of the day, that's all that mattered to me. I figured with Andover in my back pocket, if I took advantage of everything I was supposed to do at FDA, I still had a good chance to get into a good college.

The truth was, I wasn't too worried about FDA's demise because I was too busy hanging out with Nicky. Somebody told me that DiCo was now working at a high school in Brooklyn—at another predominately Black school—and had already assembled a new debate team that was, supposedly, doing quite well. That information triggered a feeling of jealousy and furthered my anger toward DiCo, but I quickly told myself it didn't matter. Nicky was enough to fill the void DiCo left.

Now that we were finally together in the same city for more than a few weeks at a time, it was perfect. Nicky attended Mott Hall Bronx High School and so knew some of my friends from M.S. 219, and I knew some of her friends as well. It was easy for us to create a daily rhythm together, and I spent most of my time with her. Being with Nicky also kept me from feeling neglected by my parents. But, for the most part, I was back to raising myself. I didn't ask for much, and my parents didn't give much. My mother barely kept food in the house, leaving me to fend for myself if I wanted to eat anything other than what they served at school. Sometimes, Nicky would take the lunch money her mother gave her and buy me dinner. Sometimes, I would go to my grandmother's house. Sometimes, I would just be hungry. The thing was, I was so used to living like that, it didn't knock me off my game. I just kept telling myself that the end was near. I had one more summer at Andover, then during my senior year I would apply to college, and that's when my real life would start. The finish line was within reach.

"Jonathan, I missed my period."

It was Nicky calling on a Saturday morning in May. When I didn't say anything, she whispered into the phone, "I think I'm pregnant."

"Have you taken a test?" I asked her out of obligation, not out of real concern. Nicky and I had had so many "pregnancy scares" that never turned out to be true.

"Not yet," she said. "I mean, it's probably just late because I'm stressed out or something."

"Probably," I said.

"But if it still doesn't come by this weekend, would you go with me to the clinic on Monday?" she asked.

"Yeah, of course," I said, "but you watch, your period's gonna come this weekend."

"Yeah," Nicky said. "You're probably right."

Nicky's period didn't come, so on Monday after school we were on the bus heading to Planned Parenthood.

I still thought it was going to be another false alarm, but just in case, I turned to Nicky and said, "If you are pregnant, you'd have an abortion, right?"

"Of course," Nicky said. "We're too young to be having a kid."

"And I'm not trying to show up at Harvard or Yale with no baby," I said. "That would ruin everything."

Nicky was silent after that.

At the clinic, Nicky went into the exam room alone. I stayed in the waiting room and read my history textbook, trying to make use of the time.

When Nicky came out of the exam room smiling, I knew I had made the right decision not to worry. Nicky always jumped to conclusions. But it was her body, so I just tried not to act ignorant when she got worried every time her period was late.

"Let's go," she said, and I packed up my books and followed her out of the clinic back to the bus stop.

On the bus, Nicky turned to me and said, "Jonathan, I *am* pregnant."

"What?!" I said. "You came out the room smiling. I thought we were in the clear."

"No, I was smiling because this is just a lot," she said. "I mean, there's a baby inside of me."

I shook my head, "No, we can't do this, Nicky. We can't. You have to get rid of it. You were supposed to schedule the abortion if the test came out positive. Why didn't you do that?"

Now, Nicky didn't look happy. "I know. I'm going to schedule it, but I just need time to think."

"Think about what?" I demanded. "There's nothing to think about. You even said it yourself: We're too young. And I can't be a father right now. A baby would ruin everything!"

"Yeah, I know," Nicky said with tears in her eyes.

Within a week, Nicky had decided that she was keeping the baby. It was a decision she came to on her own. Her mother agreed with me that Nicky was too young. We were both in the eleventh grade and nobody would ever argue that seventeen was the right age to become a parent. Nicky's mother also thought I was too irresponsible and wouldn't be available to help raise the child. Although I didn't appreciate the label of irresponsible, I agreed wholeheartedly with the idea that now was not the right time to have a baby. I begged and pleaded with Nicky to reconsider. But she refused. She told me we were responsible for the life we created, and she wasn't going to kill it.

The only life I was thinking about was mine and how a baby would ruin it. And like any person who saw a threat to their life, I immediately started fighting with everything I had. Every day, sometimes three or four times a day, I told Nicky I didn't want to be a father. I told her I wasn't going to give up my dreams for a baby. I told her *she* was ruining my life. I called her names.

I lashed out in the worst ways possible, saying anything to get Nicky to see what a mistake bringing a child into the world would be. But as desperate as I was to get Nicky to have an abortion, she was just as clear she had to keep this baby. "This baby shouldn't have to die because of our mistake," Nicky said.

Never in my life had I been so afraid. My whole life had been full of hardships. Most of them, though, had been the result of other people's poor choices. And, most of the time, by using my intelligence, and with the help of my village, I'd been able to get past any obstacle in my way. But a baby? There was no way to get past a baby. I knew I wouldn't be able to be one of those people who didn't participate in their child's life. Pretend it didn't exist. I didn't have the DNA to be a deadbeat dad. Not when my own father had never once abandoned me. Not once.

I had to be better than that. But my teenage brain could not reconcile how to combine fatherhood with the future I imagined for myself: Going to a top college, followed by medical school. Leaving the ghetto behind. Becoming somebody important and respectful. Teen father didn't correlate with that vision. The two ideas were completely paradoxical in my head. And I didn't have anybody to help me work it out. I was too afraid to tell anybody in my family, and I was still holding on to hope that Nicky would change her mind. But as every day passed, despite my constant pleading and badgering, Nicky remained resolute that she was keeping the baby.

I told my mother first because I knew she would never be upset about a baby. And I was right. My mother said she was happy for Nicky and me, which, while comforting not to be yelled at, was confusing to have my mother praise me for getting my girlfriend pregnant at age seventeen. When my father found out, he was pissed. As soon as my mother told him, he rushed into my room and shouted, "I let you fuck in my house, the least you could do is wrap it up," and then he knocked over my flimsy dresser, my clothes spilling out all over the floor. The intensity of his anger matched the fear and shame I felt.

"Clean this mess up!" he yelled as he walked out of the room. And yet, a little while later, he came back to reassure me that I still had a future and would make it to college. "It's going to be harder for you, Jon," he said. "But I know you're going to be okay. You have more options than your sister." I didn't know what to feel about my father's assessment because he had no idea what it was like to even go to college, much less the kind of school I was hoping to go to. The kind that the people at (MS)2 swore I was a shoo-in for if I kept up my grades. His predictions did nothing to quell the churning anxiety that hadn't stopped since Nicky told me she was keeping the baby.

But the fact that he didn't tell me that I had ruined my life made me pluck up the courage to call my brothers. They were the ones I was most afraid of disappointing. I had told them that going back to New York wouldn't change my chances of succeeding and that I knew what I was doing. But when I told them, they also thought I still had a chance at going to college and having the life I dreamed of. "It's just going to be harder to get there," Justin said. "But you can do it because you have no other choice." Everyone seemed so fucking okay with it, except me. And that just made me angrier. All I could see was a disaster in front of me. There were days when I would just lie in my room screaming into my pillow. I felt so helpless. I couldn't undo what I had done. This baby was due in the winter of my senior year. I couldn't see anything happening between now and then that would allow me to get back to the future I had been working toward.

Nobody seemed to notice how much I was struggling with it all. My parents and my brothers all seemed to think I'd just handle things like I always did. They seemed to think I was stronger than I really was. They didn't see that this was destroying me. They didn't hear me sobbing at night. They didn't know the dark thoughts that occupied my every waking hour. They didn't know that I wasn't looking for answers—I just wanted a way out.

The only person who seemed to understand my pain was my sister, Helena. Being a teen parent herself, she knew exactly what I was going through, and she came over to talk to me when she heard the news. "Jon, you're going to be okay," she told me as I started crying again. She was sitting on the edge of my bed, while I lay there staring at the ceiling, letting my tears run unchecked down my face. "You'll get through this," she promised.

I shook my head. "No, I won't. This baby is going to ruin everything for me, Helena. My life is over. And Nicky doesn't even care."

Like my mother, Helena never held her tongue. "Nigga, this isn't Nicky's fault. Y'all both made that baby. And your life isn't over just because you have a kid. I'm still here, ain't I? Life will go on, Jon. You gotta stop feeling sorry for yourself."

I sighed and pulled myself up into a seated position next to my sister. I knew Helena was trying to help me, but when I looked at her life, living in the 'hood, with no talk of going to college because she was too busy raising her daughter, I didn't feel comforted. In fact, it just made me feel as if I was right to think there was no way out of the mess I'd made. Of course, I didn't say that to my sister because I knew she was doing her best, and I didn't have the courage to make the sacrifices she made.

Despite the fact that everyone in my family wanted me to stop acting like the world was ending, I couldn't pull myself out of the dark hole I had fallen into. And I believed the only person who could save me was Nicky.

When Nicky said she wanted to come over so we could talk, I decided this was going to be it. I would apologize for being an ass, but I would also explain to Nicky why we were too young to become parents. I knew I had been selfish and mean, but this time, I promised myself, I would keep my cool.

I was alone in the apartment when the doorbell rang. When I saw Nicky standing outside my door with a flower in her hair, for a moment I forgot about the baby and just remembered how much I loved this girl. She smiled, and I took her back to my room so we could talk. When she walked by me, I smelled her sweet perfume and a wave of memories washed over me, reminding me of the first time we'd been in this apartment together, when I felt so safe with her. I missed those times.

"You look good," I said as Nicky sat on my bed.

"Thanks," she said with a soft smile.

I came and sat next to her on the bed.

"The reason I wanted to talk," Nicky started, "was because I wanted to know if you are still planning on going to your summer program in Massachusetts?"

"What do you mean, am I still going? Of course, I am. This is my last year," I said, slightly confused by the question. Nicky knew how important (MS)2 was for my future.

"But if you go, you'll miss all of the appointments with the doctor for the baby," she said.

I looked at Nicky like she was crazy, and all of my plans of being nice and calm flew out the window. "That's why I told you I didn't want this baby," I said, jumping off the bed. "I don't have time to be a father, Nicolette," I said. "I told you this, and this is what I meant. I can't do this right now."

"Well, I didn't make this kid myself," Nicky countered. "And we both have to take responsibility."

"No," I said as I started pacing back and forth across my tiny room so I didn't have to look Nicky in the eye. "I told you I didn't want this kid, and you made this decision on your own," I said, my voice rising in anger. "I'm not ready to be a father, and you're definitely not ready to be a mother."

"Don't tell me what I can and can't do," Nicky said. "And it's not like I'm dying to be a teen mom."

"So, why are you doing this, then?" I said. "You don't have to be a teen mom. Get the stupid abortion and be done with it. You always said you would get an abortion if we ever messed up."

"I know what I said, but I can't do it," Nicky shouted back at me. "I'm not killing this baby."

"What the hell, Nicolette," I hollered back "You're ruining my life. Everything I've been working for, you're ruining it all."

Nicky raised her hands and shook her head in disgust. "I can't deal with you," she said. "You are, literally, going to make me lose this baby by stressing me out." She paused then, as she thought about what she just said. "Yeah, you probably want to make me have a miscarriage so you can go live your perfect life."

"That's not true," I said.

"Well, it sure seems like it," Nicky said, reaching for the door. "And I don't need that from you, or from my mom, or anybody!"

"Where you going?" I asked.

"Why do you care?" she said over her shoulder.

"Because we gotta figure this out," I said, still hoping I could get her to change her mind, but feeling my chances slipping away. She couldn't leave.

"There's nothing to figure out," she said. "I'm keeping this baby, and you're an asshole."

I ran over to the door and grabbed Nicky by the shoulder and tried to force her to turn around and stay. "You can't go now. We're not done," I said, the desperation in my voice came out like a threat. "You have to listen to what I'm saying."

"Nigga, have you lost your entire mind? You better get your hands off me," Nicky said, her breath coming in shallow bursts.

Immediately, my hands fell away. Had I just put my hands on my girlfriend in anger? Was I becoming my father?

"I'll see you around, Jonathan," Nicky said. And she walked out of my room and out of the apartment.

Nicky stopped talking to me after that day. The school year ended, and she refused to take any of my calls. Our mutual friends told me that Nicolette had made the decision to stay away from me because she was convinced that my negative energy would make her lose the baby.

So, it was official and everybody knew it. I *was* an asshole.

The thing was, as much as I wanted to place all the blame on Nicky for not getting an abortion, I knew I could have prevented her from getting pregnant. I could simply have worn a condom rather than assume we could "take care of it" afterward. That stupid decision tormented me day and night. I knew that was the true source of my shame and anger. I wanted to blame somebody else. Anybody. Nicky. My parents. God. But this awful situation I now found myself in was completely preventable, and I was to blame. Which is what I was doing on a twenty-four-hour loop of self-abuse. I told myself that all the work I had done was for nothing. I wasted all of that hard work, including the work and effort that so many other people had poured into me. I let all those people down, too. I couldn't hold my head up at school, around my teachers, because I had become the worst fucking stereotype and a cliché. Another Black teen parent from the ghetto. Somebody's baby daddy. Another failure. Sometimes, the ill-timed prophecy of my Grandmother Corine, when we were about to move to New York from Virginia, would ring in my ears and taunt me: *"You take those kids back to New York, they gonna get into drugs. They gonna be in a gang. They gonna be teenage parents. Don't say I didn't try to warn y'all."* My parents should have listened to her.

Even though I told Nicky I was definitely going back to (MS)2, it started to seem like a waste of time. If this baby was coming before I graduated high school, I wouldn't have time to go to college. A baby couldn't wait four years for me to start being a dad. Pampers and milk cost money, and college students don't make money. Also, the thought of walking around Andover with everybody knowing what I'd done filled me with dread. Getting my girlfriend pregnant wasn't what (MS)2 kids were supposed to be about. Before I could change my mind, I emailed my (MS)2 counselor, Mr. Collins, and told him something had come up and that I no longer thought I would be attending college, so it didn't make sense for me to come back for the third summer.

His reply email came right away. And we jumped on a phone call to talk.

I blurted out the truth before I could chicken out.

"I'm having a kid," I said. "So, I don't think there's any point in coming back."

Mr. Collins listened to me provide all the reasons it made no sense for me to do a college-prep program when I, obviously, couldn't go to college with a kid to support. I also admitted that I didn't feel as though I could handle the workload at Andover with everything I was dealing with. Since I found out about the baby, I hadn't been able to concentrate on anything school-related.

"Jonathan, I'm not going to tell you that the path for you is going to be easy," Mr. Collins started. "But it's not impossible. But getting into college will be impossible if you don't at least try. So, why don't you just come back and finish the program. You've worked so hard, it would be a shame for you not to finish."

"But I just messed up so badly," I said, on the verge of tears.

"Jonathan, you made a mistake, but you can't let one mistake define you," he said quietly. "You're supposed to be the head of cultural sharing this year. You were selected for that role because of who you are. Because all your fellow classmates and teachers see you as a leader and as someone who cares for other people. Why don't you let that be the Jonathan you're working for?"

That Jonathan doesn't exist anymore, I thought. But, oh, how I wished he still did. If there was any way to be the Jonathan who Mr. Collins was describing, I knew I would sacrifice anything and everything to get him back. But I messed it all up being stupid.

"Jonathan," Mr. Collins tried again. "You know, you're right, maybe things will be too hard for you to go to college right away. But maybe they won't. Maybe college and being a father will be possible for you. Anything can happen between now and then, and if you come and finish the program, you leave the door open for that possibility."

Even in my darkest moments, there was still a spark of hope in me, and I decided to trust Mr. Collins. As depressed as I felt, the lessons I'd learned from my mentors and guides still resonated in my spirit. First and foremost, I would not be a quitter. I didn't have high expectations for myself, but I agreed to go back to Andover to finish what I started.

Luckily, the program was organized so well that the only thing I had to do was pack my bags and get myself to the airport. My flight was arranged and paid for, the shuttle bus from Boston to Andover was waiting for me, and once I arrived at the campus, all I had to do was follow the schedule and go to my classes. It was a relief to just have to follow directions.

I wasn't the first (MS)2 student facing teen parenthood. There had been a third-year student who was visibly pregnant during my second summer. At least nobody could see my scarlet letter. But the faculty all knew, and I told most of my friends because I couldn't act like everything was normal. Even though I was physically there amidst all the peaceful green space, my mind was in a constant state of dark thoughts. I was so depressed and agitated, I started to think that if I didn't exist, I would be free from all the pain I was in. I could just check out. I didn't tell anyone I was having these thoughts, but it was obvious I wasn't myself.

My roommate, Mike, noticed right away that I was struggling, and he talked to the new director. He told him I wasn't doing my homework, and I was just sitting in our room most afternoons staring out the window. The administration's response was to drop me down from the C-level classes to the A-level classes. I didn't really care about the "demotion" because the homework was easier, and I was now in class with Mike, Juanita, and my other good friends. After classes, when we'd all be hanging out together, my friends would tell me I was going to be a great father, and that college would still be possible, but their kind words could barely penetrate the wall of shame and anger I'd built around myself.

I felt deep in my bones that I didn't deserve to be at Andover anymore. Coming back was a mistake. I remembered the looks the pregnant girl got when she was here, and I imagined those same looks directed at me. I felt different from everybody else there. I had left Nicky dozens of messages begging her to reconsider her plans for the baby, but her silence told me she wasn't going to, which meant my future was ruined.

I dragged myself through classes, and I did all the pre-college work I had to do. I wrote my college essays and filled out the common application, but it all felt pointless. I went on the college field trips because I had to. We visited Dartmouth, Bates, and Bowdoin, but the whole time we were seeing these schools, all I could think about was the uselessness of the experience. How could I go to college in Maine or New Hampshire if my baby lived in Brownsville, Brooklyn, which is where Nicky lived with her mother and two siblings?

Somehow, I made it through all six weeks of the program, mostly surviving on the kindness of my friends and generosity of the faculty and staff at (MS)2. And then it was time for graduation.

My parents and my Uncle Wayne drove up from New York for the festivities. When they arrived on the campus, I could tell by their faces that they were as impressed and in awe as I had been the first summer I got to Andover. My mother gushed over every little detail, from the delicate dishes in the dining room to the distinguished-looking oil portraits of old white people hanging on the walls. She was in tears for practically the whole weekend, talking about how proud of me she was. Even my father was visibly impressed. Not just by Andover's opulence, but that I had succeeded there. A child of his making it through this vast sea of white privilege was validation that he must have done something right. Even if it was only providing half the DNA in my body. "See, I knew Jonathan was going to be okay," he boasted to my mother, but loud enough so I could hear. I didn't want to seem ungrateful for the vote of confidence, but all I wanted to do was scream at my father and the rest of my family members: *"But I'm not okay! Don't you see I'm dying inside? Can't you see that I need help?"* But they didn't see. And I didn't say a word.

When I got back to New York, time betrayed me. It was a countdown for when *my* life would end and parenthood would begin. And I was scared out of my mind. I never once thought that I wasn't going to take care of my child. My thoughts were centered on one question and one question only: *How do I give this kid the best life possible?* But the problem was, I didn't have the answer, and I was driving myself insane about it. I tried to run plays and scenarios of how to be a father that wouldn't mess up this kid's chances of having a good and decent life. Just looking back at my own family tree, I had a lot of examples of just how easy it was to mess up a kid's life, starting with my parents. And at seventeen years old, I didn't trust that I'd just be able to figure it out.

The baby was due in six months and time refused to slow down. The pressure continued to build. Even though Nicky still wasn't talking to me, her mother started calling me on a regular basis to ask what I was going to do to help her daughter raise this child. "You know you have to take responsibility for your child," she would say.

"You know you gotta take care of this baby, Boo Boo," my mother kept reminding me.

"Yo, you gotta be a man. It's time to grow up" was my father's advice.

All of these adults were here to tell me that I had to man up. That I had to do the right thing. That I had to take care of a baby, but I didn't know how. And nobody offered to teach me. I was supposed to be getting ready to go back to high school, but instead I started applying for jobs. And even that was new to me. The only real job I ever had had been through DFOY during middle school, and I didn't really have to apply for that. So, I put applications at the places I'd seen kids my age work— fast-food joints, retail shops, and grocery stores—and hoped for the best.

At night, I would mourn the life I thought was promised if I worked hard enough, but now knew I'd never have. I'd been to Harvard, Yale, and MIT. I'd seen the life of a carefree college student. I was a witness to the lives of the rich kids at Andover and knew what the possibilities were for people with money. I had truly believed that if I followed the right path, I would have a chance at that life, but becoming a father at eighteen erased those possibilities. "Carefree" and "easy" would never be words used to describe my future. That was the painful pill I kept trying to swallow, but, instead, it just choked me going down.

Once school started, I skipped all my appointments with the FDA college guidance counselor and soon started skipping a lot of my classes as well. It was too hard to focus on my academics when I felt like my dreams were dying and my life was ending. So, rather than sitting in class pretending to care about the origins of war and calculus, I spent a lot of time sitting on the benches up the block from my parents' apartment just trying to contain the raging emotions inside of me. There was a liquor store across the street where the owner had no problem selling me bottles of cheap E&J brandy and I got into the habit of drinking my feelings down to a dull hum. I was in survival mode again, starting over in a situation where I didn't know the rules. And there was nobody in my village who could help me navigate the world of teen fatherhood. My brothers couldn't help me. My parents couldn't help me. My friends couldn't help me. So, I was wide open to anyone who could show me the way.

Tyson was a drug dealer in our neighborhood who drove a nice car, wore nice clothes, and did nice things for the people in his life. I didn't know Tyson only by his reputation, though. We shared some close connections. Tyson was my parents' dealer, and he was dating my friend Omari's sister. So I knew who Tyson was, and he knew who I was, even though we didn't have a relationship ourselves.

"Yo, Jonathan." Tyson rolled up on me one afternoon when I was cutting school again and sitting on the benches. "Come with me, I gotta go pick up my daughter from school."

I jumped in the car without thinking.

As we started to drive, Tyson made small talk like we were old friends. "Yo, I gotta pick up my daughter, and I promised her I'd buy all her friends ice cream."

"That's cool," I said, taking stock of the interior of Tyson's car and the new kicks on his feet. I thought it was nice he was buying ice cream for all his daughter's friends, and I tried to calculate how much maintaining this lifestyle would cost. I knew how Tyson got his money, and I wasn't trying to live like that, but he was making drug dealing look real PG. Especially when he picked up his little girl and she jumped into his arms, yelling "Daddy! Daddy!" like he was her hero.

"Come on, Jon. Help me get this ice cream for these kids," Tyson leaned over and hollered at me through the car's passenger-side window.

I scrambled out, and he gave me a wad of cash like it was nothing and told me to buy a whole bunch of ice cream from the ice-cream truck that hovered outside the school building.

I did what I was told and had my own moment of feeling like a hero as all these little kids took the ice cream and popsicles I offered them, shouting "Thank you" as they took off running with their treats. Meanwhile, Tyson just stood there smiling and letting his daughter shine in front of her friends. Again, Tyson made it all look so easy, I could almost forget he was the same guy who sold crack to my parents.

Back in the car, we delivered Tyson's daughter to her mother. Then, he just started driving around the neighborhood. And talking.

"Yeah, your mom was telling me you about to have a baby," Tyson started the conversation. "What you gonna do about that? How you gonna support your kid?"

I was staring out the window watching my neighborhood go by and didn't bother to face Tyson when I mumbled, "I don't know."

"You gonna be like all these other fools out here?"

Now, I turned around. "What do you mean?"

Tyson shook his head like he was disappointed in me. "You

gonna go work some nine-to-five and make seven bucks an hour, or you gonna make some real money?"

Something about the look on my face must have made him pause. "Man, lemme stop. Your mama is always talking about 'you're a good kid,' so you probably don't even know what I'm talking about."

Tyson stopped talking then, and I didn't try to fill the silence with words I would regret.

At the next red light, Tyson told me to get out of the car.

Before he pulled away, he said, "Let me know when you're ready to make some real money." And then he drove off.

I knew Tyson wanted me to sell drugs for him. I wasn't stupid. But I wasn't ready to cross that line. Besides, I always had RJ in my ear. RJ was Tyson's older cousin, and he liked to chill with me on the benches. RJ was in his early forties and worked construction, but he had served ten years in prison for selling drugs. Without asking for my permission, RJ slid into the role of my advisor and protector in the neighborhood. I thought of him like a cross between a wise uncle and a loyal friend. RJ was always warning me to stay out of the game. "Because there's only two ways to get out once you're in," he said. "You're either going to end up in prison, or you're going to end up dead."

RJ understood that I needed money for the baby, so he taught me the art of sports gambling. The deli next to the liquor store was where we'd place our bets. Watching sports was my passion, so I started studying everything that could impact a game, from the weather in the location where a team was playing to the re-lationships between players on opposing teams. I got so good at predicting who would win, on a good day I could pocket three hundred dollars, and pretty soon I built up a reputation. People started coming to me to help pick their teams and to place their bets for them. And I was saving everything I won for the baby, hoping it would be enough, but I could just hear Nicky's mother saying, "See, I told you, you can't depend on Jonathan."

It was a Wednesday in early October and Ms. Turay, the college guidance counselor at FDA, pulled me into her office to yell at me for not coming to see her regarding my plans for college. I was supposed to have a list of schools I was applying to and a draft of my essay.

"I'm not going to college," I told her.

"Why not?" she asked.

"Because I'm having a kid," I said, even though I was pretty sure all of the faculty and staff knew that by now. Rumors spread fast.

Ms. Turay cleared her throat before responding. "I had heard that, Jonathan, but that certainly doesn't mean you can't still go to college."

I shook my head in disagreement. "I can't go to college and raise a baby at the same time," I said. "This kid is coming this winter and I gotta buy a crib and diapers and all the other stuff babies need, and none of that stuff is going to fall from the sky, so I need to find a job, not a college." I didn't even stay to listen to whatever she was going to say in response because college felt like a pipe dream by that point. A pipe dream I couldn't afford.

Meanwhile, Tyson had been showing me how he earned money and supported his child, and his way definitely looked like something I could handle, as long as I shoved the last shred of decency I had deep down into the bottom of a bottle of E&J. With the baby's due date fast approaching, I decided if Tyson was willing to take me under his wing and give me a chance to make money for my family, I was willing to learn.

At first, I kept the crack Tyson gave me hidden under my bed, but then I got worried my parents would find it and smoke it, so I started stashing my supply in Omari's sister's apartment because she lived in our building, and I knew I could trust her. She was selling, too. I hated what I was doing. Every time I sold to somebody, I couldn't help but wonder if they had kids at home, and if they were spending their grocery money or the money for the electricity on the crack I was selling them. But rather than quit selling, I started drinking more.

RJ knew what I was doing and tried to get me to stop before

it was too late. "You know your mother is always bragging on you. She said you were going to go to some fancy college because you were so smart. Well, you ain't being real smart now," RJ would say.

I heard him, but I ignored him.

When Nicky found out what I was doing, she let it be known that she would never speak to me again if I was going down this road.

I drank more after that. Nothing was right in my life. Now that I was making money, I was supposed to feel better, but I didn't. Not only because I was making money illegally and risking my life, but also because the money I was making didn't justify the danger. After Tyson took his cut, I was netting only about one hundred dollars a week. I could have been working at McDonald's and made the same amount.

Even when the cops came and kicked down Omari's sister's door and arrested her, it wasn't enough to make me walk away from it all. Omari's sister was released later the same day, but she was spooked. And so was I. Obviously, the cops were on to us. But we didn't take that as a sign to stop selling—we just found a different place to stash our drugs.

My behavior did not go unnoticed. My mother knew something was up when she saw me stumbling home drunk. She knew I was cutting school. I even suspected she knew I was working for Tyson, but we both knew she didn't have the moral authority to reprimand me. What was she going to say? So, she didn't say a thing to me about it.

Instead, she called my brother Josh and begged him to come home for Thanksgiving to try to knock some sense into me. Josh came, but when he asked me what was going on, I didn't tell him I was working for Tyson; I told him I was depressed because Nicky wouldn't talk to me. I told him I had gone to the hospital with Nicolette to find out the sex of the baby—it was a girl—but other than that, I was still on the outside of everything that had to do with the baby. I told Josh I wanted to be a part of my daughter's life, but Nicky wouldn't let me. All of this was true. I just omitted the part about also working for a notorious drug dealer, obliterating my feelings with alcohol, and giving up my dreams to go to college.

Josh got busy right away. The Monday after Thanksgiving, I came home from school and found Nicolette in my apartment with my brother. He sat us both down and told us we had to get our shit together because, when the baby arrived in February, she was going to need both of us, and we would need each other.

"Nicky," Josh turned to Nicolette, "what did Jonathan do that has you so angry?"

Nicky took a deep breath and let out a torrent of grievances. All of which were true. She started with my bad attitude and then listed all the ignorant things I'd done since finding out I was going to be a father. Many times, I tried to interject with an explanation, but Josh wisely wouldn't let me say anything until Nicky had said her piece.

I knew better than to say anything to try to defend my behavior. I think we all knew it was indefensible. Instead, I apologized and promised Nicky that I really wanted to work things out so we could do the right thing for the baby. And I didn't want her to be mad at me. I tried to explain how desperate and scared I felt, but I ended up just saying, "I'm sorry," about a million times over.

"I don't care what happened in the past," Josh interrupted my apologies. "You both need to start thinking about the future."

Nicky hesitated at first, but with Josh's urging, she turned to me and said. "I didn't want to ruin your life, Jonathan. I just couldn't make myself ruin this baby's, either. But I do want to work things out for the baby, too." We talked for what felt like hours after that, and promised we would start over. Over the next few days, Nicky and I started working our way back to being friends. I was nervous at first, afraid to say something wrong, but we both wanted the same thing—a healthy baby—so we kept talking.

Josh gave me back a piece of my life that I had really missed.

Before the pregnancy, Nicky was the only person I felt like I could be my real self with, and she always helped me see the good in myself, even when I couldn't. Having her back in my life felt like a step in the right direction. It was the first positive thing that had happened in my life since everything had turned sideways.

But I still didn't stop selling drugs for Tyson. I didn't stop gambling. And I didn't stop drinking. If anything, I felt compelled to make more money now that I'd promised Nicky I'd be there for her and the baby.

A few days later, RJ knocked on my apartment door. He was extremely drunk. He was wearing a dark suit. "My grandma just fucking died, man," he said, lurching and falling into me. Rather than bringing him into our apartment, I dragged him outside to the benches.

"Sit your ass down, man," I said.

RJ crumpled onto the bench and then started mumbling, "My grandma, man. She was, like, the only one who ever cared about us, and now she's gone."

"I'm sorry, bro," I said.

RJ looked at me and tried to focus his bloodshot eyes. "I know she's watching over us, man, so we gonna win big tonight."

"That's cool," I said, just trying to make him feel better about his grandmother.

"Give me five dollars so I can put you in," he said, holding out his hand.

I gave him five dollars.

"I got five dollars, too," he said. "Let's go."

I helped RJ stumble over to the deli to place our bets. We did what was called a ten-team parlay, which meant we picked ten different sports teams who were playing that day. If we were lucky, all of our picks would hit and we would take home a couple thousand dollars from that ten-dollar investment. I left RJ outside on the benches, and I went home to watch the games.

At the end of the night, when the Yankees beat the Oakland As, I almost peed myself. The Yankees were the tenth team we'd put our bet on. And they won! Every single team we selected won! This was incredible. I tried to do a quick calculation of how much we won, and when I hit on four thousand five hundred dollars, I kept telling myself I had to be wrong.

I ran outside to find RJ. He was still asleep on the benches. I woke him up, yelling, "We won, RJ! We hit all ten teams!"

RJ slowly came to, and I shouted again.

"RJ, we just won four thousand five hundred dollars!"

If RJ was still drunk, that information completely sobered him up.

"I can't believe it," he said, jumping up from the bench and grinning like a fool. Then, he pointed to the night sky. "See, I told you my grandma was watching over us."

"Bro," I said, "I love your grandma!"

When we got our money the next morning, it was all in cash. I couldn't believe it. Then, RJ handed me three thousand five hundred dollars and kept only a thousand dollars for himself.

"What are you doing?" I asked him. "We both put in the same amount, and we agreed we'd split anything we won fifty-fifty."

RJ shook his head. "You need that to take care of your kid. This is more than enough to buy the crib and some Pampers. And don't worry, everybody else will give you clothes. So, take this money and stop messing with Tyson. You gotta be better, kid."

I looked down at my feet because I was ashamed that RJ had to give me his winnings just so I would stop selling drugs.

RJ took my silence as proof that I needed more convincing. "If you don't stop, man, you won't have a choice about getting out. Mark my words."

I knew RJ was right, but all I could think about with that three thousand five hundred dollars burning a hole in my pocket was telling Nicolette.

I ran home and called Nicky, and before she could even say hello, I was yelling in the phone, "I hit, I hit, I hit! You gotta come over here."

Nicky came over that morning, and I gave her the money and told her, "Buy whatever you need for the baby."

Before she would take the money, Nicky squinted her eyes at me and asked, "This isn't drug money, is it?"

I shook my head no. "I swear to God, Nicky. RJ and I just hit big. And his grandmother was blessing us, I guess," I added. I told Nicky the whole story and she was laughing by the end.

"Well, I guess we need to thank RJ's grandmother," she said. And then she kissed me on the cheek. "Thank you, Jonathan. I know you're trying."

And that kiss and her words and the feeling that I had finally done something right melted away a whole layer of the black cloud that had been hanging over me for so long. It had been a long time since anybody had told me I had done something good. And I missed that feeling.

Not even a week later, RJ was knocking on our apartment door again.

Nicolette was over, and we were sitting in my room.

I went to open the door, and Nicky followed behind me. RJ was standing in the doorway, like he didn't want to come in. He wasn't drunk this time, but I could see from his face that whatever he had to tell me, was bad news.

He saw Nicky, and he pitched his voice real low when he said, "Yo, Tyson needs you to grab it. Somebody just set him up and robbed him on the street."

Both Nicky and I knew that "grab it" was code for "go get somebody's gun." Tyson lived only two buildings away, so grabbing his gun would take me about five minutes. Before I could consider the consequences of doing so, Nicky interjected.

"You better not go get that man's gun. Let him deal with his own problems. You don't need to get involved with this, Jonathan. We're about to have a baby!"

I turned to RJ. I knew, with a record, he couldn't afford to get caught holding Tyson's gun. He'd be sent back to prison in a heartbeat. In fact, it was common practice in the 'hood for drug dealers with a record to recruit young kids to hold their guns so if they ever got stopped by the cops, they'd never have any evidence on them. I had a clean record, so Tyson had asked me on a few occasions to hold his gun while we went out together.

"What does he want me to do?" I asked RJ. If he just wanted me to grab his piece and hold on to it, I could do that. But if he wanted me to go with him while he hunted down whoever robbed him, I wasn't up for that.

RJ shrugged. "I'm not sure exactly. He just told me to tell you to grab his gun. He'll probably let you know what he wants you to do next. I just know he's real mad right now."

"What do you think I should do, RJ?" I said.

"You gotta do what you gotta do, but Tyson ain't going to be happy with you if you don't do this for him. That's the only reason I'm here. I don't want you to have any beef with my cousin. You know how he is."

Nicky wasn't having it. "The only person you need to be loyal to is this baby," she said, crossing her arms across her round belly.

I couldn't think straight. I knew Nicky was right, but Tyson wasn't somebody you messed with. I hesitated for a minute trying to figure out the right thing to do.

"You better not walk out that door, Jon," Nicky shrieked. "You could get killed!"

I knew Nicky was right, but I was afraid of what Tyson would do to me; so before I could chicken out, I turned to Nicky and said, "I'll be right back," and then ran out the door.

As soon as I stepped outside our apartment building and turned to head toward Tyson's building, I stopped running. The scene before me was surreal. I saw Tyson on the ground surrounded by a bunch of police officers and police cars. His hands were behind his back, and it looked like he was getting arrested. RJ came up alongside me then, and both of us stood there as we watched the cops drag Tyson up off the ground and shove him into the back of a police car. Their lights went on and their sirens blared, and they drove him away.

"Aw, shit," RJ said, shaking his head. "They got him."

I was in shock. If I had run out of the house just five minutes earlier to get Tyson's gun, would the cops have gotten me, too? The thought sent ice-cold chills through my body.

"Holy shit" is all I could say.

I knew Tyson had two strikes against him already, so this was strike three.

"What do you think is going to happen?" I said, turning to RJ.

RJ shook his head and sighed. "What's going to happen is what I've been telling you all along, son. My cousin is going to go to prison for a very long time. His daughter ain't going to see him no more. His life is going to be lived in a cell and all for what? Nothing. Is that what you want, Jonathan? You got a kid coming. Is this the life you want her to have? Keep selling drugs, then. Do what you gotta do. I'm out."

And with that, he left me standing on the corner looking at my future.

I always prided myself on following the advice of the members of my village. It had gotten me pretty far in my life. RJ had been keeping me company on the benches, and he taught me how to gamble, but I refused to follow his most important advice. All along, RJ had been trying to help me. I just wasn't listening. The reality was, RJ was constantly telling me to get out of the game, and in his own way, he tried to show me that I had options for making money other than selling drugs. But now it was up to me to decide if I was brave enough to follow RJ's advice and explore all my options or stay mired in the muck I was drowning in.

I ran back to my apartment, went straight to my room, pulled out the stash of drugs I was hiding in a shoebox in my closet, and flushed everything down the toilet.

Nicky watched me and didn't say a word until I was finished getting rid of any and all evidence that could connect me to Tyson.

"What's happening?" she cried, her eyes wide with concern.

I told her about Tyson getting arrested and also what RJ said to me.

"I'm done, Nicky. I'm not doing this anymore. I promise you. I'm finished."

"Really?" she said, the look on her face showing me she wanted to believe me.

"Really," I said. "I promise."

Nicky hugged me then, and I hugged her back.

"You're doing the right thing, Jonathan," Nicky said. "You're so smart, and you're going to be okay. You just have to believe in yourself again."

Nicky's words hit me hard. I *had* stopped believing in me. I don't know why or when but I had given up on myself instead of trusting that I could, in fact, handle what my life had become. Everybody else in my life believed in me. My parents. My brothers. RJ. It was time for me to do the same. I remembered what my counselor at Andover had said: I needed to believe in the Jonathan who had worked hard his whole life. The Jonathan with dreams to be a doctor, not the Jonathan who made one mistake.

I grabbed Nicky and embraced her again. "Thank you, Nicky," I said. "I needed to hear that. But right now, I gotta get out of here. I can't be seen around this neighborhood. Tyson's got friends and enemies who think I work for him. I have to disappear for a while."

Nicky picked up her phone, then made a quick call.

"My mom says you can stay with us," she said, one minute later.

And so I packed a bag and went home with Nicky. I moved into her house with her family, and I got a job. My first day at Family Dollar was Christmas Eve. I was now officially one of those fools working a nine-to-five making seven dollars and twenty five cents an hour.

When I look back at this tumultuous time in my life, I recognize that I made it through to the other side because of, and in spite of, the people I chose to follow. Ultimately, it's not clear to me how or why certain people drop into my life when they do. I have simply learned to find the guides who have the best information to share. The problem is, when you're in survival mode, it's sometimes difficult to assess what is the best information. I made the right decision when I listened to Mr. Collins, who urged me to finish my last summer at Andover and fight for my dreams. I made the right decision when I listened to RJ and got out of the drug game. I knew both of these men knew more than me in their respective fields, so it made sense to follow their advice. In some ways, it was the same reason I followed Tyson. He was an expert at what he did. He knew how to survive and support his daughter, but in my book his means didn't justify the ends. His "wisdom" required me to abandon my moral code, and I couldn't do that. At the end of the day, Mr. Collins and RJ wouldn't become permanent members of my village. But like the old man who taught me how to tie a tie, I counted them as honorary village members because they helped me along my journey.

9

I Wasn't Supposed to Go to College with a Baby

Ms. Turay said I could still go to college. She said it wasn't too late to apply. Even though I had twenty-seven absences on my record since the beginning of the school year. Even though I was barely passing my classes. Even though my daughter was due to be born in less than three months' time, Ms. Turay still believed I could get accepted and attend a four-year college and then go to medical school.

I thought Ms. Turay was crazy for thinking that. But since she knew more than I did about college admissions, I listened to her and I trusted her. I reminded myself that my only job was to follow the directions of the people who knew more than me. They were my guides. Ms. Turay was providing me with step one of the blueprint to get back to my future self. The one I wanted to be, and the one I needed to be for this kid who was coming, whether I was ready or not.

"Look, Jonathan," she started when I came to her two weeks before Christmas break, asking if there was any hope for me to still get accepted to college. I assumed it was going to be a long shot, but I was still praying for a miracle. "You're lucky you have everything ready for your applications from your time at Andover. And you've taken enough AP classes and extra college courses that you could graduate tomorrow, so the only thing we have to do is find the right school for you to apply to."

"No Ivy League is going to look at me now," I said, the disappointment clouding my tone.

"Jonathan," Ms. Turay said with an exasperated sigh. "There are more than Ivy League schools out there where you can get a good education. And you need to consider going to a school in New York so you can be closer to home and available for your child. Also, you should be looking at schools that offer services that can help you as a new parent. And those programs do exist."

I was listening, so Ms. Turay kept talking. She told me I should apply to all of the state universities of New York, known as the SUNY schools, as well as the city universities of New York, known as the CUNY schools. Even though I had lived in New York for most of my life, I had no idea what the SUNY or CUNY schools were all about. Ever since my first summer at Andover, I had been focused on schools with name recognition, either Ivy League or Division I for sports. And Johns Hopkins had been at the top of my list ever since I watched *Gifted Hands* and decided that if Ben Carson could be a world-class surgeon, then so could I.

"Have you ever heard a program called 'EOP?' " Ms. Turay asked as she typed something into her computer.

"No, what's that?" I said.

Ms. Turay checked something on her screen and then turned back to me. "It stands for Educational Opportunity Program and they offer it at Stony Brook University where they identify students with lots of potential but who need a little extra help being college ready. If you complete their six-week Summer Academy before the fall semester starts, you're guaranteed a full financial package. And Stony Brook isn't too far from the city."

The only thing I knew about Stony Brook University was that my father's brother, my Uncle Yogi, had gone there. Uncle Yogi was a public school teacher, and the only one of my father's siblings who graduated from college. Like my parents, he always stressed the importance of education. But he never made Stony Brook the goal.

I shrugged. A full-ride scholarship was exactly what I needed, but before I could get excited about it, I thought about Nicky and the baby. How could I go off anywhere to college and leave them behind? It wasn't clear how the details would work out, but since Ms. Turay wasn't calling me crazy for thinking I could pull it off, I told her to add Stony Brook University to the list.

"There's only one problem," she said as she scrolled through the webpage. "It seems as though your SAT scores are too high for the program," she muttered.

"What do you mean?" I said.

"Well, there are requirements that applicants have to meet, like income level, GPA, and SAT scores. They're trying to identify a certain type of candidate, I guess, and you meet all the requirements except your SAT scores are higher than what the ideal candidate would have."

"So, I can't do the program because I'm too smart?" I said, trying hard not to let my exasperation show.

"Don't worry. I'll look into it," Ms. Turay said. "You just put your materials together and bring them to me by next week, and we'll submit everything."

"Okay," I said as I got up to exit her office, making a mental to-do list for the task at hand. I didn't allow myself to get too excited because I had lived too much in the last three months to believe that something good was due me, but there was still part of the old Jonathan in me, egging me on to believe my dreams were still possible. The fact that I was sitting in my high school guidance counselor's office, instead of a cell at Rikers, was already proof enough that miracles could happen.

And speaking of miracles.

My daughter Emily Isabella was born on February 2, 2013. I had turned eighteen just a few months before, but when I saw Emily for the first time, I knew I was put on this earth to be her father. As DiCo would say, "Emily is my why." She changed my life in an instant. She was born joyful. She didn't cry when she came into the world; instead, she just looked around like she knew she was meant to be here. She came out of the womb happy. Just like me. But I knew, as sure as I knew anything, that I didn't want Emily to have to struggle like me. I didn't want her to suffer for my mistakes and my failures. Just looking into her dark brown eyes, I knew I would do whatever it took to give her the life I didn't have. And I promised her, whispering in her tiny ear, that I would go to college, and I would become a doctor, and I would be the type of father she could depend on and be proud of, no matter what. And I swear she winked at me when I said it.

After Emily was born, I was just in a different zone when it came to planning for the future. Even though I still hated working at Family Dollar, I went willingly every day after school because I needed the money to pay for her diapers and baby wipes. We could buy formula with WIC and food for us with food stamps, but diapers and wipes had to be paid for with cash. Nicky was determined to finish her senior year of high school on time, so she had arranged with her teachers to pick up all of her classwork and do it on her own at home for the last three months of the academic year. That way, she didn't have to leave the baby. I was still living with Nicky's family in their tight little three-bedroom apartment in Brownsville, which meant I had a one-hour commute every day to school in Harlem. That commute was repeated on the way home, and I would usually go straight to Family Dollar to work.

Homework, a job, and a long commute, coupled with a new baby, tested my resolve to keep my promise to my daughter. The thought of keeping up that schedule through graduation and then college, followed by medical school, made me feel like I was standing at the bottom of an enormous mountain knowing I couldn't stop grinding until I made it all the way to the top. And I wasn't even doing the majority of the childcare. My day started at 6 a.m., and most nights I wouldn't get home until 9 p.m. When I got home, I would take care of Emily to give Nicky a break, but she was doing most of the work when it came to the baby. That's why she was so scared for me to go away for college.

If I left for college, Nicky was quick to remind me, she would be on her own with Emily. Nicky's mother worked full-time, and when she was at home, she had to keep an eye on Nicky's little brother, who had a challenging form of ADHD. I tried to manage Nicky's fears by telling her that wherever I ended up going, I would be close enough to come home to Brooklyn every weekend. But she was still anxious about me going away. She was convinced that, one way or another, college would keep me away from her and the baby for good. That's why, when I got an email from Stony Brook University in April inviting me to the campus to learn about the EOP, I didn't tell Nicky. I snuck off on a Saturday morning saying I was going to work when I was really heading into Manhattan to meet someone who, I hoped, would be my saving grace.

I had already received five rejections from the seven different schools I had applied to. At the sixth school I was waitlisted, and I was pretty sure I was put on the waitlist because I had shown up late for my interview. I arrived twenty minutes after my scheduled 9 a.m. appointment, looking disheveled and tired, and when the woman conducting the interview asked for my excuse, I told her the truth. "I was up all night with my newborn daughter," I said.

I read disappointment in the look she gave me.

I wondered if I should have lied.

So, yes, Stony Brook was my last hope.

The email said to meet in front of the 42nd Street Library in Manhattan, where the two large stone lions impressively stand guard. It was impossible to miss the group because it was a bunch of Black teenage boys standing together on the sidewalk. I joined the group, and right away, a bald-headed Black man with black Steve Urkel glasses, who looked like he might have played football once, walked up to me and introduced himself. He said his name was Jarvis Watson. "And what's your name?" he asked me.

I told him my name, and he found it on the clipboard he was holding.

He extended his hand for a firm handshake and said, "Well, I'm glad you made it, Jonathan. I'm happy you joined us. We're just waiting for a few more young brothers, and the bus should be here momentarily."

"Thank you," I said as he excused himself.

Before I could decide if I wanted to be social and introduce myself to anyone else, my phone rang. It was Nicky, and she had figured out I wasn't at Family Dollar. I had to confess where I was.

She was mad that I had lied to her. We ended up arguing. She thought I was wasting my time. I was trying to explain to her that I was doing what was best for all of us.

I must have been talking pretty loudly because, when I ended the call, a kid turned to me and said, "Hey, bro, you got a kid?"

"Yeah, I have a daughter. She's two months old."

"Wow," he said and then turned back to his friends. I could hear them talking about me. I sighed. I was going to be *that guy* to everybody. The teen father, the stereotype, and the statistic. I knew I loved my daughter, but I hated what having her tele-graphed to the world on my behalf. How smart could I actually be if I got my girlfriend pregnant at seventeen? I worried that "teen father" would be my primary identity moving forward, and I hated that.

Just then, the coach bus pulled up to collect us, and we all piled on and headed east out of the city. I thought about not getting on to avoid the questions and comments about my circumstances, but something inside me told me to see it through.

As we were driving, Mr. Watson grabbed a microphone and introduced himself again and welcomed us formally to what he said was Men's Day. "At Stony Brook, we have a commitment to bringing more Black men to campus, and we want to show you all that the school has to offer," he said.

A few guys responded like we were in church. I heard some "Okays" and "That's rights."

When he was done with his brief introduction, Mr. Watson

introduced Francisco, who worked at Stony Brook as a counselor. He also welcomed us and told us how to contact him if
we had any questions about the school.

Mr. Watson grabbed the mic one more time and finished his
little speech by saying, "Today is going to be a lot of fun, and it's
all about you. So, I hope you all have a really great time!"

People started chatting and getting to know each other, but I
just looked out the window and watched the city disappear into
the highway and, pretty quickly after that, suburban green. I had
no idea where we were going. The only thing I knew about
Long Island was what I had seen in movies like *White Chicks*,
which took place mostly in the Hamptons. As I sat there lost in
my thoughts, Francisco, the counselor, came and sat next to me.
"I hear you got a baby at home," Francisco said, getting straight
to the point.

"Yeah," I said, realizing then that my secret was out to everyone there. I prayed it wouldn't prematurely disqualify me from
getting accepted to the college. "I have a baby girl." Before
Francisco could tell me I might want to reconsider college with
a kid, I jumped in with my own explanation.

"I know it's a lot to think I could do college and raise a kid. I
probably won't be able to do it," I said, trying to make it sound
like I was okay with the idea of opting out. "Maybe I can apply
again in a couple of years."

Francisco shook his head and tented his fingers in prayer
position. "No, Jonathan, you will go to college, now. You need
to go to college. And having a kid already just means you have
even more reasons to want this and need this. That kid needs
you to get your degree."

By now, I was used to this line. Everybody had told me the
same thing. I knew Emily would have a better life with a father
who had a college education, but I was still waiting for someone
to break down the logistics and tell me how to actually make
it happen—one year to the next, one month to the next. Day
to day. Who was going to buy the baby's diapers if I was in
school trying to be a doctor? The desire was there one hundred

percent on my part, but I just couldn't see how the pieces all fit together.

"I do *want* to go to college now, but my girlfriend is worried I won't be able to keep up with the work and help with the baby," I said. "She's probably right."

"Would you believe me if I told you that I went to Stony Brook—and with my little girl—just like you?" Francisco said.

"Really?" I said, all of my senses on high alert. All I wanted was somebody to show me that it was possible, and here he was, sitting right next to me!

"Yes, really. But I was a single father because my baby's mother died soon after she was born. I had my daughter with me at Stony Brook the whole time while I was doing a master's program. So, if I can do that, you can figure out your situation. Don't make excuses for yourself. If you say you can do it, you will."

He stood up then to go back to his seat, but not before he gave me his business card. "Hit me up if you ever need to talk about anything." And then he left me to ponder that simple idea: *if you say you can do it, you will.*

Sometimes, all it takes is for someone to give you the vision that what you want is possible. Francisco had just provided that vision for me. Here was my blueprint, sitting right on the bus with me where I was feeling sorry for myself. One more guiding light on my journey.

By the end of the day, Francisco and Mr. Watson had convinced me, and probably every other kid on the tour, that we wanted to attend Stony Brook University. More than that, that it was our responsibility as Black men to get an education and give back to the communities we came from. Mr. Watson sounded like Mr. Marshall, the way he hammered us with his speeches about Black excellence and how we were the future, and we owed it to ourselves to get our degrees. He was a lot younger than Mr. Marshall, though, so his words hit in a different way. He made it sound like he was inviting us into a brotherhood of Black excellence, and the invitation was both an honor and a responsibility. "The world needs more educated Black men," Mr. Watson preached at us while we ate lunch in the school's cafeteria. "They cannot continue to underestimate us."

The program wasn't all lectures and speeches, though. To finish the day, we ended up playing basketball together in one of the school's gymnasiums. Like everything else on the campus, the building was modern and spacious and pristine. It wasn't as fancy as Andover, but it was a nice suburban college campus, and I could totally imagine myself being a student there. In fact, after Francisco and Mr. Watson kept telling me how many resources the school had to offer someone like me, including an on-campus day care, they had me believing being a student and a father was actually possible. By the time we were shooting hoops in the gym, Stony Brook was my first-choice school. My fingers were crossed that my application wouldn't be denied because of Emily. Before I could lose my courage, I ran over to Mr. Watson, who was standing on the sidelines watching us play. I cleared my throat and then spoke. "Mr. Watson," I started, "do you have any sway with the admission committee? Because I really want to go here. You and Francisco have totally convinced me I could do it."

I held my breath as I waited for his reply. Mr. Watson looked at me like I was crazy for asking such a thing, and I realized I must have crossed a line.

"Hold up," he said. And then he yelled at the other kids on the court. "Hey, you guys, come on over here."

The guys stopped playing. Someone grabbed the ball, and everyone hustled over around Mr. Watson.

"You guys know that you have all already been accepted to Stony Brook University conditional on your going through the EOP first, right?"

"Wait. I was accepted?" I said, not even waiting to see what anybody else had to say.

"Yes. We sent your acceptance letter in the mail, but you can also see it online," Mr. Watson explained. Since I'd been staying with Nicky, I didn't know if a letter had arrived at my parents' apartment and they just didn't tell me, or if it had gotten lost in the mail. But either way, I was accepted to college!

Mr. Watson said, "That's why y'all are here today. We're trying to convince you to accept your invitation for admission. You have until May 1 to accept it, or we remove our offer."

All of the other guys were cheering and celebrating, giving each other high-fives. As a group, they went back to the court and resumed their game, laughing with happiness and pride. My emotions soared right along with theirs, but within seconds they came solidly back to earth as I thought about Nicky and the baby. Would I really be able to pull this off? Would Nicky be okay? Would Emily forget me if I was gone all week?

While the other guys were busy celebrating, Mr. Watson came over to talk to me.

"What's the matter, Jonathan?" he said. "You don't look too happy with the news."

"No, I am happy," I started, and then I confessed my worries about Nicky and the baby. "Look, I can't tell you what to do with your life," Mr. Watson said. "But I know one thing. No man ever went to bed hungry because he was too educated. But many men go to bed hungry every day because they walked away from good opportunities without even trying. Don't take yourself out of the race without even trying."

I considered Mr. Watson's words. I wanted to give Emily a good life, and I couldn't do that working at Family Dollar. Even though I knew it was going to be hard, in the long run me going to college would be the best thing for all of us. Over lunch, Francisco had told me about the Long Island Railroad, which would get me back into the city in ninety minutes, and there was something called the 7Bus, which was like a shuttle bus that ran students between the university and Midtown Manhattan seven days a week for just seven bucks. Running the numbers in my head, I figured I could be back and forth from Brooklyn to Stony Brook as often as I needed to be. I ran back to join the game with the decision made in my heart and my head. I was going to Stony Brook University. I was going to be a good dad to Emily. And I was going to be a doctor. Just like Francisco said, I was saying I could do it, and I would.

On the bus ride back to the city, I called my mother before I called Nicolette. "Yo, Mom, I'm going to college," I said, feeling my heart swell up with pride as the words fell out of my mouth. I told her about my day at Stony Brook and how Mr. Watson and Francisco had made it seem completely possible for me to succeed there. Just claiming my future made it feel real.

My mother didn't disappoint with her enthusiasm. "Oh, my God. Oh, my God, Boo Boo, I'm so proud of you," she said. "Are you at Nicky's now?"

"Not yet," I said. "I'm still on the bus."

"I'm coming over," she said. "I'll meet you there."

"Okay, Mom," I said, laughing.

I decided I would wait until I got home to talk it over with Nicky. I didn't want to be yelling on the bus and embarrass myself again. Besides, I owed it to Nicky to have this conversation with her in person so we could really figure out how to make it work. For everyone. Not just me.

But when I arrived back in Brownsville, Nicky already knew about my decision because my mother had spread the news. Not only that, in conjunction with Nicky's mother, she had planned a "My Baby's Going to College" party in the short time it took for me to get off the phone with her on the bus. Nicky's mother was in the kitchen cooking. There was a cake on the table that said "Congratulations," and my father and a bunch of Nicky's cousins were there, too. Everybody was congratulating me and patting me on the back. Even Nicky seemed as though she was happy for me. And I was so happy. I wasn't expecting any gifts, but my mother surprised me with a bottle of E&J, my old nemesis. Over the course of the rest of the evening, we all celebrated and had a good time. It was the first time since Emily was born that I felt excited about the future instead of overburdened with fear and uncertainty. It was so nice to see my parents acting normal and everybody getting along. Before I fell asleep that night, I remember thinking I had survived the worst part of my life and only good stuff was ahead.

I was so naïve.

The next morning, I was supposed to be at work at 8 a.m., but I was so hungover from the E&J I drank at the party that I showed up at Family Dollar two hours late. The manager on duty was legitimately annoyed and pulled me into the back office to yell at me.

Before she could tell me that my paycheck would be docked, or that I was going to be put on probation, I stopped her. I pulled out my college acceptance letter, which I had printed out at the party so everyone could see it, and handed it to her.

"What's this?" she said, scanning the document.

"It's my college acceptance letter. I'm going to college, so I don't need this job," I said. "I quit."

"You can't just quit," she said. "You have to give me two weeks' notice."

I knew she was right, but I was eighteen years old, deeply hung-over, and feeling myself a little bit. So, I just turned around and walked out of the store, leaving my little green vest behind.

I took a taxi back home because I had a banging headache, and all I wanted to do was go back to bed. When Nicolette saw me, she said, "Why are you back here so soon?"

"I'm going to college, Nicky. I'm going to be a doctor. I'm not working at Family Dollar anymore."

"What are we going to . . ." Nicky started.

I stopped her. "Don't worry, I'll figure something out for the next couple of months. I promise," I said. "But right now, I just need to sleep." And that's what I did until Emily demanded my attention.

Throughout the final months of high school, and even past graduation, Nicky and I kept arguing about me going to school at Stony Brook. Even though Francisco and Mr. Watson had convinced me that we could make it work, Nicky still felt as though I was leaving her with all the work to take care of Emily. Stony Brook was too far to commute to every day, but I promised I'd come home every Friday. I wasn't ignorant, and I knew even twenty-four hours with Emily alone was a lot to handle, and Nicky didn't want to just be a stay-at-home mom at eighteen. She didn't know exactly what she wanted to do next, but she didn't think it was fair that I got to go off and chase my dreams for four years, while she had to stay home with the baby.

Before I left for the EOP, I told Nicky everything was going to work out. The thing was, I still couldn't tell Nicky *how* it was all going to work out because I wasn't sure myself. I started researching majors and realized how hard it was going to be to major in chemistry or biology and complete all the requirements for medical school in four years. Especially if I was going to go home every weekend to be with Emily. I read that some kids needed five years to get all of their requirements done, but asking Nicky to wait an extra year before I'd be done seemed too cruel. So, I started looking at medical-adjacent fields, thinking maybe I could major in something a little less intense. But in the end, none of it added up to me being able to parent Emily on a regular basis. So, my plan was to use the summer to buy more time to figure the whole thing out.

Out of desperation, I decided to reach out to DiCo. I hadn't spoken to him in nearly two years, and yet when I thought about who I could turn to for help and advice, DiCo's name and face kept springing to mind. Before I shut him out of my life, DiCo had always been the person who could break things down for me and help me see the bigger picture, and I needed that kind of practicality, now more than ever. Even though DiCo didn't have kids, and I knew he had never been in the type of situation I was facing, he had always been resourceful. DiCo was the person who could look at an empty bowl and figure out how to feed twenty kids with it. When I thought about who I had in my village, hands down, DiCo was the person I trusted most to help me with this problem. I had to swallow my pride and my shame and ask for his help.

As I dialed his number, I prayed DiCo still wasn't mad at me for how I had treated him when he left FDA.

"Hey, DiCo," I said tentatively, when he picked up the call.

"Jonathan?!" he said, the surprise evident in his tone. "How are you? It's been such a long time since I've heard from you."

"Yeah, I know, and I'm sorry about that," I said. "And I'm really sorry for everything I did, you know, when you left."

DiCo sighed. "It's okay, Jonathan," he said. "I know you were hurt by my leaving. But really, it's okay."

I let out the breath I had been holding, relieved to hear DiCo say that.

"So, what's going on?" DiCo asked.

"Um, DiCo, I need your help," I said.

I then poured out my entire story about Emily, Nicky, and where we were now, with me on the verge of heading to Stony Brook.

"Wow! Jonathan, that's a lot," DiCo said. "I'm kinda in shock right now."

I held my breath again, worrying I'd made a mistake in reaching out to DiCo. Maybe he would be just too disappointed in me. But then he said, "I guess I should say congratulations on having a kid *and* getting into Stony Brook."

"Thanks, but that's the problem," I said. "I don't know if I can handle it all. I don't know if I should go through with going to college."

"Why not?" DiCo asked.

"Because I'll be leaving Nicky with all the work. And I'll be leaving Emily without her father."

DiCo sighed. "I can't tell you this from experience, but I know that your daughter will never blame you for getting a college education. She probably won't even remember these first four years of her life. But she will blame you or resent you if you can't provide for her in the future because you *didn't* go to college."

"That makes sense," I said. "I didn't think about it that way."

"I'm sure you're just thinking about making it through

tomorrow," DiCo said. "But you've got to think long term. College is more important than ever with a child to support. You can offer her so much more with a college degree."

Now, it was my turn to sigh. "I guess I'm just scared I'm going to mess everything up."

"I know it feels scary, but, Jonathan, you're not alone. If you ever need anything, please let me know. Can you promise me that? Don't wait another two years to get in touch."

"I promise," I said. "And thank you, DiCo. You're the only person I could think of who could help me."

My parents rented a car and drove me to the EOP Summer Academy at Stony Brook. Nicolette and Emily rode with us. Emily slept most of the way, and we didn't talk much in the car. The whole ride there I kept thinking how unfair it was that I got to go to college while Nicky was going back to Brownsville to take care of our daughter. She had every right to feel jealous and abandoned. Meanwhile, I couldn't imagine being away from Emily for the next six weeks. I tried to remind myself of what DiCo had told me, but I was still worried that Emily would forget me while I was gone.

Mom kept trying to lighten the mood in the car and start a conversation, but I was afraid that if I opened my mouth, I would tell my father to turn the car around and take me home. It wasn't too late to just get a steady job with the city. It's not like I hadn't considered that option. But it was my father, actually, who put his foot down and told me there was no way I was going to work for the city and throw away the opportunity to get a college degree. Maybe the idea scared him because it too closely mirrored his own life path. "Just go see what it's like," my dad insisted. "Don't throw away the chance to get an education without trying first."

I didn't thank my dad for that advice at the time, even though I should have. The thing was, my parents were such a paradox in my life. They were like the alpha and the omega in all things. I could fill a swimming pool with the mistakes, missteps, and actual crimes my parents committed over the years, and yet, at the end of the day, they were always an integral part of my academic success. Even when I least expected it.

When we arrived at the Stony Brook campus, we followed the arrows to the parking lot in front of the dorms where we would be living for the summer. Everyone who was there for EOP was unloading cars and saying their good-byes. I immediately picked out Mr. Watson and Francisco in the crowd and also noticed some familiar faces from Men's Day. All of the staff associated with the school wore red T-shirts, so they were easy to identify in the throngs of people.

I tried to pull myself together and act like I was in control of my emotions. I tried to look brave, instead of showing the fear and anxiety that was tap dancing inside. It didn't help that Nicky was watching me with a look of utter fear distorting the beautiful features of her face. Luckily, Emily was still sleeping. If she started to cry, there would be no way I would have been able to hold it together.

My family and I were all standing in a cluster, trying to figure out where to go and who to talk to. I was holding Emily in my arms, trying to squeeze in the last bit of her sweetness before I had to let her go. That's when a woman in a wheelchair wearing an official red shirt rolled over to me and my family. She was a little person who looked to be in her mid-thirties. She had curly brown hair and a welcoming smile. "Are you Jonathan Conyers?" she said.

"Yes, ma'am," I said.

"Hi, I'm Pam," she said, holding out her hand. "Is that your little sister?" she said, pointing at Emily.

"No, this is my daughter," I said and watched as Pam tried to adjust her facial expression from shock to serenity.

I braced myself for something negative to come out of Pam's mouth, but it didn't come. "Oh, okay," she said without sounding judgmental. "Well, welcome to you all. I'm going to be your counselor for the summer program and all the way through your time here at Stony Brook. Mom and Dad," she turned to my parents, "we're going to take good care of your son."

"Thank you," my mom gushed. "He's my last baby, so you better."

I rolled my eyes. My mother could be so embarrassing. Pam showed us where to go to find my dorm room, and all of us grabbed some of my stuff as we headed inside.

Walking down the corridors of the building, I swore I could feel everyone's eyes on me as I carried Emily down the hall. I wondered if people were already talking about me—the freshman with the new baby. At that moment, something one of my coworkers at Family Dollar said to me swam through my mind. "I don't understand how y'all young niggas be trying to go to college, and y'all got a kid back at home," he said to me as we were standing side by side stacking cans of kidney beans on the store's shelves. "Like, how y'all just gonna leave y'all kid like that?"

Were these people thinking the same thing? That I was a bad father for leaving my kid behind? Or that I was just ignorant for having a kid at eighteen in the first place? Either way, I hated feeling judged before I could even open my mouth. Before anybody even knew my story.

We found my room, and everybody got busy unpacking my stuff. I laid Emily on the bed, and she just smiled and cooed at me, unaware, of course, that I was about to be leaving her for six weeks. Summer Academy was run like a boot camp, and we weren't allowed to leave the campus or have visitors. We weren't even allowed to make phone calls home except for once a day, and they had to be on school phones. We had to surrender all of our electronic devices to the program because they wanted us to be one hundred percent focused on achievement. So, when I said good-bye, I was really saying good-bye until August.

My mother told Nicky to grab the baby so she could make up my bed for me. I was busy unpacking my suitcase and putting my clothes in the bureau drawers. As soon as my mom was done with the bed, she left the room saying she was going to go look around.

I deliberately took my time unpacking, trying to delay the

inevitable good-bye. I couldn't even look Nicky in the eye because, if I did, I knew I would probably lose my nerve and jump right back into the car with them. Probably because he knew I was a flight risk, my father tried to keep things moving.

"Come on, son, hurry up," he said. "I gotta get the rental car back, and I don't want to have to pay any late fees."

I hurried and finished putting the rest of my T-shirts and shorts in the drawers and threw my extra pair of sneakers in the closet. I tucked my empty suitcase under the bed. With nothing else to unpack, I reluctantly announced, "Okay, I'm done."

"Alright. Let's go, Nicky," my father said and walked out of my room.

I grabbed the baby from Nicky and, together, we followed my dad.

Before we made it back to the parking lot, we heard some sort of commotion. It sounded like someone was screaming and carrying on. As soon as we rounded the corner outside the building, we saw my mother crying her eyes out, and she was hanging on to the hand of a sharply dressed Black woman who looked mildly distressed by my mother's behavior. My counselor, Pam, was right next to my mother looking deeply concerned. I couldn't imagine what in the world my mother was up to.

Nicky and I turned to each other, and I just shook my head and mouthed, "What the hell?"

We walked over to my mother, and I realized she was pleading my case to this woman. Nicky took the baby from me, probably thinking I was going to have to physically restrain my mother from doing something crazy.

"You have to figure something out for my son," my mother was saying through her hysterical tears. "He's not going to be able to focus and concentrate if he has to be away from his daughter. It's not going to work. I know my son, he loves his child and wants to be there for her. You can't punish him by not letting him see her. He won't be able to concentrate on his studies. He won't." And with that, she produced a fresh crop of juicy new tears.

The woman my mother was holding hostage with her tears turned to me then and held out her hand. She said, "It's nice to meet you, Mr. Conyers. My name is Cheryl Hamilton, and I am the director of the Educational Opportunity Program."

Even though I smiled and shook her hand, inside I was groaning. How did my mother manage to find the director of the entire program in five minutes and get her cornered so she could tell her all of my business.

"Now, Jonathan," Cheryl started, "I understand the difficult situation you're in, so I can put you on the wait list for student apartments so your girlfriend and your daughter can come live with you on campus after the summer. The rent is expensive in those apartments because they're really for graduate students, but I can arrange to have the rent covered for the first six months, but then you'll have to figure out the rest. The only problem is that there is a rather long wait list, so it might be a year or a year and a half before an apartment actually becomes available."

Waiting a year was better than nothing. That was something to work toward.

"Thank you," I said, hoping the promise gave Nicky some hope that me being in college wouldn't have to mean us being apart for four years.

But then my mother butt in again. "Is that all you can do?" she said. "We need to figure something out now. He can't be away from his little girl for a year and a half! That's crazy. That baby won't even know him by then."

"Mom, it's okay," I said, trying to calm her down. "We'll make it work."

"Boo Boo, no!" my mother said to me. "It's not okay!"

If I thought people were staring at me before for having a baby, they were staring at me now for having a loud, crazy mother. I wanted to sink into the ground and just disappear.

"Ms. Cheryl," my mother tried again, finally lowering her voice. "Isn't there anything else you can do to get him an apartment sooner? He's a good kid. And smarter than probably anyone else here."

Cheryl's eyes darted from my mother and then to me. She sized me up, and I don't know what she saw. A Black kid carrying one hundred extra pounds with an infant daughter to support and a loud-ass demanding mother? That's what I'm sure I looked like from the outside. But somehow she saw something else because she pointed a finger at me and said, "Okay, I can do something for you, but I don't know whether you can handle it."

"Whatever it is, I'll try," I said, trying to imagine what the offer would be.

"Okay," she said, crossing her arms and lifting her chin to give herself just a bit more height. "Here's what I need you to do. You get a 4.0 and be number one in all of your classes at Summer Academy, and I will make sure your name is number one on the wait list for the apartments so you can have a place by September."

I grinned like a kid in a candy store. "Really?" I said, needing confirmation for what sounded like winning the lottery.

"Really," Cheryl said with a smile.

"It's a deal," I said. "I'll totally do it." And then I turned to Nicky and said, "Get ready to move to Stony Brook in September because I'm going to get a 4.0. Bet." It never occurred to me that I should question the probability of achieving that goal, or to ask about my competition or the caliber of the classes. I saw an opportunity and simply decided I would make it work for me and my family.

"I know you can do it, Boo Boo," my mother said, wiping her tears. "If anybody can, it's you." And then she turned to Cheryl and gave her a big hug. "Thank you, Ms. Cheryl," she said. "Jonathan's going to get that 4.0. You watch. My baby is really smart."

My mother was always running her mouth, but I had to give her credit because, once again, she found a way when it didn't seem like there was one. Meanwhile, my father was just leaning against the car watching all this unfold with a look of mild exasperation on his face.

Someone in a red T-shirt came over then and told us that

it was time for parents to go. I helped tuck Emily into her car seat and I kissed Nicky on the cheek, and then hugged her and promised her everything would turn out okay. When I shut the car door, a wave of sadness crashed over me and threatened to snatch the breath from my body. As I watched my father drive away, whatever emotion elite athletes must experience before the biggest game of their career is what I felt in that moment. It was a singular all-consuming determination to succeed. And I just knew I would do it.

During the six weeks of Summer Academy, we were treated like recruits during basic training. We had a regimented schedule with little room for free time. And the one-phone-call-per-day policy was strictly enforced. I felt like we were in prison. Even our bedtimes were strictly monitored, and if we were caught with our lights on after 10 p.m., we would be written up for an infraction.

I had no idea how we were supposed to keep up with our work and be in bed by 10 p.m. Most nights, I could be found in my bed hiding under the blankets with a flashlight, studying until I was sure I knew everything that would be covered on the tests. Nobody was going to stop me from winning my bet with Cheryl Hamilton. And sure enough, on my first three tests, I got an A on every single one. That 4.0 would be mine even if I had to stay up all night, every night, for six weeks straight. Me and my flashlight were unstoppable.

During my one phone call during the third week at Stony Brook, I told Nicky she better start thinking about how she wanted to decorate our new apartment because I was going to get that 4.0 and beat everyone else in the program. I could feel Nicky smile through the phone when I told her that. "You just watch, Nicky," I said, hoping my confidence was enough for both of us. "We'll be together sooner than you know."

I went to tell Mr. Watson about my test grades but he didn't look happy to see me. I wracked my brain trying to think about anything I might have done to spark his anger. But nothing came to mind. My whole life that summer revolved around one thing, studying. I didn't cause any trouble. I wasn't breaking any rules (except for that flashlight), and I wasn't even socializing because I was one hundred percent focused on getting that 4.0, so whatever Mr. Watson had heard about me, had to be a mistake.

"I can't believe you, Jonathan," he said, shaking his head, like I had done something really terrible.

"Why, what did I do?" I said, my defenses raised.

"Don't you remember when I talked about brotherhood and your duty to lift one another up when I welcomed you all into the program?"

"Yeah?" I said, my face a mask of confusion.

"Well, did you think I was saying all that stuff for show, or because I meant it?" he asked, and then waited for my response.

"Because you meant it," I offered, meanwhile my wheels were spinning trying to figure out how I had violated the spirit of brotherhood in the last three weeks.

"Exactly! So, I'm trying to figure out why I see you studying at your desk all day and all night, without offering to help your brothers in this program. That's just selfish."

I started to explain my bet with Cheryl Hamilton and the situation with Emily, but Mr. Watson cut me off. "Jonathan, you know I've read your entire file. I've seen your résumé and your test scores. I know you went to (MS)2 at Andover. I know you're a smart kid, and you know how to study. You've had advantages other people here haven't, and it's going to cost them. Three of the guys on your hallway, in fact, are about to flunk out. You got one hundred on your Africana Studies test, they got sixties."

I tried to protest, as I felt myself getting attacked for trying to do well so I could support my family. I was already under enough pressure to get good grades, and now I was supposed to be responsible for every guy on my hall passing, too? Because I had advantages that other kids didn't? Mr. Watson was obviously confused. I was coming to Stony Brook with a deficit, not advantages.

But he didn't see it that way. "I've been watching you just

shut yourself in your room and ignore everybody else. You have a responsibility, Jonathan, because you have power."

"Excuse me? What power do I have?" I asked.

"Knowledge is power. And you have the knowledge that these guys lack. They're not stupid—they just don't know how to study in a way that's going to get them where they need to be."

"So, it's my responsibility to teach all my classmates how to study," I challenged Mr. Watson. "That's my job?"

Mr. Watson closed his eyes and pursed his lips, like he was trying to keep himself from losing control of his emotions. But when he opened his eyes, he asked me a simple question and his voice was calm. "What are you doing to uplift your brother, Jonathan?"

I shrugged and admitted the truth. "I don't know," I said.

"Well, let me ask you another question then," Mr. Watson said. "What does your success mean if those around you fail?"

When I didn't say anything in response, Mr. Watson gave a wry smile. "You think about that," he said. And I took that to mean our conversation was over. I left his office fuming and wondering if I was ever going to catch a break. How could I ever do the right thing when there was always a catch or one more step I had to complete. It just all seemed like too much.

Back in the dorm, I passed a kid named Travis who lived on my same hall. Just to assuage my guilt, I said to him, "Yo, Travis, how you doing, man?"

"It's all good, bro," he said.

"You doing good in history class?" I asked.

Travis's face fell and he admitted, "It's hard, man. I don't know how you're getting all these perfect grades."

I let out a sigh. And then I made a decision. I told Travis to come to my room during our study break after dinner. And I told him to bring anyone else on our floor who was struggling in history class.

That evening, four guys, including Travis, showed up to my room, and I told them I wanted to help them figure out how to study better. First, I asked to see how they were studying for their tests. I looked at their notebooks and realized what the problem was. They were highlighting almost every single word in the textbook and then trying to memorize all of it. That would never work.

"Yo, you guys can't study like this," I said, handing them back their books. "This is too much information, and it would take too much time to cram all that into your heads. You guys have to learn how to study efficiently."

I pulled out my study guide from the last test and showed them how I pulled out the most critical information and then organized it around key themes and essential questions. I used arrows and boxes to create a mind map that was easier to memorize than just sentences copied from a book.

"This is how you study smart," I said as they all furiously copied my notes.

For the next few days, I studied with Travis and his friends, showing them how to take notes in class that would make studying for tests easier, too. Since it had been working for me since Mr. Murphy's tenth-grade AP European History class, I showed them all how to do Cornell Notes, too, and they quickly picked up the habit. Even though I resented the responsibility at first, I realized that teaching my classmates actually helped me retain the information I needed to know. And I liked seeing the lightbulb go off in their brains when a concept clicked. As I was watching these guys do better in class and feel better about themselves and their abilities, I remembered what Malcolm always used to say to me, *"We're Black Kings, Jonathan, and Black Kings always look out for each other."* Malcolm helped me make it through FDA and (MS)2, and now it was my turn to help these Black Kings rise.

It sounds cliché, but helping my new friends made me feel good about myself. Moreover, studying with Travis and the others helped me get out of my head about my own issues for a while and gave me something else to focus on. And when all the guys I'd helped passed their next tests with A's and B's, I felt as though we all won something. And it wasn't just academic success I was celebrating. These guys became my friends and my brothers at EOP. They helped me make it through the rest of the summer when I felt depressed and lonely, or when I would berate myself for leaving Nicky to deal with Emily by herself. They would come sit in the room with me and crack jokes to cheer me up, and they would promise me I was going to make it. And just as Mr. Watson had predicted, we built a brotherhood.

"Don't think you're going to survive at Stony Brook just by getting good grades," Mr. Watson had preached at us during Orientation. "You're gonna survive because of the people you meet and the relationships you create with the people sitting next to you right now who understand where you come from. Do not underestimate your community. You will need them, and they will need you."

I had no idea how right Mr. Watson would be, not just that summer, but for my full four years at Stony Brook. Those relationships I created during EOP summer sustained me through all of the ups and downs I went through. But Mr. Watson made me realize that these friendships needed to be intentional, and they required nurturing from me. I couldn't expect to reap the rewards of community support without pouring into the community myself. That was a lesson I would continue to practice well beyond my life at Stony Brook.

I graduated from the EOP with a 4.0, and I had the highest grade in every class. All of my friends who I had helped study finished right behind me, ending the summer getting A's in every class. A few days after the EOP graduation, Cheryl confirmed that Nicky, Emily, and I could move into our one-bedroom on-campus apartment two weeks before classes started.

Nicky and I had a blast setting up our little home. We were broke as hell, but this was the first time either one of us had our own place. The graduate apartments were situated away from main campus in their own little bucolic setting with lush green grass and solid oak trees outside our windows. It felt like we were playing make-believe in an enchanted forest.

Our apartment was bigger than most of the homeless shelters I'd lived in throughout my childhood, and it was brighter and more spacious. It was anything but luxurious, but it felt like we had given our daughter a gift. Nicky and I just kept looking at each other and giggling like little kids on Christmas morning because, really, we were still kids. Kids playing house.

Even though Emily wasn't even a year old, I turned our living room into a learning center for her because I wanted to make sure my daughter had the proper stimulation for her brain from day one. I put up posters with the alphabet and numbers on the wall, and I set up a stack of the educational toys I'd already purchased for her. Nicky thought I was crazy for doing it, but I wanted everything about Emily's life to be perfect, because I was still such a work in progress.

10

I Wasn't Supposed to Be a Doctor

Pam listened to my ambitious plans and then quite politely told me I was crazy. "Sweetheart, you can't take eight classes your first semester," she said, her voice warm with concern. "That's a perfect recipe to overwhelm yourself and fail. I know you have a baby girl to support, but overloading yourself during your first semester of college is not the way to do it. Just remember, you can do it all, just not all at the same time. You have four years!"

Before I opened my mouth to make this a debate, I paused. Looking at Pam, seated at her desk in her wheelchair, I had to check my assumptions and make sure, because Pam was an Italian-American woman and a little person at that, that I wasn't dismissing her abilities to help me. Did the fact that she didn't look like me make a difference in what she could do for me? In my mind, I quickly ran through what I knew about Pam. She had multiple years of experience as an advisor for EOP students at Stony Brook and had successfully helped dozens of kids graduate and get full-time jobs. Clearly, she had more knowledge than me in this arena, so I forced myself to stop talking and listen. Let the guide lead the way.

"Making it through this place is going to take more than just studying," Pam said. "You have to prioritize your classes, yes, but you also have to find a job, and take care of that precious baby girl."

"I hear what you're saying," I said, "but I don't really have a choice in the matter. I only have four years to get this done."

Pam looked at me over her glasses, like she was trying to see if I was really serious. Then, she turned to her computer. "Okay, listen, this is not what I would suggest, but if you're bound and determined to do this, let's make sure you're doing this strategically. And for the record, you're not taking eight classes."

"Alright," I said. "How about seven?" I said with a grin.

"Okay, Jonathan. Let's see what we can do, but don't say I didn't warn you."

"Deal," I said. "And thank you, Pam."

Pam let me register for seven classes, and she hooked me up with two perfect on-campus jobs. I worked at the computer center, where all I had to do was walk around and refill the paper in the printers, and I worked at one of the science labs, where I helped clean the equipment. At both jobs, I could easily fulfill my official work duties in a short amount of time, so I could use the rest of the time at work studying and doing my homework.

The other good thing about those jobs was that I could bring Emily to work with me, which I increasingly had to do because Nicky was having a hard time. Just like back home, her days with the baby were long because I would go to class, then go to work, and if I needed to, I'd study at the library because studying at home was impossible. As soon as I walked in the door, though, I'd take over Emily's care and tell Nicky she was free to do whatever she wanted. I often urged her to get out of the house just to see something besides the four walls of our apartment.

"Where am I supposed to go, Jonathan?" Nicky would ask. "I don't know anybody here, and we don't have a car."

"You can go to the mall or something," I'd suggest.

"And do what? We don't have any money," she'd remind me. Many times, she would just hand me Emily and go to the bedroom and cry.

One time, I came home and found Emily in the crib and Nicky locked in the bathroom, screaming. I tried to coax Nicky out of the bathroom and asked her what she needed. She said she needed to be alone. She needed space. She needed peace. I was scared to leave Nicky like that, but I wanted to give her what she asked for, so I scooped up the baby and ran out of the house with the stroller. My heart was racing, and my mind was flashing warning signals. I had heard of postpartum depression on the TV talk shows I used to watch with my mother, but on those shows, the mothers suffering from this mysterious condition ended up drowning their babies in bathtubs or driving off a cliff. I feared this was what Nicky had, but I was too afraid to bring it up in case it triggered something in her. That night, I stayed out as long as possible, until Emily was in a deep sleep, before I snuck back into the house.

Just as Pam had predicted, juggling all those classes, homework, two jobs, and a baby was a lot. It was more than a lot. It was too much for me to handle. Even with food stamps, I was barely making enough money to pay our bills, but working more hours would mean more time for Nicky alone with the baby. And if I took more time to be with Emily, I'd miss out on study time and, possibly, fail my classes and lose my support from EOP. I felt like I was drowning in quicksand and desperately needed somebody to throw me a rope. But I was too afraid to tell anybody I was struggling. If I admitted to Pam or Mr. Watson that I couldn't hack it, I worried EOP would take away our apartment, or kick me out of the program. I thought about calling DiCo, but he had already given me a gift card to buy diapers for Emily before school started, and I was too proud to tell him we needed more money to make ends meet. I couldn't even ask my parents for help because they were doing worse than we were.

It seemed like as soon as they dropped me off at school, my parents' lives started to fall apart. They were evicted from their apartment in the Bronx and forced to move back to the Webster Projects with my grandmother while they tried to plot their next steps. Without any kids to claim, they no longer qualified for Aid to Family with Dependent Children, so food stamps and apartment subsidies either disappeared or were severely limited. Living with my grandmother was a temporary solution only, but without benefits and few options to find an affordable place to live, my parents decided to try for yet another fresh start by returning to Virginia. All of this turmoil was playing out like a rerun of a bad dream, adding another layer of anxiety to my already-overburdened conscience.

By the time October rolled around, Nicky and I were barely speaking to each other because we were both so exhausted and unable to feel any kind of grace for the other person. And then we turned on each other.

"You're so selfish, Jon" was Nicky's most common complaint. "Everything has to be about you. Emily and I don't matter."

"How can you say that?" I'd lash back out. "What do you think I'm busting my ass for? For Emily and for you! You think I wanna be working this hard?"

"I think you wanna do whatever you want. I'm the one taking care of the baby every day," Nicky said.

"But it's only for a little while," I begged her to remember.

"Four years is not a little while," Nicky said. And then she'd leave the room, and we'd go off to our respective corners, angry at one another.

I was failing at everything. I felt like I was a bad father, a bad boyfriend, a bad provider, a bad son, a bad employee. Everything that is, except my grades. I refused to fail in the classroom, which meant if I had to choose between studying or being with Emily, I chose studying. If I had to choose between hanging out with Nicky in the evenings or going to get extra help for my English class, I'd choose the late-night tutoring session. Always. Sometimes, if I had to study, I'd even get to work late because I knew the only currency I actually had that was worth something was my intelligence. And knowing that the people in EOP were supporting me and investing in me because they believed I was smart enough to pull this all off, I refused to let them down. I refused to sacrifice my chance to make something of myself.

Looking back, I know that I shouldn't have struggled alone. I should have reached out to my village, but my stupid pride and ego got in the way. Lucky for me, there was always somebody in my world, willing to help.

Nicky was having another bad day, and I knew she needed a break from the baby. I had already skipped English class once that week and knew I couldn't afford to miss another one, so I bundled Emily up and tried to get to class a bit early so I could explain the situation to the professor. I was prepared to sit in the back of the room so I could slip out in case Emily started to cry or get fussy. I just hoped that Professor Goldberg would be okay with the plan. She was a young adjunct professor, and she seemed really nice and just a little goofy, so I prayed she'd be okay with my plan. But she wasn't having it.

"Give me the baby," she said to me after I explained what was going on with Nicky. By now, all of the other students had entered the room and were at their desks watching this situation unfold. Luckily, this was an enrichment English class for EOP students only, so everyone knew me and my situation, but I was still embarrassed to be causing a commotion.

"What do you mean?" I said.

"I mean, you give me the baby and sit in your usual seat. I don't need my hands to lecture, but you need your hands to take notes. So, give me the baby."

I did what I was told and handed Emily over to this petite, white woman and waited to see what would happen.

Emily looked at my professor and smiled. Professor Goldberg smiled back and then said, "Kids love me. Now, sit down, and don't you ever miss my class again because of your child. Just bring her with you. Got it?"

"Yes, ma'am," I said, instantly flooded with relief.

For the next forty-five minutes, Professor Goldberg taught her class with Emily on her hip. For her part, Emily laughed and played with the professor's glasses and seemed to be having the best time of her life.

Professor Goldberg quickly leapfrogged from being just a nice professor to being a trusted member of my village.

Not only did she allow me to bring Emily to class, but she made herself available to help me with my writing assignments. Professor Goldberg would wait until I was finished with work and tutor me in the evenings because she knew I couldn't make it to her regular afternoon office hours.

And she wasn't just helping me with my writing assignments for her class. I would write my papers for all of my classes weeks in advance and then show them to Professor Goldberg, who would work with me to correct all of the grammatical errors and help me hone my arguments.

"Jonathan, you're a really great storyteller. I hope you keep writing," she would tell me on a regular basis.

It took me a while to believe her, since writing had never been something I felt I was good at, but working with her made me realize that the same passion I had for talking and telling stories could be translated onto the page. She opened up that option for me, to see myself as a writer. Which, in turn, would lead to this book one day.

At the time, I was so thankful that Professor Goldberg was willing to be a member of my village, but I could barely offer a thank-you in response to her generosity because I was desperately trying to hold the crumbling pieces of my life together. Nicky and I were on the verge of collapse.

Our petty arguments had escalated into a full-on war. The last fight we'd gotten into had gotten so loud and so out of control, our neighbors rang the bell and threatened to call campus security if we didn't shut up. We were both so angry and both so hurt; we had nothing to give one another except buckets of grief. I was selfish and Nicky was ungrateful. Emily was caught in between.

The suitcases were stacked by the door. I saw them as soon as I walked into the apartment. My heart seized with fear.

Nicky came out of the bedroom and saw the look on my face. "What's going on?" I said.

"My mother's coming to pick us up tomorrow morning," Nicky answered me with barely a hint of emotion.

"Where are you going?" I asked.

"We're going back home, Jon," Nicky said. "I gotta figure out what I want to do, and I can't do it here by myself. I want to go to college. I want to have a life, too. And my mom can help me with the baby. Since you obviously can't."

The accusation hurt because it was true, but I didn't want to dwell on that. My brain quickly shifted into survival mode to try to fix things. To stop Nicky from leaving with the baby. I hated being left. It triggered every memory of abandonment for me from my recent past. In my mind, when people left me, bad things happened.

"Nicky, you don't have to go," I said desperately. "We can work this out. I'll take fewer credits. I'll stop trying to do premed and just focus on figuring out my major so it will be easier." I tried to offer Nicky everything she'd been asking for but that I had been unwilling to give. But I was willing now if it would make her stay.

Nicky held up her hand to stop me. "Jonathan, this isn't about you. I just can't do this anymore, and I need to get out of here."

I spent the next hour desperately trying to get Nicky to change her mind. I tried to make it more about Emily needing me more than me needing her. When I saw that wasn't working, I told Nicky she was the one being selfish for taking our child back to dirty and dangerous Brownsville rather than letting her live on a suburban college campus. But it didn't matter what I said. Nicky had made up her mind, leaving me to stew in my feelings and try to figure out my role in the way things had unfolded.

Because I was too mad and anxious to stay in the house with Nicky, I went to the mall and found myself in front of one of those Build-A-Bear stores. Suddenly, I was seized with the idea that Emily might forget who I was if she didn't see me every day, so I used the last bit of money I had to build a teddy bear for my daughter, with a recording of my voice to remember me by, saying, "I love you." Even though I was furious at Nicky for taking Emily away from me, the emotion bubbling to the surface wasn't anger, it was a full-body despair. I was so overwhelmed with grief, I cried while I watched them stuff Emily's teddy bear.

The next morning, Nicky's mother showed up right on time. She and Nicky packed the U-Haul with their luggage and the baby's furniture. I made sure Emily had her new bear. And then they left.

My boys from EOP tried to get me to see the bright side of things, namely that I could now focus on my studies without guilt. They let me cry without judgment. They told me to come stay with them in the dorms most nights so I wouldn't have to sit in a half-empty apartment and beat myself up for being a failure. They tried to cheer me up by taking me to campus parties and reminding me that, even though I had a kid, I was still a kid myself. I was grateful for their care, and I went along with them, trying to appreciate the campus social life, but acting like a regular college kid was just that for me: acting. Underneath my smiles and good humor, there was always the knowledge that I couldn't relax and get comfortable. I had to keep grinding so I could support my daughter and prove to myself that I could win.

Even though the semester was almost over by the time Nicky left, I still had a few more weeks before winter break. I was doing pretty well in all of my classes, but I needed to ace the last few quizzes and tests before final exams. The only wrench in my plans was my parents.

After temporarily staying with my brother Justin when they first arrived in Virginia, my mom and dad had found their own apartment. It sounded like a step in the right direction for them; however, that's when things became problematic. That's when my mother started calling me on a regular basis and asking me for money. It was a familiar pattern.

Sometimes, she'd call me ten times in one day. Just like she used to call her mother when we lived in Virginia. I could feel red-hot anger coursing through my veins every time she'd call, but I tried to keep my tone respectful. "Ma, you can't call me asking for money and not expect me to get mad when you know damn well that if I had a single extra penny I'd be using it to take care of Emily, not your 'phone bill.' Why is that so hard for you to understand?"

"Why is it so hard for you to help your own mother out?" my mother cried.

I had to put some distance between my parents and myself. More than the physical distance between Virginia and New York, I needed to create an emotional distance as well. I needed to detach myself from the vortex of their addiction and their insatiable and myopic need. Just like Nicky had said to me, I needed time away from them so I could work on me. I didn't make an official announcement or call and declare my intentions. I did, however, block their numbers on my phone for a while and told myself that the only way I was going to make it through college was by becoming totally selfish with my time and attention. On paper, and now in practice, I had no parents.

The beginning of the second semester of my freshman year found me in Pam's office again. "If you're trying to get into this Introduction to Respiratory Therapy class, then maybe you should consider actually majoring in respiratory therapy," Pam was telling me. "Students who major in respiratory therapy are practically guaranteed a job when they graduate, and they make good money."

All I wanted to do was sign up for an extra two-credit class that would boost my GPA and counterbalance the low grade I received in chemistry the previous semester. My friend Greg told me this Intro to Respiratory Therapy class was an easy A, so I just needed Pam to okay my registration. But she wanted to use our meeting as an opportunity to help me select a major. Because Pam had proven herself to be an excellent advisor and resource, I forced myself to consider what she was saying.

"What is respiratory therapy, exactly?" I asked, settling into my seat.

"Respiratory therapy is a solid field to get into," Pam said. "The easiest way to explain what a respiratory therapist does is that they help people breathe. You work in the hospitals alongside doctors and nurses, and it's a very hands-on and in-demand profession."

"Pam, I came to Stony Brook to be a doctor," I said, reminding her of my goals.

"I'm not saying you can't be a doctor," Pam responded. "I'm just saying you should consider all of your options."

I smiled at Pam so what I was about to say didn't come off sounding like I was a snob or something. "No thanks."

"For the record, majoring in respiratory therapy isn't easy," Pam said. "It's one of the toughest science majors at the university." Pam pulled a document from a pile of papers she had on her desk. "Look at all the required classes for the respiratory major," she said, pointing at the list of classes on the right side of the page. "And now, look at all the prerequisites to go premed." That list was detailed on the left side. "There are only two classes that are different. If you major in respiratory therapy, two things happen: One, you have almost everything you need to get into medical school. And two, you have a viable career option, should the need arise."

"What do you mean 'should the need arise'?" I asked.

"Jonathan, you have a sweet baby girl at home," Pam said patiently. "In four years, she's going to be a real human who needs you around. She is going to be starting school and wanting ballet classes and swimming lessons. You may want to take a break and be with her for a few years before you start medical school and all that entails."

I didn't interrupt her flow, so Pam continued.

"You'll walk out of here with a job by graduation. And we're talking about starting salaries above seventy thousand dollars. It's way more money than you'll be making if you major in chemistry or biology, which pretty much only qualifies you to clean test tubes in a lab if you're lucky."

I could feel the gears in my mind shifting, and I told Pam that I would give it some thought.

Pam folded the paper in half with the list of requirements and handed it to me. "You have to make a decision pretty quickly," she said. "If you apply to the respiratory program while you're still a freshman, it's easy to get in. After that, though, you have to wait until you're a junior to apply, and then the program is very competitive to get into it. So, don't think too long."

Pam got me into the Introduction to Respiratory Therapy class, and as soon as I looked at the syllabus, I knew I could get that A. Just like Greg told me, basically, we just had to show up and listen to the professor explain to us what respiratory therapy entailed. The professor made it sound like a respiratory therapist had the most important job in the world. On the first day of class, he made the whole class hold our breath as long as we could. We did until we were all panting and gasping for air.

"Now, what were you thinking about when you weren't able to take a breath?" the professor asked.

The room was silent. Nobody raised their hand.

"Exactly!" the professor crowed. "Because if you can't breathe, nothing else matters."

Attending that class was a game changer for me. I immediately fell in love with the idea of being embedded in the most important aspect of human life, breathing. Like the professor said, if you're not breathing, you're dead. By the time the second week of class was over, I returned to Pam's office and told her I was going to take her advice and declare my major in respiratory therapy.

Pam beamed and clapped her hands. "Good for you. I think you're making the right decision," she said.

"Me too," I said. "But I'm still applying to medical school."

She smiled. "I know you will, sweetheart. I wouldn't expect anything less from you, Jonathan."

While I was grinding away at school, Nicky was spending her time figuring out what she wanted to do and become in the world. Having Emily obviously forced her to get clear sooner rather than later, but once she was back in Brooklyn, it didn't take her long to decide to enroll in community college so she could start to explore her options. Once she started school and discovered what types of classes she enjoyed and what she was good at, she was much happier, and we started talking again. Regardless of where we stood as a couple, we were both committed to supporting one another through our studies so we could be better parents for our daughter.

However, in what was both a blessing and a curse, Nicky's mother had to retire early because of medical issues, so she was around more to help Nicky with Emily. But that meant money was now extra tight in their household. Nicky now depended on me to send money on a regular basis for diapers and other necessities. I tried to send Nicky as much money as possible, and as often as possible, but my bank account always seemed to be empty. My two part-time campus jobs were barely enough to buy food, pay my phone bill, and buy my train pass and expensive science textbooks and other school supplies. To save money, some of my friends and I would buy one textbook and share it. Or, I would simply skip buying food and scavenge in the dumpsters by the cafeteria to find something to eat. There were days when I didn't have any money, and Nicky would call me crying because she was, literally, using the last diaper for Emily at that moment and didn't have the money to buy the next package. The first time that happened, I wanted to cry, too, because I had only fifteen cents in my wallet at that moment. I knew crying wouldn't solve anything, though, and I promised Nicky I would take care of it.

After I hung up the phone, I thought about my own father and all the times in Virginia when he'd get on his bike and ride to the grocery store, choosing a store far away from Holly Cove so he wouldn't be recognized. And he'd come back home with his coat stuffed with stolen bologna and white bread so we could eat. Even though it was his fault we didn't have money in the first place, he was willing to do whatever it took to feed his family. And so, with a heavy heart, I decided if I had to be like my father, then that's what I would do. I put on my coat, went to the store, and stole a package of diapers for my daughter. I did what I had to do.

I tried not to let my money troubles stop me from concentrating on my classes. I kept hearing Dr. Hodge's voice in my head reminding me, *"If there is no struggle there is no progress,"* and I would tell myself that the suffering I was enduring to get my degree would result in having the means to pay for whatever my child needed, whatever Nicky needed, and whatever I needed in the future. But the struggle was always there. It seemed to be getting harder and harder as winter carried on, and I could neither see nor feel any signs of relief. I was now taking five hard classes, working two jobs, and commuting back to Brooklyn every weekend to help take care of Emily. When I was back in Brooklyn, I couldn't study in Nicky's crowded house, so during the week, I'd have to cram all my studying into the scraps of time between classes and my jobs. My friends would sometimes have to remind me to eat, often buying the food for me to eat because I never had any money. The little I had would always go to Emily's care.

I was used to living in poverty, so it wasn't the lack of food or money that was bringing me down, it was the feeling that I was running like a hamster trapped in a wheel and I wasn't getting anywhere. And, no matter how fast I ran, how hard I studied, how many hours I put in at my job, it wasn't enough. I was still failing. The last time I'd stolen a package of diapers, I almost got caught. My refrigerator was empty. And Nicky still felt as though she was doing the majority of the parenting. Which she was. Every day, my drive to keep going grew weaker and weaker. I would just sit in my apartment at night and try to find the light, but there was just a growing sea of darkness.

And then, one evening, I decided just to give up. I was done running.

Before I could change my mind, I pulled out my phone and sent an email to Pam, requesting a meeting for the next morning. I was going to tell her I was dropping out. I hit send on my email and immediately felt a sense of relief wash over me. No more racing toward a four-year finish line. I could just go back to the city, start working, and build a life from there. Nicky wouldn't be mad at me. I could see my daughter every day, and I wouldn't have to work so freaking hard for so long without seeing any results. Just imagining that simple life allowed me to fall asleep that night, and for the first time in a long while, I slept peacefully.

The next morning, I woke up knowing this would be the last day I would wake up at Stony Brook University. Instead of packing my backpack, I started packing my suitcase with all my clothes, but as I packed, the consequences for what I was about to do flooded my brain. I tried to imagine what Pam would say. I could already feel the sting of my brothers' disappointment and my father's anger at me for dropping out of school. Meanwhile, Justin's warnings not to be a quitter rang in my ears. I could see my mother's tears.

"But I can't do it!" I shouted aloud to the voices in my head. I cursed my parents for being too broke to help me. I cursed myself for getting Nicky pregnant when I was seventeen. I cursed both my ambition and my inability to succeed.

I threw the rest of my things in my suitcase. I just wanted the whole thing to be over. I checked my watch and realized I had just enough time to make it to Pam's office, which was located in the Melville Library in the center of campus. I started practicing my "I'm dropping out" speech as soon as I walked out the door, trying to prepare myself for Pam's reaction. But I was already on my way out.

As I approached the graduate housing complex entrance, I decided to check my mailbox before heading to the library. It was just an excuse to stall so I wouldn't have to face Pam and her arguments to make me stay.

I didn't expect to find anything in my mailbox, but when I opened the little metallic door, I saw a single, white envelope in there. I pulled it out and saw that it was from DiCo. Seeing his name on the letter made me cringe because I hadn't reached out to him in a while. I didn't want to tell him how badly things were going with Nicky and Emily, and I had kept promising myself I'd call him when things were better. But things hadn't gotten better. I hesitated before opening the envelope, thinking whatever was inside might be an angry note, chastising me for ghosting him, but I tore it open anyway. Inside, I found a note that read, *I haven't heard from you in a while. I hope everything is okay. I thought you might need this to keep going. Don't forget, I'm always around if you need to talk.* I peeked inside the envelope again, and there was a check for five hundred dollars! Five hundred dollars. I felt like I had just won the lottery.

I held that note in my hand and re-read it three times to make sure I wasn't dreaming. It was like DiCo knew what I needed even when he wasn't around. He knew me well enough that he understood my silence was not a rejection; it was just me being afraid to ask for help. And he sent the help without me having to ask. That five hundred dollars meant I could buy diapers for Emily for months without having to risk going to jail. But more than the money itself, just knowing that DiCo was thinking about me, and that he cared enough about me to send help, was the lifeline I had been waiting for to pull me out of the quicksand. I started crying in front of the student mailboxes and couldn't stop.

Then, before I could change my mind, I ran all the way back to my apartment and canceled my meeting with Pam. I realized I had to stop thinking that I had to do everything on my own. That I was alone. I was angry at my parents, but that didn't mean I couldn't depend on other people in my life. My village was there for me, and I had to keep reminding myself that asking for help didn't make me weak. On the contrary, it helped me get the resources I needed to survive.

I never told Pam that I had come so close to giving up on myself.

I didn't bother going home for the summer after I finished my first year at Stony Brook. The truth was, since my parents were shuttling in and out of homelessness in Virginia, I didn't have a home to go to. I could have gone to Nicky's in Brownsville, but it was too crowded and chaotic there. I stayed at Stony Brook all summer and took classes so I could stay on track for graduation. Plus, I had applied for and been accepted into one of the school's summer research programs known as the Undergraduate Research and Creative Activities (URECA) program. I got to work with some of Stony Brook's top research scientists who were studying the connections between brain function and different aspects of the respiratory system. Now that I had made the decision to major in respiratory therapy, I figured, why not get a jump-start learning more about what my future held. The scientists I was working for were examining brainstem sites and neural mechanisms responsible for shifts in respiratory patterning. My job as the research assistant was to attach electrodes onto the diaphragms of mice and cats, and test their strength and monitor their central nervous system sites simultaneously. It was fascinating yet tedious work, but it only served to get me more excited about a career in medicine. I felt as though I was totally in my element, and I loved geeking out in the labs. It was intriguing to me to see how every part of the body worked together. Sometimes, I would stop in the middle of a procedure and just dial back my memories to eighteen months prior when I was hanging with RJ and Tyson on the benches, thinking my life was pretty much over. The distance between then and now had to be more than mere months, but I felt like I had lived a lifetime and then some.

By the time sophomore year officially started, I felt like a racehorse tethered at the starting line, just raring and ready to be let loose to see how fast I could go. I missed Nicky and Emily, but I learned how much I could get done alone. I was able to keep up with all of my classes and responsibilities. The pace I was maintaining was insane, and the struggle was very real, but I refused to let up on the gas. I knew that all I had to do was get through the required classes on my list, do the right amount of extracurriculars, get the degree, and I would have the keys to the kingdom. And once I had them, nobody could take them away from me. Nobody else would be in control of whether I won or lost. There was no room for failure, and there was no way I was going to quit. The only thing standing in the way of getting to the finish line was one class. One class that everybody feared, including me: BIO 203 Cellular Organ and Physiology.

It was one of the critical prerequisites for the respiratory therapy program. If you couldn't pass BIO 203, you couldn't be a respiratory therapist. Therefore, BIO 203 was the class that weeded out the people who weren't truly up for the task. My friends and I called it the class meant to separate the weak from the strong.

I got a nineteen on my first test.

When the professor handed back the tests, I just stared at the number nineteen like it was written in a foreign script. I had never earned such a low grade. Without moving my head, I tried to see what the people sitting around me had gotten on their tests. I couldn't make out anyone's scores, but judging from the sad looks on the faces of half the class, I wasn't alone in my despair.

So, I doubled down on my studies. I quit one of my three jobs and put in as much time as possible studying for that class. I think I averaged only four and a half hours of sleep the week before the second test. I did everything I knew how to do to memorize everything I thought would be covered on the exam. But when I saw what was on the test, I knew I was in trouble. Even though I had studied so much, the questions on the test were completely confusing to me. I felt like I hadn't studied at all. I sighed and started filling in answers, hoping and praying that what I did know would at least be enough to pass.

It wasn't. I got a thirty-three.

That's when I really started to panic. When I looked around the lecture hall the week before the third test, I saw a multitude of empty seats. We went from nearly 350 students to 100. People were dropping like flies. I didn't have a Plan C. If I couldn't pass this course, I couldn't major in respiratory therapy or be a doctor. I simply had to study harder.

So, that's what I did. I studied like my life depended on it. When my friends Doug, Craig, and Greg tried to entice me to go out for just an hour during the week, I'd refuse. If I wasn't in class, working, or visiting with Emily on weekends, I was studying. I didn't even go to the dorms to sleep during those days, preferring to be alone in my apartment so I could take advantage of every single waking hour to cram information into my brain.

Even still, I failed the third test.

This time, I didn't even bother to try to hold it together in class. I just put my head down on my desk and let the tears leak out of my eyes. I wasn't alone. I could hear other people sniffling and sobbing around me.

After class, I plucked up my courage and asked the professor if there was even a chance for me to still pass the class. I needed to know whether, once I walked out of the classroom, I still had a chance to fulfill my dreams, or whether it was time to give up. I didn't care if I passed with an A or C, I just wanted to know if there was even a reason to keep trying.

The professor had to look up my scores on his computer. He then looked up at me and said, "Listen, Jonathan, you can still pass the class if you get a seventy or above on the final. You're not out of the game yet."

Normally, I would have taken the professor's words as an exciting challenge, but a seventy in this class seemed as close to impossible as me flying a spaceship to the moon. I mean, technically, it was possible, but it was highly unlikely.

As I walked out of the science building that day, I reviewed the facts. I knew that whatever methods I'd been using to study for this class, obviously, weren't working. And I knew that if I kept using those same techniques, even if I studied until I made my eyes bleed, there was no guarantee I'd get a passing grade. It was clearly time to ask for help. It was my only option if I wanted to succeed.

There was a kid named Chad who lived in the Stimson dorms with Craig, Greg, and Doug, and he was also in BIO 203. He hung out with us sometimes, and he seemed like a nice guy, but more important, he was passing the class. I knew for a fact that Chad got a seventy on the test that I got a thirty-three on, so, in my mind, that made him the perfect candidate to ask for help. One day after class, I asked him if we could study together.

"I haven't passed a single test this semester," I confessed and then said, "Whatever you're doing, I need your help."

"Dude, two heads attacking this stuff has got to be better than one," he said. "Let's do it."

Chad and I started studying together that evening. We started out with Chad explaining his technique when he took the tests.

"The answers they're looking for are in the questions themselves," Chad explained to me. "You have to analyze the questions first before you can work on the answer. It's almost like they're trick questions to see if you truly understand the concepts," he said. "Most people mess up because they're not answering the right question."

I showed Chad my last test and, sure enough, when he explained what the questions were actually asking, I realized why I was scoring so low. My answers didn't address the problems.

Once Chad explained that to me, I felt like I'd been walking around with blurry vision, and he just provided me with a pair of prescription glasses.

"This totally makes sense now," I said, cackling with glee like I had just discovered the holy grail. Chad helped me go over all my tests until I understood how to decipher the questions, but then we still had to study to know how to answer them.

Three weeks before the final exam for BIO 203, I let everyone in my life know that I would be unavailable until the exam was over. I, literally, shut myself off from the world. I didn't go to Brooklyn to see Emily. I put minimal effort into my other classes, and I just studied and studied for that one test. I studied with Chad, and then I studied even more on my own. Even when I was eating and sleeping, I was going over the material in my mind.

When the day finally arrived for me to take the exam, I was calm and as confident as I could be because I knew there was nothing else, short of not sleeping, that I could have done to be more ready. I gave it up to God whether or not I would pass, but I wanted that seventy so badly I could taste it. I knew that if I could just get into the respiratory therapy program, I'd be set because, the way the major was set up, it was designed so students couldn't fail once they were in the program officially. It was a cohort-based program, and there were lots of built-in supports for the students. Because I was used to disappointment, though, I prepared myself for the worst.

When the professor handed out the tests, I took a deep breath and I looked at the questions, remembering everything Chad had taught me. I took my time deciphering the questions and then did my best to answer each one thoroughly. I sat in my chair for the full two hours until the professor called time. I handed in my test and then held my breath for the next seven days.

When the grades were posted the following week, there was an eighty-three by my name.

I couldn't believe it. I refreshed my computer screen just in case. But it still said eight-three. "I did it," I whispered to myself in my empty apartment, and I started to cry. I had never worked so hard or wanted anything so badly and felt so afraid I wasn't going to get it. But I did it. That eighty-three percent meant I had earned my place in the respiratory therapy program, and I could officially say I was premed now, too. I was well on my way to the finish line.

At the end of my sophomore year, I invited DiCo to come to the Stony Brook campus. I was receiving a handful of awards for my high academic achievement, and I wanted him to see the ceremony. Not because I wanted to show off, but because I wanted him to know how much his continuous care and investment in my education mattered. And it wasn't just the monetary support he gave me; it was the fact that he made himself available to me if I ever needed to talk or needed advice. He was neither my mother nor my father and yet he poured into me like I was his child. And the only way I felt like I could repay him was to invite him to see how seriously I was taking my education, so he could see the impact of his support. I was still avoiding my parents, so DiCo's support was even more significant to me at that time.

The ceremony was held on a Saturday in May, so DiCo took the train out to Stony Brook. I found him after the service was over and he gave me a great big hug. He wore his new signature look, khaki pants and a short-sleeve button-down shirt. One of the awards I won was for having one of the highest GPAs out of all of the EOPs in the entire SUNY system.

"Jonathan, I am so proud of you," DiCo gushed as I walked with him back to the train station later that day.

"Thanks, DiCo," I said. "You know, I couldn't have done it without you."

DiCo stopped walking. "Of course, you could have. You would have figured something out—you always do. But I am glad I've been able to help you a little bit."

"It's so much more than a little bit, DiCo," I said. "You've, literally, saved me from giving up more times than you know."

"Well, you know you're helping me, too," DiCo said then.

Now, it was my turn to stop walking. "How am I helping you? I feel like I'm always coming to you with my problems to solve."

DiCo paused and took a deep breath. On the exhale, he said, "I'm applying to law school this year."

"So, does that mean you're going to quit teaching to be a lawyer?" I asked.

DiCo sighed before answering. "I mean, that's the plan because, according to my family, I wasn't supposed to be 'just' a high school teacher at a public school. You know, because I went to Yale. I was supposed to do something 'more important with my life.'" He grimaced and made air quotes as he said the words.

I didn't say anything because it looked like DiCo was fighting against something in his mind. I just gave him space to process whatever he was trying to figure out.

"You know what?" DiCo asked while turning to me with a glint of determination in his eyes. "What I do as a teacher is important."

"I agree one hundred percent," I said.

"Thank you," DiCo said. And then he continued. "When I saw you up on that stage today, Jonathan, I was so proud of you, and I realized that you are my why. Students like you are my why. And if I can be part of your success and other kids who don't get a fair share in life because of their race or their gender or their sexuality, then that's what I'm going to do. It's what I'm good at, and it's what I love. I don't need to go to law school to prove anything. Law school is not my dream."

DiCo's cheeks were now flushed with color, and he was breathing heavy, like he'd just run a race. The satisfied grin on his face made me want to smile in return.

"You always told us to stand up for what we thought was right, DiCo," I said. "And it sounds like you're taking your own advice."

"Damn right I am," DiCo said. He seemed really pumped by the decision he just made and I was happy for him. DiCo was one of the best and most passionate teachers I ever had. I hated to think of him taking those talents away from the kids who would really benefit from his passion.

I laughed and gave DiCo a hug. "DiCo, you're an excellent teacher, and you know it. So, it sounds like you're making the right decision."

DiCo returned the hug. "Thanks, Jonathan. And I mean it, you don't even know how much you inspire me with your determination to do what motivates you, no matter what anybody else says. Watching you soar here at college these last two years, with everything you've accomplished, it makes me want to try harder and do better myself. Honestly. I want you to know that just by being you, you are helping me and so many others who you probably don't even realize."

11

I Wasn't Supposed to Win

My first trip outside the United States began with a cupcake purchased outside the Student Activity Center at Stony Brook. It wasn't an actual purchase because I couldn't afford to spend a dollar fifty on a cupcake. One of the requirements of the Respiratory Therapy program was that we weren't allowed to work. The program was designed to be so rigorous with classes and clinicals that, in theory, we shouldn't have any extra time for outside jobs or activities. Nicolette had graduated from community college and got a job running a medical office in Queens, and now she was the primary breadwinner in our family. She and Emily had moved back to Stony Brook to live with me, and we were surviving, but money was tight. With my refund checks from my loans, I could afford to eat, pay my cell phone bill, and help with Emily's day care bills. But I didn't have a penny extra for a cupcake.

"You can have one anyway," the girl told me as she handed me a cupcake.

While I munched on my cupcake, the girl, who told me her name was Samantha, started telling me about her organization. "Our group is called Students Helping Honduras, and we raise money to send Stony Brook students to Honduras as part of a work exchange program. We're helping to build a school for the local children in a small village there. The kindergarten was completed last year, so this year we're going back to help build the first-grade classroom."

"How many students do you send there?" I asked.

"Usually, we can sell enough cupcakes to send everyone in our group. Last year, everybody went, and we were about ten students."

"Wow! How many cupcakes do you have to sell to send that many people to Honduras?" I asked.

"We do have to sell a lot of cupcakes," Samantha said, laughing, "but the real challenge is finding a kitchen on campus we can use to bake them all. Selling them isn't really the problem."

"I have an apartment with a nice oven, and my girlfriend is a great baker," I said as my wheels began to turn. Even though I was supposed to be singularly focused on finishing my degree in respiratory therapy, I was still one hundred percent committed to going to medical school, and I knew I needed to pad my résumé with extracurricular activities that proved I had a real interest in serving humanity and that I was more than a minion who could get good grades. I wasn't allowed to have a job officially, or even do an internship during the school year, but there were no rules against participating in school clubs. Going to Honduras sounded like it would tick off a lot of items from my "To Accomplish Before Graduation" list, including seeing more of the world. I had watched some of my friends jet off to places like Florida and Mexico for spring break. A couple of people I knew were studying abroad in Europe and Asia. All of it sounded so exciting to me, and I yearned to take off and travel, too, but having no money and the weight of all the classes I was carrying, and Emily waiting for me at home every night, had made me think that dream was impossible. Until I ate that cupcake.

Within a couple of weeks, I was a full-time member of Students Helping Honduras. I told Samantha that the group could use my apartment whenever they needed to make the cupcakes. Nicky and Emily loved participating in our cupcake crusades, and I loved that this was an activity we could do together as a family. Nicky helped with the baking, and we would take Emily with us when it was time to sell. It was criminal, actually, to deploy my adorable, two-year-old daughter as our secret weapon. I would hold her, or she would stand by the table and shout, "Buy a cupcake for the kids, please." Literally, nobody could say no to my little girl selling cupcakes for the children in Honduras.

That fall, we sold enough cupcakes to send our group of ten students to Honduras during winter break. I felt like I blinked, and then I was on a plane to Honduras with Samantha and the rest of the group members.

Despite the fact that we left brutally cold winter weather in New York, when we arrived in Honduras, it felt like summertime. The air was warm and dry, and the temperatures hovered in the mid to high seventies. When we arrived in Villa Soleada, a settlement in a rural region of the country where we would be staying, I was shocked at the conditions in which people were living. On paper, when I read that there was no electricity or running water and that the area was rife with poverty and gang violence, it didn't sound much different from the neighborhoods I grew up in, but it hit different in a rural setting with red dirt and palm trees dotting the landscape. I felt like I had stepped back in time and into a different dimension.

As American volunteers there to help continue progress building the school for the local children, we were treated like special guests in Villa Soleada. We stayed in a hotel that was heavily protected by armed guards. The organization we were working with had to make sure that volunteers were safe during their time in-country, so security was at the highest level. The local residents did not have such protection and weren't ever seen at the hotel. It didn't sit right with me that we were being treated better than the local population just because we were Americans, but the organizers of the program told me that the government would never allow the liability of American volunteers coming to Honduras without such protections.

I didn't know how we would be treated by the local people. I tried to imagine how I would feel if a bunch of foreigners showed up in the South Bronx, speaking a language I didn't understand, saying they were there to help us. I might have been happy for the new building, but I assumed I would be suspicious of their motives or jealous that they got to stay in nicer accommodations than the projects where I lived. So, I was both humbled and surprised at how kind and generous the people were to all the volunteers. Many of them worked alongside us at the construction site and some wanted to practice their English with us and hear about our lives in the United States.

Since we were scheduled to stay in Honduras for only a week, we were eager to get to work. Every day there were activities planned for us, from touring all of the ongoing project sites, to meeting with the local people. The majority of our time, though, was spent at the construction site. We spent eight hours a day working on the school building with professional masons and other local volunteers. I was either laying bricks, mixing cement, or digging trenches to help construct the first-grade classroom for the children. It was hot, sweaty, backbreaking work, but the pressure was on to work quickly and efficiently because these kids, who had started kindergarten the year before, couldn't continue their education until we finished building. When we left, another group of students from another American university would pick up where we left off. As I worked, sweating under the tropical sun, it occurred to me that this was the same work my father made my brothers do to ensure they would go to college. I now understood why he made them do it. Every brick I laid, or trench I had to dig, sparked a level of gratitude in me for all of my blessings, which I'd never felt before. I felt it on a physical level that actually made me work harder. The gratitude fueled me to do as much as I could for the people in Villa Soleada, who continually showed us how much they appreciated the work we were doing.

Early in our stay, a little boy who looked to be about five years old came up to me with a shy smile on his face.

"*Hola,*" I said.

He poked my belly and said, "*Gordo.*" And then he laughed. I knew "*gordo*" meant "fat," so I laughed, too, and patted the kid on the head. But then, out of nowhere, one of the local volunteers came over and smacked the crap out of the kid. He smacked him so hard the child's feet lifted off the ground. The guy had a tattoo on his face that we were told was a marker of gang affiliation, so I was worried about getting involved. But then the guy started yelling at the kid in Spanish. He kept pointing at me and I heard the word "*gordo*" over and over again. I figured the kid was being yelled at because he called me fat.

The man raised his arm to smack the kid again, and without thinking, I grabbed him and said, "No, no, no. Please don't hit him again." I assumed he spoke some English because most of the adults working with us did.

The man took his hands off the little boy and said to me in heavily accented English, "You guys come all the way over here to help us. You don't have to do this for us. And he disrespects you. It's not okay," he said, still fuming.

"No, it's okay," I rushed to assure him. "I'm not offended. I am '*gordo*,'" I said, patting my stomach and smiling, trying to break the tension. The man grudgingly accepted my words, but he still made the kid apologize to me.

"*Lo siento*," the little boy said in a quiet voice.

"It's okay," I said, patting him on the back and smiling to show him and the man that I was truly not offended.

Satisfied, the man walked away, and I turned back to the little boy.

"*Como te llamas?*" I asked him, using the little bit of Spanish I had learned ahead of the trip.

"Diego," the kid replied.

I told him my name was Jonathan, but Diego preferred to call me *Gordo*.

And for the rest of the trip, Diego and I became best friends. Every morning he would be waiting for me at the construction site, sometimes with a piece of mango or some other fruit he picked for me. In exchange, I would give him a dollar to take home to his family.

During my time in Honduras, I learned so much more than how to build a classroom out of cement blocks. I learned how to kill a chicken with my bare hands. I learned how to play soccer on a dirt field. I learned how to draw water from a well, and then what it felt like to get violently ill from brushing my teeth with that water. I learned that on the days he didn't show up to play with me, five-year-old Diego spent twelve hours in the fields with his family picking coffee beans or bananas. Being in Honduras forced me to re-evaluate my entire life. What I grew up believing was a hard life with two drug-addicted parents, being homeless and living in poverty, could have been much harder if I didn't have safe water to drink, a school to attend, or I had to work twelve hours a day like Diego. And yet, Diego didn't act like he felt hopeless. He still found reasons to laugh and smile and make friends with a stranger. Like the rest of the families in Villa Soleada, he was grateful for our help, and he was generous with the little that he had. Diego showed me what it looked like to wake up every day and believe that something better was always possible.

Before I left Honduras, I told Diego that just because I was leaving didn't mean we couldn't still be friends. I told him he better go to school when the building was finished. And he promised he would. I'm happy to report that Diego is eleven years old now and heading into middle school, so he kept that promise, and for my part, I've tried to keep my promise to make sure my trip to Honduras wasn't just an experience to pad my résumé. Diego and the people in Villa Soleada deserved more from me. They had invited me into their community and taken care of me, and like Mr. Watson taught me, it was my responsibility to help nurture that community in return. When I returned to Stony Brook, I continued to work with Samantha and the Students Helping Honduras to continue raising money for the school. I encouraged other students at Stony Brook to join the group and go to Honduras, and I eventually became the vice president of the organization.

But Diego's influence on my life extended beyond the group. Even at five years old, that child taught me how to look at my life and focus on the opportunities instead of the obstacles. That's how Diego managed to wake up every day with a smile on his face, coming to me excited about whatever adventures we could have together. I vowed to do the same. How could I not, when at baseline, as a struggling college student, I already had so many more opportunities than Diego. I had my own challenges and obstacles to conquer, but I also had a strong village supporting me. It was simply up to me to decide which one of those things to focus on, the opportunities or the obstacles.

After my trip, I promised myself that whenever an opportunity comes into my life, I will pluck up my courage and activate the same curiosity Diego used to walk up to a strange American man and call him *gordo*. Even when I don't see the immediate benefit. Because you never know what can happen. And that's how I ended up in a conference room full of Stony Brook's star students and members of the administration, not long after my return from Honduras.

I looked around the conference room and thought, *What the hell am I doing here?* I did not belong in this place with these high-achieving people. But when a woman from the university's president's office had called me to ask if I would come to a meeting of specially selected students, I agreed, telling myself it was "an opportunity to exercise my courage and curiosity." But when I showed up to the meeting, I felt like my invitation to this gathering had to be a mistake. These "special" students were some of the most impressive kids on campus. I was way out of my league.

There was an Indian girl there who was a senior, but she had already created some kind of specialized mosquito spray meant to help stop the spread of malaria in a village in India. The other students were all white; one guy was on his way to Columbia Law School, another kid had already been accepted into NASA's space program to train to be an astronaut, and there were a couple of guys who had job offers to work at Google after graduation. What did I do besides get my girlfriend pregnant in high school and get good grades? I didn't see that as particularly special, and I tried to avoid talking about myself to any of the others, but I still had to share the details of my Stony Brook experience with a film producer who was circulating around the room, talking to all of the students. He had been hired to make a promotional video featuring one or more of us from this group, for the university's new Far Beyond marketing campaign.

I stayed only as long as it seemed necessary and then went back to my apartment to study.

I immediately put the whole experience out of mind, so when the producer from the event called me the following week to tell me he'd decided that I was the one he wanted to feature in his video, it took me a moment to connect the dots.

"Why me?" I blurted out.

"Because I thought you had the most compelling story," the producer said.

"Did you speak to the other students?" I asked. "There was a girl there who was on her way to eradicating malaria in India! She was amazing."

The man chuckled. "I did talk to the other students. And you know what? They were all doing exactly what they were supposed to be doing with their lives. That girl you're talking about, both of her parents are doctors. She was groomed to be a high-achieving scientist or doctor from day one. There's no story there. Nothing unusual. The kid going to law school in New York is going to be the fourth-generation lawyer in his family. All of those kids are, literally, following the path that was set for them at birth.

"Meanwhile, you may not know this, but your GPA is better than all of theirs. You have one of the hardest majors at the university, and you are doing all of this while raising a daughter. You've won almost every academic award possible from what I can see on your transcript. You're the one who wasn't supposed be in that room, young man. You weren't supposed to be here achieving at these levels, given where you started and the challenges you've faced. You have defied the odds. You have the story I want to tell. They don't."

"What does this mean, exactly?" I said. "What do you need from me?"

"It means I would like to make you the face of Stony Brook's Far Beyond campaign. The administration gave me the choice to decide who it would be, and I'm choosing you, if you're up for it."

"What do I have to do?" I asked.

"Nothing, really," he said. "We're going to make a video of you for the university to use to showcase the caliber of students at this school and, hopefully, inspire more kids to want to attend Stony Brook. All you have to do is tell your story."

The video got made over the course of one rainy day. And then it seemed like, overnight, my face and name were everywhere—a giant poster of me was hung on the exterior of the Melville Library building in the center of campus. I was asked to speak at important university galas. My friends started to call me to tell me every time they saw a poster of me somewhere out in the world. There was a giant poster of me in the Chelsea neighborhood of Manhattan and at the airport in Washington, DC. National media outlets reached out wanting to write about my life. I could no longer walk on campus without being recognized or having people clap me on the back and shout out my name.

But online, where people could be anonymous, I found all kinds of negative comments criticizing me for everything from my weight to the fact that I was a teen father.

It was a lot.

I didn't want all the negative online bullshit to bother me, but it did. The truth was, I hated the attention. I was upset because I still didn't feel I truly deserved to be celebrated. I felt like the only reason I was getting attention was because my parents were addicted to drugs, I came from a bad neighborhood, and I was a teen father. I understood that I was shattering stereotypes of Black men from the 'hood, but I didn't have any pride around that. In my mind, I was fighting against being seen as a statistic. The reason I worked so hard was so I would be judged by my current achievements, not my past or where I came from. My whole life, I struggled to hide the ugly parts. I'd been trained to keep the family's secrets, and now everybody knew my truths.

I felt exposed, and all I wanted to do was fade into the background and be anonymous again.

It wasn't until summer, when most kids had left the campus, that I learned the upside of sharing my story.

As was my custom, I planned to stay on campus for summer to take classes. Plus, I wanted Emily to spend her summer in Long Island surrounded by nature, rather than in Brownsville where the rumble of the subway accompanied her lullabies. But as always, I needed a job.

Pam was ready with an opportunity. She told me she had the perfect job for me.

"What's the job, Pam?" I asked. Then quickly added, "Whatever it is, I'll take it. You know I will."

Pam laughed at my enthusiasm, and I laughed with her. By this point, Pam and I were friends. She wasn't just my advisor anymore.

"I know you will, Jonathan, and this job is perfect for you. And only you can do it."

Now, I was intrigued. "What is it?" I said.

"Okay, so I don't know if you know this, but you were the first EOP student we ever had at Stony Brook who had a child. And because you've done such a good job here, we decided to take a chance on another student, a young woman this time, who has a baby. But we want you to mentor her during EOP's Summer Academy. Help her get acclimated, and make sure she doesn't fall behind in her studies. Show her where the day care is, that kind of stuff."

My mind was spinning. "Wait, I was the first EOP student to come in with a baby?"

Pam laughed. "Yeah, you were, and somehow I didn't know that until you got here. Remember, I thought Emily was your sister?"

I laughed at the memory. "I do remember that," I said.

"Well, you showed us that we should be extending offers to more kids who are teen parents because we have the resources on campus to help. So, basically, we're going to replicate what we did for you—get the girl an apartment in graduate housing, help her with child care, and see if she can thrive, too."

"So, tell me again, exactly what I'm supposed to do for the job?"

"Basically, we're going to pay you to be this girl's friend. You're not responsible for her success; we just want to provide her with a mentor who's been there and done that. Now, granted, you've set the bar pretty damn high." Pam laughed. "So, don't make her think she has to win every single academic award and be at the top of every one of her classes, just show her the ropes."

I didn't say it out loud to Pam, but I understood the assignment only too well. Stony Brook wanted me to be for this girl what Francisco had been for me—visual proof of what was possible.

When I met my new mentee, Tiffani, at the beginning of the summer, she told me right away that just hearing about my success had given her the courage to go through EOP. The more I hung out with Tiffani and shared my experiences with her, the more I realized that sharing my story and letting her see my flaws was actually motivating for her and healing for me. I couldn't be ashamed of my background or the fact that I was a teen father because my journey—even with all of its challenges—landed me in a pretty good place. I remembered Mr. Collins's message to me back at Andover: one mistake doesn't define you, and I shared that with Tiffani, but I added my own learning to the message. What you think is your biggest mistake can turn into your biggest blessing, like Emily had for me. It was a full-circle moment for me to become a member of Tiffani's village, and I was ready to do my part.

I didn't feel like a college student by the time I hit my senior year at Stony Brook. My final year in the respiratory program meant I was doing clinicals at different hospitals all over Long Island. I did a rotation at Stony Brook University Hospital, but I also had to work in places like Jamaica, Queens, and Port Jefferson, New

York. Basically, I was working the same twelve-hour shifts, three days a week, as the on-staff respiratory therapists at the hospitals. We didn't get paid, but we were doing the same work as the professionals. I really enjoyed my rotation working with the tiny babies in the Neonatal Intensive Care Unit (NICU), and decided, after that rotation, that working in the NICU would definitely be my specialty.

Once I experienced the adrenaline rush of working as a respiratory therapist and got the hands-on experience with patients, saving lives and, literally, helping people breathe, an idea crystalized in my mind: I didn't want to be a doctor anymore.

Or maybe the realization was that I didn't *need* to be a doctor anymore.

Being in the hospital every day, it became clear to me that doctors weren't the only ones saving lives and truly helping people. The therapists and the nurses were, more often than not, right there in the center of the action, often providing lifesaving procedures needed by the patient. I always wanted to be a doctor to help people who were sick, and that's what I got to do every day as a respiratory therapist. It was fast-paced. I got to interact with many different types of people, and the work was challenging enough to keep my brain stimulated and functioning at high levels. I had to assess the needs of my patient and diagnose the root cause of their problems before performing any treatments. Each patient presented like a complex puzzle that had to be solved. And when I got the right solution, and the patient could breathe again, I felt such a rush of satisfaction. Every day, with a new patient, I felt like I was learning something new.

So, I had to ask myself, if I was this happy working as a respiratory therapist, why was I still pushing myself to go to medical school? I didn't need to be a doctor to add value to people's lives. And I didn't need to chase the doctor title to prove that I added value to the world. Every day, I was realizing that, just by being me, I was adding value to the world, and I didn't need seven more years of school to claim my worth. At the end of the day, I came back to my why to make the decision. Emily was my why, and being a respiratory therapist meant having to work only three days a week instead of five or seven, so I could be an active participant in my daughter's life, rather than just the guy who pays the bills. The only person who really wanted me to be a doctor was young Jonathan who thought being a doctor was the only way to outrun his past. But that Jonathan no longer got a vote in the matter.

Because Stony Brook had such a well-respected respiratory therapy program, hospitals came recruiting with job offers in hand. I received invitations from several hospitals to come check them out. Before graduation, I had job offers from three hospitals. Ultimately, I chose the offer at New York University Hospital Langone Medical Center in the city because it was a prestigious hospital with a generous starting salary, and Nicky wanted to be close to her family in case my workload was really taxing and she needed support.

The only thing left on my to-do list was to graduate.

"Boo Boo, I want to be a part of your life and Emily's life," my mother said. My parents moved back to New York City in the spring of my senior year of college. In what seemed like a crazy twist of fate, they found a nice one-bedroom, rent-controlled apartment in Midtown Manhattan, and my father found a job in the food services industry. It appeared they had finally gotten their lives together, and my mother wanted to reconcile with me. She understood why I had stayed distant these last four years, but she wanted to reconnect and make amends.

I had to ask: "Are you still using?"

"Oh, we're done with all that," she said dismissively. "Daddy and I are doing really well. Why don't you come see us at the apartment, and bring Emily. It's real nice."

I was wary at first because I still didn't fully trust my parents, but I started accepting my mother's invitations to come see her in the city, and I would bring Emily with me. My mother's face lit up with joy whenever she saw Emily, and it made me happy to see the two of them together.

I had a choice to make. Holding on to anger served no one and took up space in my body that I'd rather reserve for pleasure. In the four years that we'd been estranged, I had done a lot of learning and processing of my feelings about my parents. I'd even spoken to a therapist at Stony Brook, and I'd come to forgive my parents for what they did to me because of their addiction. I made a choice to accept my parents for who they were and be grateful for what they were able to give me, rather than focus on what they could not. My parents planted and nurtured the seeds of my educational journey, and for that I am extremely grateful. In many ways, they made my journey much harder than it needed to be, but I also know they are responsible for giving me my wings.

I was ready to have my mom and dad back in my life, especially because I wanted them to be there for the day they seemed to always know would come—my graduation.

On graduation day, I woke up in my apartment with Nicky asleep next to me and Emily softly snoring in her bed on the other side of the room. I technically still had two more weeks to finish my clinicals, but I had passed everything, submitted all my work, and was about to walk in the graduation ceremony with the rest of the class of 2017. I rolled over and hugged Nicky, but she was sleeping too hard to feel it. It felt surreal that this day was actually here. This day. The finish line I'd been running toward. I made it.

I climbed out of bed quietly and headed into the shower, being careful not to wake Nicky or Emily. I wanted to be ready before my family started arriving. This would be the first time we were all together in a long while.

Everybody met up at my apartment. My parents arrived first, and I was relieved to see that both my mom and my dad looked healthy and happy. My mother rushed to hug me tight while screaming about how proud of me she was. I showed my parents around the apartment, showing off Emily's learning center in the living room, and told them how well Nicky and I were doing. "I'm proud of you, son," my father said. It was enough to make me glow inside.

"You had to do all of this on your own, Boo Boo," my mother said, waving her arm to showcase everything in the apartment. "We should have been here to help you. We should have done better." She started to cry.

"Ma," I said, "I'm fine. Emily is fine. I'm graduating, and that's it. There's nothing you can change about the past."

My mother's tears continued to fall, and Nicky handed her a box of tissues. I watched as she pulled herself together and then gave me a brave smile. "I'm okay, Boo Boo," she said, sniffling. "I'm just so proud of you and Nicky."

Jay, Justin, Josh's wife, Laura, my sister, Helena, her husband and two kids, plus my Uncle Yogi, all came to celebrate me: the youngest Conyers child graduating from college. Fulfilling the family legacy.

The ceremony was held at the Kenneth P. LaValle Stadium. There were some four thousand students graduating that day and the crowds around the stadium were immense. Since my face was still plastered all over campus, a lot of people approached me to congratulate me. But the attention didn't bother me this time.

Our graduation speaker was the actor Michael J. Fox, and he talked about how his experiences as an actor in Hollywood with Parkinson's disease proved that, with the right attitude and determination, anything was possible. I completely agreed with his assessment, but in my mind, I had to add the caveat "with the help of a dedicated village by your side." I knew I wouldn't have made it through these four years without DiCo, Pam, Jarvis Watson, Professor Becky Goldberg, and all of my friends from EOP and the Stimson dorm who helped hold me down and lift me up when I couldn't do for myself. Which was often. I knew that without Nicky's love and support, I wouldn't have made it past my first year of college, and Emily wouldn't be the happy and healthy child she was. And there were countless other members of my village, from Marquise to RJ, Malcolm and Mr. Marshall, Diego and Dr. Ubinto, who participated in my evolution, protected me, planted seeds for my success, and pushed me to try harder and do better than I was willing to do for myself. There was no way I would have made it to this moment, to my graduation, without all of those people in my corner.

"I want to highlight one particular student," President Stanley was saying as I tuned back in to the activities on the stage. "This student is an amazing person who has gone far beyond the expected during his time here. He came from a difficult background but today is graduating in four years with a 3.7 GPA in respiratory therapy and will be beginning his professional career at New York University Hospital Langone Medical Center, one of the finest medical institutions in the nation. Jonathan Conyers, please stand up!"

Even though, by this time, I should have been used to the attention Stony Brook brought to me, I was still embarrassed to be singled out like that in front of all those people in the stadium that day. When I stood up, my image was projected on the jumbotron screens so everyone in the audience could see me. The applause was deafening, but my family told me later that when Emily saw me on the screen, she started screaming, "That's my daddy! That's my daddy!"

After the ceremony, my family and I piled into three different cars and headed back into Manhattan for dinner at Dallas BBQ on 42nd Street. Emily was thrilled to be surrounded by all of her family. I couldn't remember ever feeling so calm and content. I didn't need to fixate on the future to find my joy. I didn't need to start planning my next conquest to get through the day. I didn't need to focus on the finish line anymore because I was already there. Sitting in that restaurant surrounded by my village, with the people who loved me the most in the world, I felt like I was exactly where I was supposed to be.

Epilogue

Jonathan, wake up," Nicky hissed in my ear.

"What's the matter?" I said, pulling myself out of sleep. I knew something must be wrong for Nicky to wake me up when she knew I had to be at the hospital early in the morning.

We were temporarily staying at my parents' Midtown apartment with them so we could save money to get our own place in the city. That night, Emily was sleeping over at Nicky's mother's house, and I immediately thought something must have happened to my child. But before I could formulate the right question, Nicky whispered, "Your mother keeps calling your name, but your dad is telling her not to bother you. They woke me up."

I turned my ears to the sounds coming from the living room, and, sure enough, I heard my mother, and it sounded like she was gasping for air.

"I can't breathe, get Jonathan," my mother moaned.

"Kimmie, leave him alone," my father responded, trying to shush her.

I scrambled out of the bed and went to see what was happening. Nicky followed right behind me.

As soon as I stumbled into the living room, I saw my mother sprawled on the mattress on the floor struggling to breathe. "It's my asthma. My asthma," she was saying, but as my eyes swept the room, I saw all of their paraphernalia on the table. And my father was obviously high.

I wasn't an angry and disappointed kid anymore, so I didn't get mad or cast blame. I was a respiratory therapist, and it was my job to help people breathe. And my mother was desperately struggling to pull in air. The sound of her raspy gasps frightened me.

"Call an ambulance!" I shouted at my father.

He looked at me with fear and indecision in his bloodshot eyes, and I knew he was worried that if he called, their secret would be exposed.

He was worrying about the wrong thing.

"Call the ambulance or Mom's going to die," I shouted, trying to make my father understand the gravity of the situation. The tone in my voice spurred him to action, and he made the call.

I found my mother's nebulizer and tried to get her asthma medicine into her, but she was just getting weaker and weaker. She mumbled something about getting tired, and then she just passed out in my arms. I couldn't feel her breath anymore, so I started to administer CPR, hoping I could breathe for her until she could breathe on her own. "Come on, Mom," I demanded. "Don't do this to me," I said, trying to remain calm while I continued to count and breathe.

I kept doing mouth-to-mouth while Nicky and my father stood by helpless, but urging me to keep going. "I can't lose my wife," he started to cry. "I can't lose Kimmie."

Within just a few minutes of my father's call, the ambulance arrived, and I told the EMTs everything. They quickly got an oxygen mask on my mother and got her breathing before they whisked her off to the hospital. Before they left, they told me that I had saved her life by administering CPR.

My father went with my mother in the ambulance, and Nicky and I stumbled back to our room in a daze. But I didn't have time to process what had just happened. I looked at my watch and realized I had to be at work in less than an hour. So, I threw on my scrubs and headed out the door. I thought I had graduated from this type of drama in my life when I graduated from college. I guess I was wrong.

A couple of days later, my mother was back from the hospital, but she said nothing about what had happened. And I didn't, either. We never spoke about it. I didn't even tell my brothers about the incident. That's how things still worked in my family, and I assumed they would never change.

But *I* changed. I knew if I wanted to remain a part of my parents' life, I had to do things differently. My parents would always be my parents, but it was up to me to define the boundaries of our relationship, and I would do so in a way that put my mental health and safety, and that of my children, first. I would keep their secrets, but I would always lead with the truth when it came to making the choices of how and when we would come together as a family. My children would never be witness or victim to my parents' addiction.

A few weeks after I saved my mother's life, Nicky and I signed the lease on our first official apartment as husband and wife. It was a spacious two-bedroom apartment in Queens, and we could afford it on our salaries without having to worry about making rent. It was the perfect size for our family of three, which would soon be a family of four because Nicky was pregnant. This time, we were all elated, especially Emily, who was overjoyed to have a little brother or sister. And Nicky and I finally felt like we had everything we needed to bring a new life into the world with the proper resources and support.

When I think about where I came from and where I am today, husband, father of three children, a successful and internationally recognized respiratory therapist, debate coach, and youth mentor, I realize it doesn't benefit me in any way to fixate on the struggles of my past because I love where I am in the present, and I'm excited to see what the future holds. And I have to thank my parents and my village for helping me get here.

I have come to believe that gratitude shouldn't come with caveats. Just because my parents and some members of my village didn't come in perfect packaging, I still benefited from their care. In order for me to live unburdened by my past, I have to remind myself of that truth often.

I tell myself on a regular basis that some of the greatest advice, protection, and unconditional love I ever received came from imperfect individuals. These reminders free me from the past, and they help me see most people today as good, or at minimum, good enough. I don't ever want to block the blessings from people who may not come with a superhero's cape, and I won't judge an individual because of their origin story, or where they sleep at night. This doesn't mean I put myself in dangerous situations, or I leave myself, or my children, vulnerable to other people's bad behavior. I am discerning, but I try to keep an open mind and an open heart, so my village continues to grow and expand.

At the end of the day, I'm really happy that all three of my children—Emily and her little sister and brother—have grandparents on both sides of the family who love them and want to spoil them. I'm grateful that I am now in a position to give back to the members of my village, and I try to pay forward what they did for me. Before I even graduated from Stony Brook, I started volunteering to help DiCo with the debate team at his new school, and, today, DiCo and I work together at the Brooklyn Debate League trying to help as many kids as possible from underserved communities find their voice and find their why through debate. I also serve on the alumni board of (MS)2, and although it pains me that Dr. Ubinto doesn't work at the school anymore, I am so happy to be a part of the organization that was pivotal to my survival. Like Mr. Marshall, Dr. Hodge passed away before I could thank him sufficiently for the difference he made in my life, but I have returned to FDA—with Malcolm— on numerous occasions to speak to the current students, to show them what their future could look like. I am also usually the only person who visits Marquise in prison, talks to him on the phone, and puts money in his account. Because I am still his friend. And he is still part of my village.

I remember how important it was for me to find mentors and guides to show me the way to the finish line. I remember yearning to see visions of what was possible, after my brothers were no longer in my life on a day-to-day basis. So, I try to be that for the next generation of young people who don't know where they fit in or where they belong in a world that makes them feel unseen or as if they don't matter. Showing these kids that they do matter and that they belong at any table they choose is my new why.

My village gave me the blueprint for success and survival. I hope this book can do the same for you.

Acknowledgments

I'm humbled and grateful to all of the individuals who have played a role in bringing this book to life. Thank you for your support, your guidance, and your belief in me.

This book would not have been possible without an amazing team of women who supported me, championed my story, encouraged me to be vulnerable and honest in sharing my truth, and helped me to see a vision for this book that was bigger than anything I had ever dreamed of.

First, I have to share my immense gratitude to my agent, the incomparable Johanna Castillo. Because of Johanna, my journey into the world of publishing has been an exciting adventure knowing she always has my back and my best interests at heart. She has been an incredible guide and protector throughout this whole process.

Next, I have to thank my amazing editor, Krishan Trotman, who gave me the opportunity of a lifetime with this book. From the first day we met, she was passionate and steadfast in her commitment to me and my story. Thanks also go to Amina, Maya, Tara, and all of the wonderful team members at Legacy Lit who have made me feel comfortable and confident in a world that was all brand new for me. Their commitment to excellence set the tone for this entire project and I appreciate them all for that so much.

I don't even know how to say thank you to the woman who truly made this book possible for me. The woman who became a mentor, a friend, and, in my eyes, a second mom to me. Lori Tharps, I thank you. You held my hand throughout this entire process, and you have made me a better writer, a more courageous speaker, and I thank you for being side by side with me in this journey.

To my parents. I am so grateful that you did what most people would not or could not have done. You gave me permission and your blessing to tell my story, even though it would expose some of your lowest moments. You told me to tell it all and let the skeletons out of the closet, so I could be free. Your courage and your selfless act humble me, and I'm so thankful I have your blessings and your consistent care in my life. I love you both.

To my mentors and village members: You are highlighted throughout the book, and I hope I have done you all justice. I hope the world understands that without you, there would be no story.

To my wife, Nicky, you are the kindest person I know. You taught me the true meaning of unconditional love and I thank you for being my biggest cheerleader and best friend all these years and especially through this process. I'd like to promise that I'll never write another book about our family, but I think we both know that's a promise I cannot keep.

Finally, I want to express the gratitude to the readers who have taken the time to engage with this book. Your interest and enthusiasm for the ideas it contains are what make writing so meaningful, and I hope that this work will have a positive impact on your life.

And of course, I have to thank my three children—Emily, Sophia, and Junior—because at the end of the day, you are all my why.

READING GROUP GUIDE

DISCUSSION QUESTIONS

1. How do Jonathan's parents challenge stereotypes about people suffering from addiction?

2. In the book, Jonathan attends M.S. 219 and FDA, schools that are historically under-funded and under-resourced. What is the value of educators in these spaces, particularly in under-funded schools?

3. Throughout the book, Jonathan finds himself in precarious and grave situations that require quick decision-making. Name one of these situations, and how Jonathan exercises autonomy and choice despite his extreme circumstances.

4. Jonathan often disagrees with both Mr. Marshall and Dr. Hodge, and is resistant to their encouragement. How do these teachers' strict approaches impact Jonathan despite his not seeing their importance at first?

5. Name one way that Jonathan turns adversity into motivation.

6. How did the diversity of people in Jonathan's village contribute to his coming of age and the way he sees himself in

the world? How does the village he chooses early on differ from the village that has a positive impact on his life?

7. How does joining the debate team alter the course of Jonathan's life? In what other areas does his new skills help him thrive?

8. How does Jonathan learn to combine forgiveness and boundary setting to forge a lasting relationship with his parents?

9. Surmise two lessons that Jonathan learns from becoming a father. How does his village contribute to his journey at that stage of his life?

10. Visit Jonathan's website (https://www.jonathanconyers.com) to see what he's up to today. What are three ways that he is engaging with his community in the same way his community engaged with him growing up?

YOUR
BOOK
CLUB
RESOURCE

VISIT
GCPClubCar.com

to sign up for the **GCP Club Car** newsletter, featuring exclusive promotions, info on other **Club Car** titles, and more.

 @legacylithbg

 @legacylitbooks

 @legacylitbooks